The Director

in the Theatre,

BY MARIAN GALLAWAY

DIRECTOR, UNIVERSITY THEATRE

UNIVERSITY OF ALABAMA

THE MACMILLAN COMPANY, NEW YORK

COLLIER-MACMILLAN LTD., LONDON

First Printing

PN
2053
63

Library of Congress catalog card number: 63-8429

The Macmillan Company, New York
Collier-Macmillan Canada, Ltd., Galt, Ontario

DIVISIONS OF THE CROWELL-COLLIER PUBLISHING COMPANY

Printed in the United States of America

Preface

Since several excellent texts on directing already exist, a new text must justify itself by presenting new material or a new point of view. I hope that I have done the latter, in emphasizing the director as a person dealing with people. By working in college and community theatres in eight states, from Maryland to Arizona, from South Dakota to Alabama, I have learned this point of view the hard way because my training in middle-western universities conditioned me to expect easy acceptance of the theatre by the public as an art and by the students as a professional way of life. It has been shocking and heartbreaking to me at times to realize that the dearth of theatre experience in many parts of the country has resulted in an apathy toward theatre that only a crusader can penetrate. I certainly do not presume to have many solutions, but I believe some energy can be saved by revealing the problems ahead to the young people going out to direct plays. The stars in their eyes are good, but if there is also in them a slightly frosty glitter of recognition when difficulties loom up, it seems to me that is good, too.

Because my love of the theatre and my joy in it have come mainly from my work with playwrights and actors, I think of that part of the director's work as the most important and have

iii

devoted the most space to it. But it should be said that public relations and bookkeeping are also part of the director's responsibility, and I have given these matters the prominence I think they deserve by dealing with them first. A theatre artist is so dependent on the regard of people who hold the purse strings and the power of sanctioning his plans that he must win respect in their terms if he hopes to ever convey his purposes to them. This is not what horrifies some young people as compromise; it is a necessary means to an end.

In the plan of the book, I have been guided by students and performances I have seen, by the texts I have studied, and by directors I have seen at work, from B. Iden Payne to Alan Schneider and Vincent Donehue. It seems to me that an elementary text in directing should drive home the most basic principles that a director will need as he begins to practice his art because if one deeply understands principles, he can formulate effective techniques. In watching high school, college, and community theatre productions and even children's plays, I have been impressed with the general lack of this basic understanding. I have seen excellent productions, of course, but I have also seen merely excellent scene designs, sprightliness, correctness of detail, so that I often thought of Cicero's hurt and angry *"Quo tandem usque ruimus?"*, whither are we tending? The content of a play is so compactly, so economically provided that its values must be clearly and fully understood by the director before he can select the techniques that will communicate it. This is the hardest part of the director's job, and the one most sedulously avoided by beginners. Since, like the playwright, his work must be completed by others, the director must also be able to communicate clearly and vividly. And since his medium includes not only the actors but also the physical stage and all the people responsible for arranging it in the communication of the play, he must be a highly efficient planner and executive. It is my hope that this book will help the director in these basic tasks of thinking, planning, and communicating. Such "techniques" as I have included are only those very basic ones that, in the breach, obscure the communication to the audience.

If it is possible to name the few "most formative" influences on my point of view, I should have to acknowledge Hegel's *Philosophy of Fine Art* and John Howard Lawson's *Theory and Technique of Playwriting* as books most congenial to me. I think Marcel Proust's *A la recherche du temps perdu* has been more illuminating about the working of the human mind than most of the psychologists I have read, from Watson to Kris. Perhaps Kenneth Macgowan was the first to show me the power of the theatre as a means of communicating feelings. A long succession of anthropological readings touched off by *The Golden Bough* and Allardyce Nicoll's *Masks, Mimes and Miracles* have put my hand into the hands of a long, long line of fellow workers stretching back into the most ancient past and forward to the unpredicted future.

Wherever it has been possible to recall specific books that have helped to fashion my point of view, I have included them in the bibliographies. But after more than thirty years of voracious reading it is inevitable that I now quote and misquote out of my subconscious. I must therefore conscientiously avow my obligation to people and authors whose names have slipped from my conscious memory to become a deeper part of my thinking.

My major source, I suppose, is Stanislavsky, though I particularly treasure his own statement that to found a method was not a part of his intent, but that he expected the actors and other directors to adapt his teaching to their own needs and personalities. And I also treasure the reports of Gorchakov and Norris Houghton to the effect that at show time Stanislavsky suppressed any superfluous "creativity" in the interest of making the play acceptable to the audience. For the practical purpose of preparing actors in their roles, "the method" enlists the greatest cooperation of some actors. However, when an actor is unable to respond to "method" directing, the director has other means, not wholly mechanical, and indeed often productive of credible and moving results. In educational and community theatre, he needs both means.

Two chapters have given me some trouble — Chapter 4, Starting the Promptbook; and the part of Chapter 13, which deals with the actor's speech.

In Chapter 4 I have perhaps risked swamping some students in a morass of technical material which a skilled director handles as a matter of course. This material is almost *de trop* to students who know stagecraft and have been on crews and in plays, except insofar as they are now asked to recognize, as part of the director's complex responsibility, the necessity for complete and early planning. On the other hand, the technical material is hardly adequate for a student who enters the course without preparation, from another academic area, because he expects to coach plays in high school. If the student is not prepared, he must study to repair his deficiencies. Even if he knows stagecraft, he should read theatre history and the exciting works of modern designers, in order to vitalize his already somewhat sophisticated approach to play production. The text might well be supplemented by student reports on all of the books on design and staging mentioned in the bibliography, and by varied crew assignments.

The sections on speech have necessarily been limited to general problems that might arise in any amateur company anywhere. Speech sounds have interested me since my father teased my Brooklyn mother for [fʌ] and [gɔɪl], and she avenged herself on me for [hæʊs] and [ɑ] for [ɑɪ], while all of us teased my German grandmothers because they could not pronounce [θ] or [w]. In my work in the theatre, I have found the worst vowel distortions in the southern states, but also the most beautiful modesty, so that a reasonable standard of intelligibility and acceptability has not been impossible to achieve. People from western Connecticut, New York, and New Jersey have an incredible number of consonant elisions due to speaking too rapidly. They are the least speech-conscious people I have met, and for me they are the hardest to motivate to improvement. "General American" seems to be closer to Middle Western than to any other regional speech, with energetic consonants, few vowel distortions, a lively rate, and support from the heavy abdominal muscles. Obviously it would be impossible to discuss all regional peculiarities in a text on directing. I have, therefore, dealt only with the basic problems of intelligibility and audibility that a director will face wherever he goes.

There is another conspicuous omission, a discussion of styles. I omit this material because I sincerely believe that only glibness can result from a cursory presentation. It is my conviction that to understand a style, the student must read copiously in the history of the era that produced it. The Expressionism that came out of Germany after World War I, the Bolshevik conditions that evolved a Meyerhold from the Moscow Art Theatre, are to me incapable of brief definition. I think that anyone who attempts to produce "The Flies" without understanding Sartre's particular existentialism can be at best shallow, at worst false and boring. I admit that the possession of labels may stimulate a student to seek the *ding an sich,* but I also fear the possibility that the label may tend to replace the thing in itself.

It is desirable for everyone entering a course in directing to have had some theatre experience, perhaps at least a course in stagecraft and one in acting. Unfortunately, many students who enter the course do not have time in their programs for this preparation, yet need help toward one of the many tasks of a high school speech teacher, that is, the coaching of plays. Many community theatre workers, too, possessing only a modicum of experience, are eager to direct plays. For these people, one must present those elements of the director's task that are most basic and most likely to be of immediate and permanent use — methods of analyzing the theatre situation in which the student will have to work, the script he must present, and the people with whom he will have to deal. An understanding and some use of these matters is a semester's work, after which the student is ready for a more detailed study of techniques and styles.

Another problem in writing the book has been the matter of assignments. Although I subscribe to the belief that one learns best by doing, I do not know of any college or community situation where it has been possible or indeed desirable to put into an actual directing situation everyone who, after acting in a few plays, or none, would like to try his hand at directing. To direct means to command the time of a company and at least a small critic audience. To direct with any prospect of success means, especially to the inexperienced young director, competent actors, who, in most college and community theatres are already giving all the time they can afford to major programs for the entertainment of the public; and who, even when forewarned, sometimes resent the mistaken directions of, or take the reins from, the beginner's hands. Given a less competent cast, it is a serious question whether director or actors learn enough to justify their rehearsal time. With these reservations, I try to find directing opportunities for perhaps half a dozen young directors a year, whom I think promising, and to secure audiences for them. As the rest of the directing class must not be neglected, I have devised exercises from what I feel to be my own most fruitful training — watching rehearsals and trying to understand what I saw, an experience I welcome even today. Since many directors will not use the means described here, the student may find it difficult to report on some of the assignments. But in these cases he will have the advantage of seeing in action another point of view from that of this book and will thus be able to formulate a more individual and personal approach of his own.

In order to understand all of the illustrations, it will be necessary for the reader to have constantly at hand four plays:

The Playboy of the Western World by J. M. Synge,[1] *The Glass Menagerie* by Tennessee Williams, *The Importance of Being Earnest* by Oscar Wilde, and *Romeo and Juliet* by William Shakespeare. My reasons for selecting these are, first, they are all classics in their respective genres; second, they are conventional enough to be easily comprehended by any educational or community theatre group; third, they are as diverse as four plays could possibly be — an Irish folk comedy, a realistic modern drama, a comedy of manners, and a Shakespearean romantic tragedy; and fourth, all are available in paperback editions.

In conclusion, I want to acknowledge the help of Phoebe Barr for writing exercises to train the actor's body; of Dr. Allen Bales for criticising the material on voice training; and of Dr. Albert Griffith for suggesting fruitful readings in psychology. I am, of course, deeply indebted to my editor, John Dennis Moore, for his meticulous criticism of the whole manuscript.

[1] In *Five Great Modern Irish Plays* (New York: Random House, The Modern Library, Inc., 1941).

Table of Contents

xi

Chapter 1

What Is Theatre?

Coming out of a movie or matinee in the afternoon, one is sometimes surprised that it is still light outside. The buildings in the
street seem for a moment to have changed, as if one were in a
strange place. Then one remembers an errand, perhaps, and the
world outside looks normal again. This experience is the result
of "losing oneself" in the play. A stage director learns to seek
evidence of this feeling in the faces of the audience after the
play.

The Audience at the Theatre

It is interesting to watch the process by which a group of
widely diverse individuals become an audience. Of course the
process starts some time before they come to the theatre. A
striking poster or well-written news story commands their attention and they decide to come to the play. Instead of settling
down in their slippers, they freshen up, put on rather festive
clothes, and drive from all quarters to one place. They meet
friends in the lobby and talk about their personal concerns as

1

they stand in line, first for tickets and then for the usher's attention. In the theatre aisle and increasingly, as they enter their row, they unconsciously give up fragments of their personal liberty; but they seem to have a feeling of satisfaction, even though conversation becomes difficult as they sit shoulder to shoulder. Lights on the curtain draw all of their eyes in the same direction, and when the house is darkened, conversation stops as if turned off by a dial. Their identity is now reduced to eyes upon the stage and an attitude of waiting for the curtain to rise.

It seems to be chiefly this unanimous and willing, though unconscious, loss of identity that distinguishes an audience from a mere gathering. As a play progresses, personal identity is further submerged as the stimuli from the stage initiate interest, direct sympathies, and eventually create in the audience a mass wish, the same wish that the protagonist has as he pursues his objective.

"Empathy" is the word commonly used to describe the behavior of persons viewing art — though the term is properly applicable to human responses to all sensory stimuli, ugly as well as beautiful. The theory originated with two German psychologists, whose empirical data led them to postulate that perception has a motor content; that is, when we see or hear or otherwise experience a sensory stimulus, we always respond with our muscles in some way. Another German psychologist, Theodor Lipps, used the word *Einfühlung* (a feeling into, or a tendency in some way to duplicate) to describe the experience. E. B. Titchener, in his *Experimental Psychology of the Thought Processes,* first brought the word into English as "empathy," and it was adopted by Herbert Sidney Langfeld. His *The Aesthetic Attitude* applied the work of Lipps and others to perceptions of beauty and ugliness. Langfeld was concerned with the degree to which one identifies oneself with the object of aesthetic contemplation. He availed himself of E. Bullough's term, "psychical distance," to describe the way in which one loses awareness of himself in an aesthetic experience.

Let it be supposed that an individual is on a ship during a storm, and there is serious danger of shipwreck. It is quite possible that a man of artistic temperament would admire the movement of the waves, and the dash of the spray, entirely oblivious of danger, and with no concern as to what the high seas may ultimately do to the ship . . . . Suddenly, however, a wave larger than any previous one approaches and the artist's muscles set in preparation to meet the blow . . . at that instant he has entirely lost . . . his aesthetic attitude." [1]

Langfeld showed that empathy in a play does not mean complete identification with any single character, but with each of the characters in turn, as they provide kinaesthetic stimuli. If the audience identified with only one character, they would attempt to participate in the action and, using their own personal will and understanding, would carry the plot in a direction other than that intended by the playwright. Langfeld cites an occasion when an actor was playing a poor inventor who was unable to buy fuel in order to fire some pottery; if he could finish this task, his future would be made. Excited by the suspense of the situation, a man in the gallery threw down fifty cents, shouting, "Here, old man, buy wood with it." Obviously this man's identification became too complete, and hence, unaesthetic.

The problem of the extent to which one "loses oneself" in contemplating a work of art has been phrased by Ernst Kris in terms of the play of children as they make believe: "A firm belief in the 'reality of play' can coexist with a certainty that it is play only. Here lie the roots of the aesthetic illusion." [2]

Iredell Jenkins, in *Art and the Human Enterprise*, clarifies the matter of identification by distinguishing three modes of perception: that which recognizes an object in its particularity (the

[1] Herbert Sidney Langfeld, *The Aesthetic Attitude* (New York: Harcourt, Brace, 1920), pp. 55 f.
[2] *Psychoanalytic Explorations in Art* (New York: International Universities Press, 1952), p. 42.

aesthetic mode); that which recognizes use in the object (the affective mode); and that which attempts to understand the object in its connectedness (the cognitive mode.)[3] He grants that the aesthetic experience is "intimately entangled with our cognitive and affective undertakings and cannot be discussed intelligently in isolation from them." [4]

The last step of casting this dual theory *in aere aeterno* of terminology for students of the theatre is the work of John Dolman, Jr.,[5] building upon Langfeld's discussion of E. Bullough's "Psychical Distance as a Factor in Art and an Aesthetic Principle." [6] The new word was "aesthetic distance," and it means the gap between full identification with a stage event and full realization that it is merely a stage event.

Most of this thinking was done on the basis of empirical observation and report. Yet anyone who has worked in the theatre can add corroborative data. One has heard the respiration of the audience controlled from the stage and released as an actor reaches a point of release. One has observed motionless silences and slight general moves to relax as an event on stage permitted. One has seen strain in faces. There are many photographs that show the tense absorption of audiences.

As members of audiences, we have also experienced moments when "aesthetic distance" was broken either by a too complete yielding to the events of the stage or by the full realization that it was all make-believe. What seems to happen in either case is that we become aware of ourselves; through a breach of "aesthetic distance," the audience becomes a collection of individuals again.

More important for the student than to remember these words and their history is the recognition of the fact that when the

[3]Harvard University Press, 1958, p. 20 ff.
[4]*Op. cit.;* p. 70.
[5]*The Art of Play Production* (New York: Harper and Bros., 1928, revised edition, 1946).
[6]Langfeld, *op. cit.,* pp. 52 f. and 72 f.

audience "loses itself," or better, "gives itself," to whatever degree, it places a responsibility upon the theatre. We take a whole evening of the lives of these people, and we demand their belief. If we give them false and cheap stimuli, we can pervert them momentarily to the cheap and false. The least we can pay them for their irreplaceable time is an image of truth, an experience of excellence.

The Theatre as an Art

In the creation of a work of art there are always three elements: first, some experience — an image, an idea, a feeling — so potent, so pressing, that the artist cannot rest until he has got it outside of himself; second, the means he employs to externalize his experience, his medium, that gives him a body for the experience; and finally, the beholder, someone for whom the artist's experience is approximately duplicated in the externalization.

An artist seems to be distinguished from other people primarily by his need to externalize his experience of beauty. In at least some respects, his perceptions are extraordinarily keen, and he may have the frightening gift of insight, which enables him to sense in the world forces that affect men's lives, to draw upon his deepest subconscious self in the service of his conscious artistic aims.[7] Moreover, no matter how conventionally he behaves, he works from a set of values that differ from those which motivate other people. He finds life, as a time to be lived, more important than the magnitude of business enterprises or the pride of possessions. He does not punch a time clock or count in any way the hours he spends making his product, for he is happier working than idle. He makes — not refrigerators or automobiles or any tangible consumers' goods, not plans that will eventuate in practical conveyances to outer space, not lethal

[7] Ernst Kris, op. cit., Chapters 13 and 14.

weapons, or gardens to feed people — he makes something intangible, a feeling, beauty. Even when he produces a sculpture of solid marble, it is the sculpture, not the marble, that has value — the intangible beauty that he has put into the marble. Finally, his reward is ordinarily more the pleasure of the purchaser than the price his creation brings.

He selects for his externalization a medium in which he enjoys working — paint on canvas, prosody, musical instruments, living human beings — and so molds his medium that it embodies and recreates his experience, which then stands outside of himself, a work of art, the form as inseparable from the content as the body is from the personality of an individual.

The medium that an artist chooses somewhat reflects the complexity of his aesthetic experience. Perhaps basically a work of art expresses release from tension. In seeking his medium, the artist wishes to express more or less stringent tension and more or less complete release. He can express these in space or time, or both. The painter and the sculptor use mainly still forms in space, the musical composer mainly sounds in time, and the dancer moving forms in space and time. The medium of the lyric poet and the novelist is words in time. The dramatist uses both still and moving forms in space, and all sorts of sounds as well as words in time, for the purpose of recreating his aesthetic experience. The musical composer and the dramatist have one further distinction in common in the selection of their media: they do not finish the work themselves, but create a set of directions, a score, a script, which is not music or drama until performers complete it in the light of their understanding. In sum, the medium of the dramatist is considerably more complex than those of the other artists, reflecting his complex intellectual and emotional experience of life.

The third point of the aesthetic triangle is the receiver, who enjoys the poem, painting, symphony, drama. The receiver is the gauge of the artist's success in externalizing his aesthetic intent.

If the work of art evokes in the receiver something comparable to the feeling which originally motivated the artist, or which evolved as he probed his feelings during the work of composition, he has satisfactorily completed his work. It is not the number of beholders, but the accuracy with which the feeling was transmitted which attests his success.

Yet in his choice of a medium, the artist selects, to a degree, the extent to which he wishes his work to be shared. A literary work or a painting, however many people behold it, is almost always enjoyed by an observer in solitude, perhaps solely by the artist himself. Even a symphony can sometimes be best enjoyed as a recording by a single listener in his own living room; but generally a group audience listens to symphony in a concert hall, and the environment actually creates a part of the whole feeling which is evoked. A drama, too, owes much of its impact to the fact that it evokes a group response from a shoulder-to-shoulder audience. A lyric poet may declare that he writes for a small coterie or for his own self-expression; a novelist must sell out an edition. A symphonic composer would like to fill a hall several times; a dramatist whose work is seen in the commercial theatre must play to many thousands or not at all.[8]

A drama as a work of art may not differ in its inception from other kinds of impulses to create. It may be, perhaps, more complex than the impulse to create a short poem or a representational painting. Like the novel, its materials are the subtleties of human relationships and the eternally changing conditions of human society. Like the novelist, the dramatist is trying to tell a story and perhaps to make a comment, but his impulse is also rather close to that of the symphonic composer, to release powerful feelings. In formulating his experience, he seeks one

[8]*Sunrise at Campobello* by Dore Schary opened in January 1958; in June *Variety* reported that it would begin "paying off" in September. At 10,000 to 12,000 customers a week, this would be 360,000 to 432,000 customers.

action, the whole story of which will, in itself, express his feeling and his comment.

His medium is vastly more complex than even that of the composer of symphonies, for his written words do not have fixed values like musical notes. Their meaning depends on the actor saying them. The playwright uses a few stage directions, comparable to "adagio," "capricioso," but there are a dozen ways to execute a stage direction, depending on the performer's grasp of its intent. Also, the playwright describes a setting in more or less detail, but his image is made concrete to the limit of the practicable by the work of the designer, the lighting artist, and even the costumer. He orders music, but specific music must be selected or composed; and sound effects, often copiously described, can only become possible and credible through the work of another special artist. In other words, the playwright works in a medium that is complex, alive, and independent, and that actually creates a large part of his externalization.

Moreover, the finished work is not complete *ad aeternitatem* so that it can be enjoyed again by merely taking it out of the files like the recording of a symphony. So far, no means has been found to repeat a play except alive in a theatre before an audience; and no two performances of a play are quite alike, even when the same company presents it; for the audience, as well as the changing condition of the performers, affects what is done on the stage. The whole visible and audible portion of the externalization is thus beyond the playwright's control at the moment when, his script complete, the curtain rises.

There is another way in which a drama differs from other works of art. The playwright has a long testing period in which to discover whether the aesthetic experience has been conveyed clearly and movingly. Agent, producer, director react to the script, and the playwright has the opportunity to revise. The close daily study of the company probes each moment of the play for possible lack of clarity or ineffectiveness. Finally, a road tour subjects the play to the reactions of audiences, and again the playwright has the chance to shape his work more and more closely toward a perfect communication. A novel is printed once and for all; it cannot be changed if a reader falls asleep during a certain passage. A play can be and often is changed in response to its first audiences. The receiver thus helps the dramatist to finish his work.

Thus, from the earliest moment of working with his material, the dramatist makes something to be widely shared, for the work is not complete until it is shared. It is not merely a script, not merely actors on a stage, not merely three hundred full houses. It is something that happens in the fusion of all of these, in the darkened theatre, between the audience and the stage. With all its weight of equipment and its incredible expense, the play is an intangible.

The Director in the Aesthetic Triangle

A theatre director is, in a sense, merely part of the playwright's medium, for he is one of the agents who helps to complete the externalization projected by the playwright in his script. Yet, in a sense, the play is more than just a job to him; it is a response to a need of his own, a feeling that unites itself to the playwright's material and in a way uses it to express his own artistic impulse. On a new play, the director does a great deal of initial work on the script itself, helping the playwright to emphasize and subordinate, clarify, sharpen, and avoid redundance. In the process of creating a new play, his contribution to the script is sometimes so great that legally his name must appear as collaborator, as was many times true of the late George S. Kaufman. Even in working on a finished script, the director's influence on the other elements of the medium would be disruptive unless he finds in the script itself some core of idea or feeling compatible with that of the playwright that he himself wishes to express.

The sources of an artist's impulse to create are legion — an experience, something he heard or read, a sudden intimation from a place he has visited, a poem, a piece of music, a face he saw "out of the rolling ocean the crowd" and never saw again. Any of the images and thoughts and feelings and relationships that may occur in a human life may provide the aesthetic experience that sets an artist to work. The director's aesthetic experience is a union of something in the script with something he has already felt the need to express. In this sense he must be considered an artist.

The main function of the director in producing a play is to make bridges between the playwright's conception (as understood by the director) and the eventual sharers. The "share" component is actually large in the director's original impulse to form his aesthetic experience into a play. In his dealings with the actors and other artists who contribute to the production, his work is almost wholly to determine and to increase the sharing values of their contributions. If he is working with a completed script, he may be concerned solely with sharing values. In this case, he is merely a part of the medium, the servant of the playwright. But to the extent that he incorporates a live experience of his own, even if it be only his deep personal appreciation of the playwright's aesthetic experience, he is an artist as he tries to externalize the play.

Indeed, it is the presence of this personal inspiration, derived in part from the script and in part from their own reactions to some aspect of life, that makes artists of and demands respect for actors, designers, and all of the component elements of the playwright's medium. This point has serious implications for the non-commercial theatre.

Theatre for the Audience

There is a certain justice in the view of some educators and newspaper editors that a play is merely a means whereby a small group of people amuse themselves and show off to their families and friends. In essence, actors are obeying a primitive impulse that goes back to their childhood and to the dimmest prehistory of the human race, the pleasure of being gathered in, exhibitionism as a bid for approval. People who are cold to the theatre are perfectly right in finding this manifestation of the age-old need unimportant, even repellent. Very often the persistence of this attitude and behavior in the performers is the fault of the director, as leader, who may not have a genuinely artistic approach himself, or may not know how to bend his medium (script, stage, and actors) to his artistic objective. Until he can do so, and create a whole and beautiful production of a play, he can scarcely hope to change an opinion of the public based on their experience.

People who produce plays merely for their own amusement, yet ask an audience to view them, not only end with no audience, but actually do much harm to themselves. A director should understand this, particularly a director who plans to use the theatre in the training of young people. For in the month or so in which they work together, the director has access to the deepest motives of the performers. He can and does give them a great deal more than theatre skills. He can help them to understand, to evaluate, and to live the life that is ahead of them, provided he has a true artistic purpose and the determination and skill to reach toward excellence.

When their own pleasure is the most important concern of the performers, the result is inevitably shoddy. Even the potentially artistic participant learns in a shoddy play to be satisfied with shoddy work. If his goal is his own pleasure, he works only as long as the play is fun for him, thus acquiring a totally un-realistic notion of life situations. He may also be deceived by a mirage of success in the purring compliments of his friends and relatives, blinding himself until the inevitable moment later in life when he will have to face his own shortcomings. He learns, too, the delights of exhibitionism, which, while giving him tem-porary pleasure, may recoil to mar his character and his social acceptability outside of the theatre.

When the play is produced for the audience and everyone is striving for excellence, beneficial effects on the performers are manifold. The first time the audience sniggers because a cigarette lighter or a seltzer bottle does not work, the embarrassed prop-erty man learns that one careless worker can ruin the work of a group. The "leads" also come to recognize their dependence on the rest of the players and the crews. Striving toward perfec-tion creates a sense of social responsibility and the mutual obli-gations of real comradeship. This pulling together for a common end is one of the greatest character-building experiences of the participants in theatre for the audience.

Few people outside the theatre realize the tremendous self-control that an actor must acquire in preparing for a play. Not only must he learn the lines and business of the play, but he must learn to move and to speak appropriately, and to take criticism — above all, to be self-critical. Whatever his whim or his real need, he must discharge his responsibility to his mates. He must keep a careful and rigorous schedule in order to main-tain the great vitality needed in rehearsal and at the same time meet his other obligations outside the theatre. He learns to plan his life.

He must stretch his imagination to understand the character he plays. By probing his own experience, his reading, his ac-quaintance with other people, he gains insight into human nature from associating with a play that reaches toward perfec-tion.

All of the participants learn to praise the artist among them and to respect the sincere efforts of each other. In other words, they learn tolerance and generosity.

Having done their best, they come out of the experience bigger persons than they were a month earlier, and they sense this. The demanding work of making a play for the audience forces them to exceed their previous accomplishments, so that they cease to be afraid of more and more difficult tasks.

Thus, whether or not the players and crew members intend to use their training in professional careers, audience-centered theatre — theatre which aims at perfection for the enjoyment of somebody else — tends to foster a sense of social responsibility, to create positive and useful self-discipline, to increase understanding of life and respect for art, and to make the participant generally a more useful person.

Many young directors begin their work in situations where the public, including their employer, have thought of the theatre merely as an innocuous pastime and, accordingly, do not give it hearty support. They do not really value it, because no one has given them reason to do so. A resourceful, skilled and determined director coming into the situation may be a shock to this public. The upholders of the *status quo* often think of suggestions for improvement as a challenge. Because of the general lack of understanding, theatre people have to accept conflict as an inevitable part of their way of life and to recognize that the burden of proof is on them.

The burden is on us to show community theatre boards and school administrators that theatre productions deserve serious effort; that when an audience is inveigled into seeing a shoddy and boring play, the waste in manhours is equal to the number of people in the audience multiplied by the two-hour length of the play — perhaps between a thousand and two thousand manhours. Worse, the effect may be not only viciously to kill time, but also to instill cheap and ugly attitudes in those who have not yet developed sufficient critical judgment to be bored.

The director must work to establish that a play well chosen and well presented is a peculiarly vivid art form which affects its beholders more strongly than reading. What is seen on the stage appears as visible evidence of some aspect of human life. The theatre, therefore, must speak accurately and truly. By reinforcing knowledge from other sources, competent theatre can help to create a thinking and sensitive community.

A civic or college orchestra, a football team, a library are recognized means of enhancing the prestige of a community. In marshaling support for theatre, one can ˋpoint out cities that have well-established community theatres and colleges where first-rate plays are done. In these places, the theatre is regarded not only as a mark of cultural superiority and pride, but also as a selling point to induce others to come there. To cite only two examples, the town of Abingdon, Virginia, certainly owes a large measure of its growth to the presence of Barter Theatre, and Roanoke Island can actually present figures showing how *The Lost Colony* has increased the economic well-being of the island.

Especially in communities where public entertainment is limited, the college or community theatre must be depended on to fill a portion of the need for adult and tasteful entertainment. And as the working day becomes shorter, communities must consider constructive entertainment as one of their responsibilities. The theatre at worst is a change from the sordid jukebox roadhouse and the monotonous sex and violence of the cinema; at best it is illuminating and moving; it can widen and deepen the bond of man to man in the community.

Reading List

DeMille, Agnes. *And Promenade Home.* Boston: Little, Brown, 1958.
Dolman, John. *The Art of Play Production.* New York: Harper and Bros., 1928, revised, 1946.

Gibson, William. *The See-Saw Log.* New York: Alfred A. Knopf, 1959.

Hattwick, Melvin S. *How to Use Psychology for Better Advertising.* Englewood Cliffs, N. J.: Prentice-Hall, 1950.

Jenkins, Iredell. *Art and the Human Enterprise.* Cambridge: Harvard University Press, 1958.

Kazan, Elia. "He's the Director." Syndicated article, *Tuscaloosa News,* June 25, 1961.

Kris, Ernest. *Psychoanalytical Explorations in Art.* New York: International Universities Press, 1952.

Langfeld, Herbert Sidney. *The Aesthetic Attitude.* New York: Harcourt, Brace, 1920.

Poffenberger, A. T. *Psychology in Advertising.* Chicago and New York: A. W. Shaw, 1925.

Rice, Elmer. *The Show Must Go On.* New York: Viking Press, 1949.

Starch, Daniel. *Controlling Human Behavior.* New York: Macmillan, 1936.

PART ONE

Preliminaries

Chapter 2

Selecting the Play:
Practical Considerations

A theatre will thrive or fail according to its ability to find the right plays to make up a season.

The late Margo Jones[1] used to say that the main reason to produce a play is that the director is in love with it. But several other considerations must influence his choice. First, the play must be pleasing to the audience. With this as its primary qualification, the play selected must also be one that the director and the working force of the theatre can do reasonably well with the facilities at their disposal. And, except in unusual circumstances, the season's program must be selected in accord with a specific budget. Finally the play must be worth working on. All of these requirements must be considered as the director plans his season.

The Audience

The director, as an artist, may find his sympathies a bit out of line with the prevailing attitudes of the community. He may

[1]Founder and director of the Dallas Little Theatre and author of *Theatre-in-the-Round* (New York: Rinehart, 1951).

17

going to move because "those people" (Negroes) were moving into her neighborhood, and the young sociologist reminded her that there was a time when Jews were regarded in the same light. This planting was essential to the main theme of the play and could not be avoided. The "curse" was taken off it by casting the neighbor as cute and harmless. But the feeling of shock in this particular audience was marked, and there was a restless moment or two before they returned to the play. Another audience not preponderantly Jewish might not have been so shocked.

Anything that affects the audience so strongly that they become aware of their own persons breaks aesthetic distance. The movie version of *The Green Pastures*, for example, contained a scene in which Moses, forbidden to enter the Promised Land, sat on the side of the mountain, his white beard blowing in the mist, while the children of Israel marched past him, each laying a hand on his shoulder in wordless farewell — old, gnarled hands of his comrades, the pitying little hands of children, the strong hands of young men and women. It was an extremely tasteful and moving scene until some members of the tight-throated audience began to gulp audibly. The scene went on for fifteen or twenty seconds more, but those who were not wiping their own eyes were amused at the sounds of weeping around them. For these seconds, there was no audience.

The response to heavy sex on the stage is comparable. When the audience becomes uncomfortable, the play stops. There is another reason to be wary of licentiousness in the plays selected for the non-commercial theatre. The players are our neighbors' children, for whose behavior we are somewhat responsible. Without embarrassment, we can watch Bergman, with her colorful history, in the most intimate scenes; little Mary Smith makes us uncomfortable. Still another reason can be found for caution in selecting plays that center around the physical aspects of sex: the unskilled stage lover does not make love convincingly. A passionate scene that can be done with finesse by skilled actors may be awkward, shamefaced, lewd, when embarrassed young actors try to play it.

Respect for local attitudes, local prejudices, local mores is thus more than a negative, "thou-shalt-not" point of view; it is a practical evaluation of what will break the empathic bond in a particular audience. One is still left with the responsibility for finding excellent plays that will be acceptable.

The director's paramount task is to evoke in the audience emotions proper to the play. All his techniques exist only to this end, and none has more than half a chance of being effective unless he understands the people to whom he wishes to deliver the play. Yet with patience, courage, friendliness, and respect, he may be able in time to increase the range of their taste, as well as his own, and to learn to say what he thinks the audience needs to hear.

The Participants

The choice of plays is also to some extent governed by the capacities of the participants, beginning with the director's. His experience, knowledge of the background of the play, access to research materials must be important considerations. For the workers in the theatre assume that the director is correct in his interpretation of the play and will assert his teachings, right or wrong, both in the theatre and out of it. For their sake as well as his own, he must be rich in knowledge of the play. Yet the mere fact that one does not know a period or a genre need not fatally limit his choice, for scholarship is attainable, given the will to acquire it. Rather than fall into the dreary groove of knowing all the answers to such few questions as he asks himself, it is a wise principle for the director once in a while to try to stretch himself by producing a play of a kind new or difficult for him.

After weighing one's own capacities to direct a possible play, one must consider the actors who may be available. Since much more is to be said of them later, only a few cautions need to be mentioned here. Even though it is unwise to precast before considering all possible talent, it is reckless to settle upon a play before being fairly sure that the most vital roles could be cast. In the first place, the play should be one which the available actors, with their particular cultural background, could understand. Rural young people, for example, might have a hard time playing crisp city characters; urban actors tend to caricature folk characters. If a play requires special skills such as dancing, singing, playing a musical instrument, the director must be fairly certain that he can secure someone who can do these things while presenting the character acceptably in other respects.

While the community theatre has the advantage of being generally able to cast to type, the educational theatre director must cope with young actors, not only lacking in basic theatre skills, but also naïve about human relations. Makeup may change the appearance of a young actor, but a young voice is almost impossible to change in a few weeks and is often very unconvincing. Yet generally a good college actor has intelligence, energy, imagination, and enough analogies in his own life, if they can be found, to understand the character in which he is cast; and the college audience is reasonably conditioned to accept truth of interpretation, even though people of twenty or so play roles of all ages and descriptions. This does not mean that the college theatre director may cast carelessly, or that he may blind himself to vocal and visual inadequacies. It means that he needs to work with great diligence and imagination to convey the spirit of the various characters through the behavior of the student actors.

Not only must the cast of a play be considered in selecting a play, but also the number and quality of other workers needed to produce the play. In a well-organized theatre the number of workers on various crews is usually two or three times as large as the number of actors. For a quick summary of the manpower needed backstage and in the front of the house during a production, the following table has been included. The first column shows how many people are needed in addition to the actors in order to produce the simplest play. The second column shows a reasonable average for a play of more than one setting:

JOB	MIN.	AV.
Stage Manager, curtain puller	1	2
Stage Crew	0	8
Lighting technician, helpers	1	5
Property crew	2	6
Sound operator	0	2
Costume crew	1	5
Bookholder, callboy	1	2
Doorman	0	1
Box office clerk	1	2
Ushers	4	8
	11	41

These estimates do not include the builders and painters, the maker of the sound tape, the seamstresses for a costume play, or the publicity workers, who might increase the totals by twenty to forty. Often, too, one must consider the availability of special help, such as musicians, choreographer, or fencing master.

The director must understand all of these jobs thoroughly by doing them himself in his apprenticeship; and often, when he is responsible for the whole play, as director, he must either be able to do them himself or help someone else learn them. A good time to begin learning the necessary and often pleasant chores of the theatre is in high school, where unfortunately, many students learn only acting. There, some teachers, in their concern for excellence, build and dress the scenery themselves and gather the properties and serve the production up to the actors on a silver plate, so to speak. This practice results in the students' missing some of the main lessons of play production, and in the director's being too frantic and fatigued to perform the critical task of coordinating during the last rehearsals.

In planning any non-professional production, the date of performance has considerable bearing on the number of people available to serve in cast and on crews. The determining factors vary from one group to another. December is likely to be a bad time in community theatre, because Christmas shopping, Christmas parties, and church Christmas festivals make strong claims on people's time. Any established examination or holiday periods will deter college students; and in spring, they want to spend their leisure out-of-doors. The beginning of a season is likely to be an auspicious time, because it draws into the theatre a goodly number of new recruits who will continue working throughout the year.

The Facilities

One important consideration in the choice of plays is the adequacy of the physical facilities. The audience is ordinarily pleased or bored with the play without knowing precisely why. Although they freely discuss the quality of the acting, they actually do not often distinguish between the actor and his role. But the physical production is something that they can make definite and sensible evaluations about, and these evaluations set them at once for or against the play. A makeshift setting, poorly lighted, leads the audience at once to expect that the performance will be equally unfinished. On the other hand, delight and respect can be evoked by the setting, so that the audience anticipates a competent production. The actors, too, are stimulated to a good performance by a good setting.

Many amateur theatres, both college and community, are technically far superior to the old, out-moded professional theatres in New York. However, there are also a great many amateur theatres that were never designed for stage productions. The audience can sit down in them more or less comfortably, but they cannot see, from some of the seats, and often there are acoustic dead spots. The stage house may extend only three feet beyond the acting area and have hardwood floors, certain doors built in, and no grid on the ten-foot ceiling. There is often no way of lighting from the front and no lighting control at all. It takes a really keen designer and technician to produce acceptable looking plays in such a theatre. But no theatre is hopeless, and often the challenge of an inadequate building stimulates the imagination and develops ingenuity in the workers who must use it.

In any case, in selecting a play, one must be sure that the theatre provides enough space for the storage and efficient shifting of the necessary scenery and properties. A tiny stage house cannot accommodate a mammoth production.

When facilities are lacking, it is almost always possible to produce plays in arena style. A suitable room for arena productions would seat sixty to a hundred or more people around a fifteen- to twenty-foot acting space. Such a room would require access from at least two sides and a simple lighting installation independent of the house lights. Of course this minimum requirement is a makeshift until excellent performances have justified the provision of better facilities.

However simple the plan of staging the play, some lighting equipment and control are needed. Probably no element of staging is more influential in creating illusion and in affecting the mood of the audience than the amount, color, and location of light on the stage. If it is important to the play to indicate a change of time of day or season, if the play contains any night scenes, or even the switching on or off of a lamp, then the question of adequate lighting facilities must affect the decision to produce the play.

If a proscenium stage is to be used, ordinarily one needs a stock of scenery, some flats for interior settings, a cyclorama for exteriors, and a few platforms. If the height of the flats and the sizes of door and window openings and of platforms are standardized, all of these elements can be used together in various combinations for many plays. A cyclorama can be made at negligible cost of tobacco cloth that will give a good effect and last fairly well if properly handled and stored. At the other end of the scale is a Hansen cloth scrim thirty feet from floor to top batten without a seam and costing several hundred dollars. The lighting equipment for a cyclorama is also expensive and, of course, requires additional electrical circuits. If the play requires any illusion of atmospheric changes these items of equipment are essential.

Properties are an important item in the selection of a play. A well-designed setting is ruined by inadequate furniture; but good furniture is almost always hard to come by, and certain realistic plays would have to be rejected if the proper period furniture were not available.

A carefully designed basic wardrobe also extends the range of the director's choice in selecting plays. Costumes can be rented for ten to twelve dollars each, with such things as boots, capes, and wigs extra. Excellent costumes can be made for little more, and they remain in stock for the next production, if there is someone to supervise their construction and handling, and if the theatre has storage space.

The more one knows about stage design and about simplification, the less he is bound by the cumbersome requirements of realism in a difficult stage. A wide knowledge and deep understanding of theatre history are of the greatest help to the director in utilizing his facilities to increase the range of his choice in selecting plays.

The Budget

A student director is often shocked to learn that money must be spent to produce plays, and that his range of choice is limited by the money available. As an artist, characteristically lacking economic interests, he tends to choose the play, spend the necessary money to produce it, and then gasp at the deficit. In nearly every theatre, the director is ordering the expenditure of money belonging to others — the membership, the college, the tax payers who support a university. It is essential that he select plays that can be adequately produced without running the organization into debt.

One glance at the costs of a play will convince him of the need to interest himself in money.

Production costs vary in different places and at different times, and a wise designer can scale the play to the money at his disposal. But production costs are only a fragment of the overall expenses of operating a theatre.

Expenditures begin with the purchase of a play worth doing. As with other commodities, one gets about what he pays for. A non-royalty play is usually a classic (requiring expensive costumes) or a piece of junk "for the amateur market." The usual royalty for a new play is fifty dollars for the first and twenty-five or thirty-five for each subsequent performance. A play several years old costs a little less. A young director must learn to think of a play as property, and of the royalty as payment for work done by the author. The ethical obligation is thus no less stringent than the law. Legally, infringement of copyright makes the offender liable to (1) injunction restraining from the infringement; (2) payment of damages to $100 for the first infringing performance and fifty dollars for each succeeding infringement; (3) imprisonment not to exceed one year, or a fine of $1000, or both, where the infringement of the copyright is willful and for profit.

However economical the production, some money must be spent for a program and tickets. The program should be as attractive as the organization can afford, for it suggests to the audience the quality of the play and may also serve as an advertising mailout. Advertisements in it can cover the cost of the program; but, if many illustrations are used, the program is expensive — a commercial type of program costs several hundred dollars — and careful bookkeeping is needed to collect the advertisers' accounts. Also, the size and nature of the audience must justify the purchase of space in the program, or the theatre loses prestige and becomes to the advertisers merely an object of charity.

Customarily, a theatre is required to use tickets so that a record can be kept of the money taken in. Sometimes the cost of the tickets can be covered by an advertisement printed on the reverse side. Standardization of programs and tickets for all plays somewhat reduces costs.

Money is also spent for advertising. Posters are generally used to advertise the play. Their quality will be taken as a promise of the quality of the play. A few handmade posters, however well designed, suggest that the producing organization feels that the play is not good enough to advertise widely; they are bad business. If posters are to be used, they should be well designed and professionally duplicated.

One of the most effective (though expensive) ways of reaching customers is mailing. To the cost of duplicating the message must be added stamps, and stamped return envelopes for the greatest return on the outlay. Many colleges have a franking permit that the theatre is entitled to use for bulk mailing. This makes direct mail promotion more feasible and inexpensive for educational theatre.

Newspaper advertising is expensive; moreover, if the theatre pays for newspaper space, it is understandable that radio and television station supervisors will expect to be paid for air time. News stories, on the other hand, are free and very helpful, especially if they include pictures.

Handbills, table tents, window displays, banners, and all sorts of promotional gimmicks run up the cost, but may bring in enough customers to justify the expenditure. A good rule of thumb is that any expenditure for publicity should bring in at least double the cost.

Some costs that are of major importance in the community theatre are frequently not computed by the college theatre director, but he should compute them, in order to understand his relationship to the college. First, the college directorial and technical staff are hired to teach, but part of their teaching load is usually remitted in order to give them time for productions. Thus, perhaps as much as one-fourth to one-third of these salaries must be regarded as production costs. From departmental funds or scholarships come the stipends for various assistants. Janitor service is also generally paid by the college rather than by the theatre. Regardless of whether these funds come from the theatre account or from some other source, they make up a significant percentage of the cost of producing plays.

Other costs met by the community theatre are rental or mortgage payments on the theatre space, capital improvements, repairs and maintenance, taxes and insurance, and utilities, including the telephone. A college director can understand the real assistance given him by the administration by recognizing that these bills, generally paid by the college, amount, in some cases, to about as much as the production expense of the theatre.

Once convinced that he needs money to produce plays, the director will study the actual and potential sources of the theatre's income. This is particularly necessary in high schools where often no money is allocated for producing plays. A teacher is assigned the task of finding a non-royalty play and producing it without spending any money. The high school teacher who takes pride in his productions often resorts to the chaotic and deplorable practice of spending his own money on the play. If admission is charged, many times the income is turned over to the school for band or football uniforms or some other established activity of the school. Any high school director who believes in the value of the theatre will resent this injustice and will work to put his theatrical productions on a sound financial basis.

A theatre's operating income is primarily derived from subsidy and/or box office.

Many college theatres operate solely on departmental funds furnished on the ground that the college must educate both the participants and the members of the audience. This policy may insure against cheap programs, but, even if the departmental funds are unlimited, the arrangement has two drawbacks: It does not permit the theatre's income to reflect the achievement of its workers; and it tacitly denies that the audience is the final, if not the sole, test of training.

A second means of securing money for college theatres is a per capita levy on the student activity fee. This must, of course, be justified by the attendance of students at plays. This is a somewhat more realistic subsidy than complete departmental support. Like the community theatre's season ticket sale, it guarantees the theatre a specific amount of money and enables the director to budget his season so that he can buy needed equipment from year to year. There is, however, one disadvantage. Since a committee of undergraduates generally allocates the student activity fund, the director may find himself at the mercy of the uninformed taste of the undergraduate student body and may feel afraid to experiment, lest he lose his popularity, and with it, his theatre income.

Some college and most high school and community theatres depend mainly on ticket sales for their operating income. This is a very real gauge of the theatre's effectiveness; however, it is an unsure source of money, unless a good system of public relations is always operating.

Foundation grants, endowments, scholarships, patron- or life-memberships can increase the theatre's income substantially. A good bit of money can be made by selling refreshments or programs in the lobby, by renting costumes and equipment, by showing movies or presenting other entertainments, but the cost of these in time and money must also be reckoned. Other ways of raising money have been found in particular situations, but the most common ways of meeting production costs are subsidy and ticket sales.

One other point must be made. It frequently happens that a director must seek to augment the theatre's income by talking with administrative purse holders. His best argument is in accurate and complete records of income and expenditures and of manhours spent on the production of a play. Indeed, the sooner a young director learns to keep records of every sort, the sooner he can reduce to routine the chores that distract him from his main job, that of directing plays.

Play selection is thus more than a matter of the director's enthusiasm. It is first of all a practical estimate of the capacity of the audience to enjoy and of the players to present the program. It is also an evaluation of the efficiency of the plant to house the play well. And it is the methodical balancing of costs and income. The selection of a program involves all of these considerations because plays cannot be produced single handed. They require the labor of many people, the money of many people, and they must create enjoyment for many people.

Assignments

1. Analyze your hometown audience:
    A. What is the population? Percentage urban? Percentage suburban? Percentage rural?
        List the chief sources of wealth.
        What percentage of the population is indigenous?
        How many car licenses do you see from other parts of the state? From other states?
        How many hotels are there? Motels? When built?
        How many wealthy people live there?

   B.   How many events are there in the concert series?
        How many volumes in the public library?
        How many book stores? Is there a museum? Art shows?
        How many writers or other artists live there?
        How many night clubs are there with live entertainment?
        How many movie houses? How many "art" movies? What
        television programs are popular with the adults? What
        other kinds of entertainment are popular?
        How many community theatres are there? What is the age
        of the oldest community theatre? How large is the mem-
        bership? Does it own its own building? Does it employ a
        director?
        How many professional plays come there in a year?
        Of what kind: Musicals? Dramas? Hit comedies?
   C.   What racial components live there?
        What are the church preferences? Which church has the larg-
        est congregation? The richest?
        Are there strong political convictions?
        Are there any special characteristics or prejudices?
   D.   Would you say that this is a good community for a com-
        munity theatre to thrive in? State your reasons.

2. Analyze your stage:
   A.   Dimensions of proscenium opening?
        Dimensions of stage floor?
        Describe any fixed equipment that takes floor space.
        Height of grid? Number of sets of lines?
        Number of counterweighted lines?
   B.   Dimensions of scene shop? Accessibility?
        List power tools:
   C.   Is there a light bridge? Control board? Where located?
        Number of dimmers? Kind of dimmers? Number of outlets
        for front lighting?
   D.   Locate and describe the dressing rooms.
   E.   Number of seats in auditorium? Any bad seats? Is the
        floor raked? Is there a balcony?

F. Is the theatre in an accessible location? Plenty of parking space?

G. List the inadequacies of your theatre. What could be done to remedy these faults? List their cost.

3. Describe a time when you felt strong empathy in the theatre. Anywhere else?

4. Describe a time when empathy was broken for you in the theatre or movie by (a) shocking material, (b) too much emotion, (c) some incongruous detail.

5. How many crew members worked on the last play with which you were connected? How many actors? Who built the set? Who gathered the properties? Who supervised the costumes? Who accounted for the money? To whom?

6. Tentatively cast *The Glass Menagerie* from your own group and justify your selection. Can you think of any inadequacies of these actors for the roles in which you have cast them? Would you have a good casting for Juliet? Who would play Capulet? What qualities would be needed in an actor who was to play Friar Lawrence? Is there someone who could provide music for *Romeo and Juliet?* What other special help would you need for this play?

7. Estimate the facilities of your theatre for producing *The Glass Menagerie. Romeo and Juliet.*

8. Do you know a space where you could produce arena style? What changes would have to be made in the room? How much would these cost?

9. Using lighting catalogues, list prices of spotlights, cyc floods, striplights, fresnels. For what is each useful in the theatre? How would you find out what a control board would cost?

10. From what sources does your theatre get its money?

11. Can you think of other ways it might get money?

12. Devise a bookkeeping system for your theatre.

13. What insurance can you get on stage properties? How much does this cost?

Reading List

Dolman, John, Jr. *The Art of Play Production.* New York: Harper and Bros., revised edition, 1946.

Gassner, John. *Producing the Play.* New York: Dryden Press, 1941.

Gillette, Arnold. *Stage Scenery: Its Construction and Rigging.* New York: Harper and Bros., 1959.

Heffner, Hubert C., Samuel Selden, and Hunton D. Sellman. *Modern Theatre Practice.* New York: F. S. Crofts, revised edition, 1960.

Hughes, Glenn. *The Penthouse Theatre.* New York: Samuel French, 1942.

Jones, Margo. *Theatre-in-the-Round.* New York: Rinehart, 1951.

Plummer, Gail. *The Business of Show Business.* New York: Harper and Bros., 1961.

Young, John Wray. *The Community Theatre.* New York: Harper and Bros., 1958.

Yeaton, Kelly. "Arena Production." In Gassner, *op. cit.,* pp. 542-600.

Chapter 3

Selecting the Play:
The Merits of the Play

In the Broadway theatre, perhaps, the audience comes to see the "star"; but in college and community theatres they come to see the play. A highly skilled company with limitless facilities sometimes makes a poor script look fairly good. But the less skill a company has in playmaking, the more they must depend on the script itself to hold interest. Moreover, in asking numbers of people to contribute their energies and irretrievable time toward making and seeing a play, the director has an ethical obligation to select something worth doing and viewing.

There are no rules about what makes a play good or bad. Discrimination is learned in a slow and hard way. Only a wide and deep background of life and art enables one to feel a degree of certainty of the value of his choice. Certain plays, like certain poems, can scarcely be enjoyed at all without specific background information about the era in which they were presented or the particular philosophy of the writer. This is true not only of historical plays, but also of plays of our own time. The startlingly new and different play may be merely a shallow stunt, or it may be a vital expression of the changing modes of thought behind today's behavior.

Where to Find Plays

The most pleasant way of finding plays is, of course, to see plays produced professionally or non-professionally. A good production reveals the merits of a play better than the text does. Even poor productions help an inexperienced director to see things that are not apparent to him as he reads the script.

Besides seeing plays the director must read them. Many fine anthologies introduce one to plays of all kinds and periods and lead one to read more of the work of playwrights who interest him. *Theatre Arts Magazine,* to which every director should subscribe, contains a complete play each month. The Grove Press, Doubleday Anchor Books, Hill and Wang, The Modern Library, and many other publishers publish recent or unusual plays in inexpensive editions. A director should get on their mailing lists as well as on the lists of Samuel French, Inc., and Dramatists Play Service. It is a good plan to order a number of plays that might be interesting and read them during a summer vacation, so that there will be time to reflect on them before making a final choice.

In seeking plays, one should investigate a few sources of new plays — plays unproduced on Broadway. A play which, for many reasons, may not have had a hearing in a commercial theatre may be very attractive to a non-commercial producing group and its audience. Efforts have been made by the American Educational Theatre Association through its Manuscript Play Project to encourage the production of new plays. The project circulates to its members about forty new plays never produced in New York, though some of them have been successfully produced in colleges over the country. New Dramatists Committee, a group of established playwrights organized to help apprentice playwrights learn their craft, occasionally releases one of their manuscripts for non-commercial production. Southeastern Theatre Conference also has a New Play Project, the purpose of which is to find and produce widely in college and community theatres one new play a year. Producing a new play is the most challenging and rewarding task a director can undertake.

Evaluating Plays

One's search for a play often begins with reading catalogues from publishers of plays. Of course the publisher is anxious to sell the plays on his list, and one can expect catalogue copy to be a bit colored. Here, for example, is an entry that describes an "all-girl" show:

The Girl With Two Faces. A 3-act mystery-comedy by Jane Kendall; 9w. Time, full evening. Scene 1 int. — A group of attractive girls, strangers to each other, are brought together in the mountain home of old Miss Runyon. She tells them she has chosen them at random from newspaper clippings to be her heirs, so that her niece will not inherit any of her wealth. Suddenly she launches into a furious tirade, for she has detected her niece among them, masquerading as one of the invited girls. Before she can reveal which girl it is, the lights go out, Miss Runyon leaves the room, and a moment later, lies dead on the stairs! The frightened girls would gladly leave but a storm renders the mountain roads unsafe. They try to protect themselves against a killer in their group, not knowing from which direction danger may next strike. To add to the mystery, a dazed girl is brought in out of the storm, and the group hardly knows whether she is to be protected or feared. The question is quickly solved, for the girl herself is the next victim of the killer. Through scenes of increasing tension, the play mounts to an utterly unforeseen and impressive climax. Yet there are plenty of passages full of humor to lighten the tension, as when Delphine, the pretty maid, shows up in Act 2, rigged out in an old-fashioned nightgown and curlpapers! Plenty of wisecracks and perky business add to the lighter mood and keep the play from becoming too terrifying. Cast: the pretty maid, the athletic tennis champion, the Cuban dancer with the Carmen Miranda accent, the prim honor student, the breezy waitress, the cute farm girl, the baby-doll, the girl out of the storm, and grim Miss Runyon herself. Seldom does any play achieve such an admirable balance of parts, with such an opportunity for clear-cut, impressive character work, and a lot of laughs. A big hit to begin with — and increasingly popular. Non-royalty to amateurs for first performance on purchase of nine copies. Repeat performances $2.50 each.

                                                    Price, 75 cents.

This description of *The Girl With Two Faces* stimulates some questions:

1. Can one believe the premise — that old Miss Runyon, to prevent her own niece from inheriting her fortune, selected heirs at random from newspaper clippings?

2. Can one believe the circumstances attendant upon the murder — that Miss Runyon, upon discovering her niece, delivered a tirade without letting her eyes fall upon the girl and thus revealing her identity? That she would not state immediately who the girl was and take steps to have her removed? That she would leave the room without making the revelation? And that the lights would go out at this crucial moment?

3. Is there really "an opportunity for clearcut, impressive character work"? Note that the first words of the description emphasize the attractiveness of the roles, and the summary of characters stereotypes each character with an adjective that might be agreeable to the actress.

4. Is the "humor" likely to be humorous to the viewers? The curlpapers and old-fashioned nightgown of the maid, the "perky business," and wisecracks to keep the play from being "too terrifying" may also prevent the "impressive climax."

5. Who is Jane Kendall, the author? What else has she written? Where could one find critical reviews of her work?

Why is it not stated that this "big hit" had a successful Broadway run? With what groups has it been "increasingly popular"?

Questions like these have to be asked of any play one may consider producing.

Another publisher, who carries some fine plays and also caters to the "amateur" market, offers *Night Must Fall* in the following terms:

Night Must Fall   Melodrama. 3 Acts
Emlyn Williams.   4 m., 5 f.   Int. Mod. Cost.
Produced in London and New York with Emlyn Williams in the leading role. It is no secret that Danny, a bellhop who arrives at the Bramson bungalow, has already murdered one woman, and there is little doubt that he will soon murder another — the aged owner of the house. He gradually insinuates himself into her affections in a skilful manner, at the same time managing to prevent her niece — who has guessed his previous connection with the murder — from giving him away. For Dan is a dashing young assassin whom she firmly believes she hates, but as a matter of fact she is fascinated by him beyond measure. Dan is a completely selfish, self-centered psychopath with no feelings and a vast imagination, who is perpetually acting for his own edification the part of a murderer, and is only unhappy because he cannot share his secret with the world. This play offers an excellent opportunity for some fine acting and should prove extremely popular with Little Theatres because of its unusual character.
$1.00.   (Royalty $25.00)

Of course Emlyn Williams is a Welsh playwright and actor, whose name could be found in *Who's Who in The Theatre,* along with some information about his accomplishments. The description states that *Night Must Fall* was produced in London and New York, and the reader may remember the movie. Since the date of this play is earlier than 1940, it could not be found in *New York Theatre Critics Reviews* but it would certainly be in Burns Mantle's series of *Best Plays* (Dodd,

Mead), an annual publication which includes accounts of all plays in New York as far back as 1919.

Like the other catalogue note, this one promises fine opportunities for actors. It is only fair to ask whether one can believe the character of Danny, of the girl who refused to give him away, and of the gullible old lady who "fell" for him. Can it be that the advertising copy is laconic because the play is well enough established to need very little promotion?

Another of Emlyn Williams's plays is presented as follows:

A Murder Has Been Arranged   Melodrama. 3 Acts
Emlyn Williams   4 m., 5 f.   Int. Mod. Cost.
A novel and unique thriller that held the English play-goers gripping their seats when it was presented three years ago. Sir Charles Jasper, an eccentric who delves into the mystic, is to come into a fortune of two million pounds on his fortieth birthday. To celebrate the occasion, Sir Charles plans a party on the stage of the St. James Theatre, supposedly haunted because of several mysterious deaths years ago. The merriment is interrupted by the appearance of Maurice Mullins, the hitherto missing nephew of Sir Charles and recipient of the legacy in the event of the latter's death. Maurice, who claims to be a novelist, induces his uncle to write in longhand what he declares to be a chapter for his new book. It suddenly dawns on the uncle that he is in reality writing a suicide confession, but too late, for he has just drained a fatal drink concocted by the nephew. With the rise of the curtain on the third act action of this thriller, we are concerned with the subtle and ingenious manner in which the guests, skeptical over the apparent suicide, force Maurice to confess. The play is packed with all the elements that are sure to hold and entertain any audience. $1.00. (Royalty $25.00)

This item uses slightly more sales talk — "playgoers gripping their seats." Compare "Should prove extremely popular" with "sure to hold and entertain any audience." Look at "an eccentric who delves into the mystic," the birthday party on the stage of a haunted theatre. What kind of audience could believe this? The third act, however, might be rather good — the guests forcing a confession — with Emlyn Williams himself as the murderer. But does not this look as if the playwright were capitalizing on his former success?

Here is another item from the same catalogue:

Jane   Comedy. 3 Acts
S. N. Behrman, based on an original story by Somerset Maugham. 5 m., 4 f. Int. Mod. Cost. Produced by the Theatre Guild, Inc. "Jane" has to do with a dowdy, middle-aged wealthy widow from Liverpool who startles her smart London relations by marrying an impecunious architect 20 years her junior. The ambitious, calculating young artist transforms her into an attractive woman, à la Shaw's "Pygmalion." She becomes a reigning celebrity because of her disarming honesty and very lack of brilliance. But the social pace soon palls, and Jane yearns for the comforts of placid domesticity. She releases the architect so that he may realize his ambitions, and reforms a brash, restless, amorous newspaper tycoon into the pattern she really wants for a husband. Having had an exciting fling, tranquility seems most desirable to her. "A civilized comedy written with wit, grace, taste and intelligence." — Atkinson, *The New York Times*. "Nothing like it is to be seen on Broadway. Mr. Behrman himself has not written anything else half so good in many years. And Mr. Behrman's best is very good indeed." — Joseph Wood Krutch, *The Nation*. $1.00. (Royalty $50.00)

What is the significance of the names mentioned in this copy? Why should production by the Theatre Guild create interest for the play? Does this copy suggest the Cinderella story, or is there a difference? Is the synopsis credible or plausible?

One learns not to depend on catalogue accounts of plays as critical statements, but to use them in determining what plays might repay examination. Catalogue copy supplies a label for the kind of play offered — "comedy," "melodrama," "drama," etc. — a statement of the number of characters, the number and kinds of settings, a short résumé of the story, a little comment on its success, and the cost of book and royalty. It never tells enough about the play to enable one to select it without reading it.

The next source of information is reviews. These give the reviewers' impressions of the production and the actors and sometimes tell a little about the play. The main source of reviews of recent plays, a source to which every college library should subscribe, is the *New York Theatre Critics Reviews,* a periodical which contains all New York reviews of all plays produced in New York since 1940. In this periodical one can look up any play he is interested in and find out what impression it made on the New York critics when it was first produced. Parenthetically, this publication is a great help in writing publicity stories after a play is selected. The reviews, however, are someone's opinions of the plays, and, though these are often persuasive, they may not coincide with one's own opinion upon reading the play. The only way to find out whether a play is any good or not is to read or see it oneself.

The prestige factors surrounding a play tell something of its quality. A well-known playwright, a producer of established reputation such as Roger Stevens or Kermit Bloomgarden or the Theatre Guild, actors who are high enough in their profession to choose the roles they will play, the length of the New York run, the awards the play has earned — these factors have some, but not absolute, value in declaring its worth. On the other hand, fine playwrights backslide, producers are not infallible, and actors are often mistaken in their decisions. The play that runs in New York may have little to say to another community, while a play that fails in New York may be of the greatest interest elsewhere.

For evaluations of older plays, there are the considered opinions of such men as John Gassner, Barrett Clark, Allardyce Nicoll, Brooks Atkinson, John Mason Brown, Eric Bentley, and a host of others. Writing, usually, at a distance from opening night, they are able in their books and articles to assess the significance of the plays they discuss, often apart from the New York production.

Since one cannot wholly believe the catalogues or the reviews, one is thrown back upon his own growing ability to compare plays with other plays and with life.

What is expected of a play is that it be "moving," that it evoke some kind of emotion in the audience. A play that is built for suspense in any degree usually evokes hope or fear about the fate of some of the characters. Some recent plays have been designed to evoke pity or disgust. Some plays are built around the thinnest story thread, with no other intent than to keep the audience laughing. In considering a play for production, a director is swayed first by the kind and amount of feeling the play induces in himself and then by his estimate of whether the audience will feel as he does.

Then, for inexperienced actors, at least, it is often wise to ask if the play has a firm story thread: a character whose understandable need for something initiates and brings to a focus the events of the play, and whose fate the audience can care about. Such a story thread may be made up of overt actions, or it may be largely psychological, but it is one of the main bases of sustained interest and suspense.

Before making a decision, one should challenge the credibility of the play. Is it believable throughout? Whether the author is Gore Vidal writing realistic family comedy, Ionesco writing of the banalities of bourgeois marriage, Odets suggesting a panacea for the ills of labor, or Strindberg unveiling the wastelands of the human soul, one has the right to ask that the play fairly mirror that aspect of life which it undertakes to reveal. Could the story happen? Is it merely plausible? Is it so familiar as to be trite? Do the characters chosen and defined by the playwright react believably to the situations into which he has put them and to each other in terms of any logic the audience might understand? Do they behave as such characters might behave in those circumstances? Or are they stereotypes that have been seen in the movies or in other plays *ad nauseam*? Does the ending seem inevitable, in the light of the particular events that brought it about? Is the action integral to the characters in their situation, or is it mere unrelated activity designed to keep things lively? Are the steps in the action clear enough for comprehension? So clear that they creak? Above all, one must believe a play.

The young director in a community with scant theatre background will be dealing mainly with realistic plays rooted in the logic of everyday experience. Yet a work of art sets up its own logic, and, because of their inner consistency, one can believe in such widely different plays as *The Playboy of the Western World,* a folk comedy; *Romeo and Juliet,* a romantic tragedy; and *The Importance of Being Earnest,* a comedy of manners with elements of both satire and farce. In each of these plays, a specific situation drives certain individuals to actions one feels they would or must take under their particular conditions of place and time. The motives are credible human motives, and the actions are believable in terms of the conditions the playwright sets forth and in terms of the relationships of the characters.

The Playboy of the Western World deals with the need of the underdog to find respect. The protagonist is an Irish country lad who never had any advantages at all and who is therefore very willing to accept the admiration of the people of Mayo. They, on the other hand, are credible in their admiration of a supposed murderer, because of their craving for heroes and the dullness of their lives. Although the people of Dublin originally rejected the play as satire, Synge himself called it a simple comedy.

Romeo and Juliet is based on the universal desire of lovers to be together and upon the rash actions that young people take even today in pursuit of love. Some of the actions could be taken only by Elizabethans, and the director must amplify his imagination by research in Elizabethan social life in order to understand and believe in the play.

Wilde's play, *The Importance of Being Earnest*, satirizes the tastes and behavior of certain Victorian *élégants*, who attach importance to nothing but manners, and whose solution to problems must be a theatrical *deus ex machina*, for they are too shallow and flaccid to make their own adjustments.

The behavior of each of these protagonists is rooted in a social life that is partly an accurate picture of their world, and partly the playwright's notion of their world. But given a credible motive and a consistently conceived world, one can believe the imaginary crime of *The Playboy*, or the sleeping potion of *Romeo and Juliet*, or the weathered handbag of *The Importance of Being Earnest*.

Whether a play is romance, tragedy, satire, farce, or comedy depends on the purpose of the playwright, and one can hardly be sure what this is unless he knows something of both the playwright and the people he writes about. The director must study these matters faithfully, for in terms of the aesthetic triangle, his artistic purpose cannot diverge very far from that of the playwright or the result is certain to be confusion.

The playwright's intent may be simply to invoke pity, terror, or laughter. But sometimes he wishes to stimulate thought. In this case the play is said to have a theme, which can be stated in a simple declarative sentence of a philosophical, social, or ethical nature. In a skillfully written play, the theme is made clear through the action. Instead of preaching, a playwright presents evidence in the characters and their actions, which are arranged so persuasively that they oblige the audience to draw the playwright's conclusions. Like the pulpit, like the table around which the advertising campaign is planned, the stage presents its message through the feelings, not through logical debate.

In considering a play for production, one wants to be sure that the meaning of the play does not deny his own ethical values, for in the non-commercial theatre the director is not only held responsible, but also, in a sense, is responsible for the thoughts he promulgates through a play.

One person's scruples may not be the same as another's, of course. Certain directors in certain situations may feel it is un-important if a play oversimplifies human problems or presents human life as mean or hopeless. One very popular play much produced in the non-commercial theatre, for example, is *Harvey*, in which the amusing protagonist refused to cope with real life, preferring to remain in a drunken fantasy. Many community theatres have laughed over *Light Up The Sky*, built on the self-ishness and fear of certain commercial theatre people, and even over *The Torch Bearers*, which ridicules the ineptitudes of community theatre people. High school teachers unaccountably select plays in which school teachers are ridiculed. *The Little Foxes*, with its pessimistic point of view, has been a community theatre staple.

A play creates a world pervaded by the playwright's view-point, and is subtly compelling because it presents this viewpoint in terms of the evidence of eyes and ears. No one would assert that the effect of a single play is to impress that viewpoint im-mediately upon the belief and behavior of a whole audience. Yet the cumulative effect of many impacts of life, epitomized in literature and the theatre, upon thought and behavior cannot be denied. Without committing himself to "sweetness and light," the director must recognize the potential effect of the plays he produces. Insofar as he selects the program, he cannot think of himself as a mere mouthpiece.

In the non-commercial theatre, the selection of the play is determined partly by its function of training the participants. Professional theatre people receive money as payment for their labors; amateurs work only for some kind of personal satisfaction. The play can do more for them than simply add to their theatre skills; it can give them some insight into humanity. It can exercise their imaginations a little beyond the needs of their everyday life and, perhaps, extend their appreciation of and joy in life.

Whether or not the play has a theme, a few questions may be asked about its significance. Does it have anything important to say? Does it illuminate human relationships? Does it increase the sum of human understanding and pity? Is it interesting or challenging in its point of view? Is it timely? Merely timely? Does it appeal to the spirit or the appetites? Does it leave a final impression that there is a marvelous power in human beings, or a feeling that life is trivial or sordid and that there is no hope for the human race?

Is the laughter in any sense a comment on human foibles, or is it evoked by cheap ridiculous surprises or by jibes at things that are fundamentally admirable? There is no need to be snobbish about comedy as mere entertainment, for laughter, in itself is a blessing. But good comedy has a cleansing effect on the audience. Indeed, the classic notion of comedy is that it purges vice and folly through laughter.

The answers to these questions determine the significance of the play and indicate what final impression it may leave with the audience.

One other criterion might be considered in the selection of a play — the language in which it is written. In judging the language of a play, however, one comes up against problems, since the play is written in dialogue, the language proper to the characters in their various situations. Often, therefore, it is not grammatical, often it is slangy, even profane. In *Candida,* for example, Shaw uses some illiterate Cockney in the lines of Burgess, although the other characters speak in a language that reflects their more ample education. Eugene O'Neill's *The Hairy Ape* is written in the language of a brutal stoker of a ship's boiler. Maxwell Anderson uses both profane and obscene language to give flavor to Trock's personality in *Winterset,* and yet he has been criticised for the unreality of the poetic dialogue in this play. Some of the most boring dialogue ever written is the perfectly correct English of *Ah, Wilderness!* Shakespeare's blank verse is often also great dialogue, but George Henry Boker's blank verse in *Francesca da Rimini* is seldom either poetry or dialogue, though it is good English.

If, then, good English does not necessarily make good dialogue, what qualities should one look for? Perhaps the first essential is that dialogue should seem to be authentic — that is, proper to the person speaking, and only to him. Next, dialogue should be to the point, as terse as possible under the circumstances of the scene, not merely pretty or redundant for the sake of the sound. It should be from heart to heart, even when the matter is intellectual. It should be fresh, not banal, unless the banalities are the idiom of the character, e.g., Miss Prism in *The Importance of Being Earnest* or Amanda in *The Glass Menagerie.* The director must try to refine his critical faculties by listening to all kinds of people and by varied reading, in order to distinguish between the stupidities and illiteracies proper to the character and those inadvertently introduced by the author.

Raising Standards

It makes sense to enter any job with the notion of staying in it the rest of one's life. This attitude gives one a deep interest in making it exactly the job one would like it to be. It makes one strive for fuller and more catholic audiences, well-disciplined and skilled actors, artistic and dependable crews, and the best theatre plant that can possibly be secured in the course of time. It is the director's function to bring about this desirable situation as fully as he can. And one of the strongest means of improving the situation is through the selection of plays that increase the range of the audience's taste, increase the skills and knowledge of the participants, and utilize the available facilities to the point of strain.

Perhaps the first need is for a varied program to broaden the taste of the audience and the appreciation and skills of the participants. Even one or two plays a year can help, if one plans ahead. In the course of a four-year period of two-play seasons, one might present the first year a light modern comedy and a classical tragedy; the second year a murder-mystery (there are some excellent ones) and a comedy of Shakespeare; the third year a Restoration comedy and a modern drama; and finally, a nineteenth-century melodrama and a play that illustrates one of the non-realistic styles — such as *The Skin of Our Teeth* or *The Ghost Sonata* or *The Adding Machine*. A plan such as this gives a purposeful variety to a meager yearly schedule and extends the experience of everyone concerned, director, participants, and audience.

A four-play season can be more varied, with some froth and some serious experiment each year. One might include annually a new play, with the idea that the best training for a director is the challenge of making an imperfect script into an audience-worthy play. One might include something definitely *avant-garde* in either content or staging. Plays by Brecht, Koestler, Genet, or Ionesco are almost out of the question for an audience that sees no more than two locally produced plays a year. In a four-play season one might also include a musical (these are very expensive because of high royalty, large casts with costumes, and generally several sets, but are so popular that prices can be raised to meet the greater cost.)

Planning a long-range program, even though tentatively, gives a sense of purpose beyond the particular play of the moment. It serves the end of training both participants and audience, and it lends the spice of variety to the work.

By now it must be fairly clear that a great theatre leader like Margo Jones was probably holding something back when she said one selects a play because he loves it. Obviously thought and judgment are needed in selecting plays, not mere inspiration. Nor is this judgment acquired over night; it develops over a lifetime. One comes to feel very wary of spreading low standards of acting, production, even thinking, through selecting trivial plays. Because the director loves the theatre, he wants it to foster the morale and the intellectual growth of the people he works for, and to stand for strength, honesty, and courage in the entertainment of the public.

Assignments

1. List ten anthologies of modern plays.
2. Use publishers' catalogues and list six to ten plays you might consider in planning a four-play season.
3. Summarize what you can find about these plays by reading accounts of them in *Theatre Critics Reviews* and *Best Plays*.
4. What conditions of Elizabethan life must you understand in order to believe all that happens in *Romeo and Juliet?* List several books that would help you to gain this information.
5. Upon what grounds could you believe in the *dénouement* of *The Importance of Being Earnest?*
6. State in one declarative sentence the *theme* of *The Glass Menagerie,* or justify your conviction that the play has no theme.
7. Which of the plays in your list from Question 2 seems to have "significance"? Upon what do you base your opinion?

8. Use the questions on page 47 and discuss the "significance" of *Romeo and Juliet*. Of *The Importance of Being Earnest*. Of *The Glass Menagerie*.

Reading List

Bentley, Eric. *The Playwright as Thinker*. New York: Meridian Books, 1946.

Clark, William Smith II. *Chief Patterns of World Drama*. Boston: Houghton, Mifflin, 1946.

Gallaway, Marian. *Constructing a Play*. Englewood Cliffs, N. J.: Prentice-Hall, 1950.

Gassner, John. *A Treasury of the Theatre*. (2 Vols.) New York: Simon and Schuster, Vol. I, 1935, Vol. II, revised, 1960.

Mantle, Burns (ed.). *Best Plays* and The Yearbook of the Drama in America. New York: Dodd, Mead, published annually 1909-1961. (Now edited by Louis Kronenberger.)

———. *New York Theatre Critics Reviews*. New York: Dodd, Mead, 1940-1962.

Rowe, Kenneth. *A Theatre in Your Head*. New York: Funk and Wagnalls, 1960.

Steinberg, M. W. *Aspects of Modern Drama*. New York: Henry Holt, 1960.

Whiting, Frank M. *Introduction to the Theatre*. New York: Harper and Bros., revised edition, 1961.

Chapter 4

Starting the Promptbook

Once the director selects a play, he gives it long and careful study before commencing work with the actors. The apprentice director has usually seen something of rehearsals and may have marveled that the director knew what effect he wanted and how to get it. What the apprentice has never seen is the painstaking private work of analysis and imagination that must always be done if the play is to be consistently moving — and complete — on opening night. Largely because he does not know anything about this part of the job, the apprentice tends to find it difficult and even to reject it, until his own experience shows him the need for careful planning. This chapter, therefore, is designed to give him an overview of the problems he will have to solve before going into rehearsal.

Everyone studies somewhat differently, of course, and each play requires some modification of basic procedure. If the play deals with familiar material or is impeccably constructed, or if one is highly experienced, he can do some of the planning in his head. However, for a beginner, it is wise to commit plans to paper. A written plan enables one to avoid inconsistencies and to make careful preparation for all the minutiae of the production. A plan saves a great deal of time in rehearsals. It is also a record of instructions to cast and staff, which avoids confusion and argument.

The written plan of a production is called a promptbook. It consists of the whole text of the play, plus all of the director's notes regarding the entire production.

When to Start the Promptbook

Every theatre faces the date when the curtain must rise for an audience, and there is probably not a director who does not say at this time to anyone who will listen, "If we only had another week!" Even if one has a whole semester or a whole summer to prepare a play for rehearsal, he probably feels this. But many directors must prepare the second play of the season while rehearsing the first and at the same time discharging the other responsibilities of a faculty member and a member of the community. Therefore it is vital to find ways of saving time without skimping on quality.

A careful plan of the whole organization of the production enables one to work efficiently at every step of the process of producing a play. It should be started as soon as possible after the decision has been made to produce the play, and it should be relatively complete before tryouts are called. Indeed, some directors, facing a difficult play or one to which they attach great importance, begin to study the play many months before they go into rehearsal.

The sooner one has a promptbook, the sooner he can begin to pigeonhole the many minor details that occur to him as he reads the play again and again to assimilate it and formulate his own point of view toward it. He may note a need for music or special lighting at certain points; he may have a clear image of some detail of scenery or costume that will affect the playing of a scene; he may see a way to save rehearsal time. As a matter of fact, although one cannot force the assimilation of a play, he can often save time by attacking specific technical problems on each of several readings. Merely to note the problems sometimes brings into focus things that help one to understand the play as a whole.

Perhaps it should be said at once that while one tries to make the plan as complete as possible, it must never be thought of as unalterable. Since one's knowledge of the play grows as he works with the actors, since the understanding of the other workers also throws light upon it, and since circumstances sometimes prevent carrying out parts of the plan exactly as it was conceived, changes inevitably occur. The plan must remain flexible to the last possible moment. Thus, although for convenience one starts the promptbook as early as possible, it is not complete until the performance puts the seal on what was actually done by every member of the staff and cast.

The Form of the Promptbook

Directors use any form for their promptbooks that is convenient for them. One requisite, often ignored, is that the promptbook be easily read by the director in rehearsal, by the prompter during the line-learning stage, by all of the crew heads who find their agenda and cues in it, and by the stage manager, who directs the performance from it.

There are several common forms for promptbooks. One may simply use the printed acting edition. Although this saves time in the beginning, it has one insuperable disadvantage: as too much print is crowded on each page, the margins are hardly wide enough for even technical directions to be written in; and by the time a few explanatory notes have been added, the page is unintelligibly messy.

Some directors buy two copies of the script for themselves and paste each sheet on an 8½ by 11 (typewriter-size) sheet, which

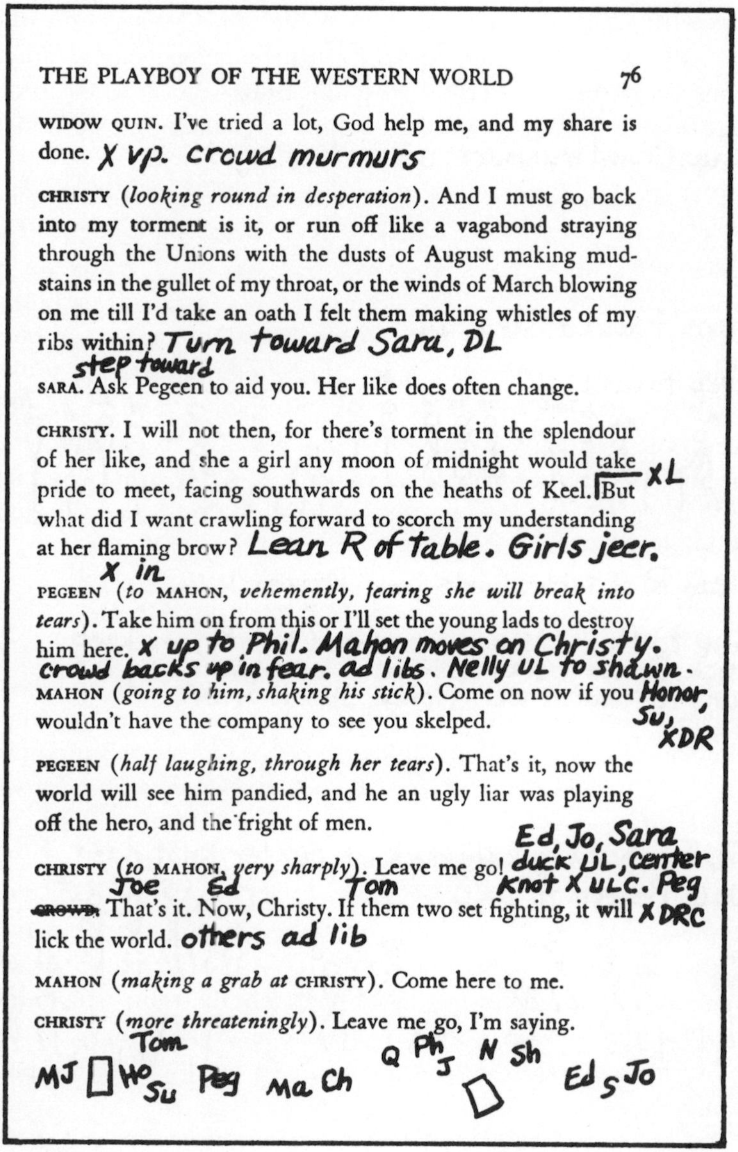

THE PLAYBOY OF THE WESTERN WORLD   76

WIDOW QUIN. I've tried a lot, God help me, and my share is done. *X vp. crowd murmurs*

CHRISTY (*looking round in desperation*). And I must go back into my torment is it, or run off like a vagabond straying through the Unions with the dusts of August making mud-stains in the gullet of my throat, or the winds of March blowing on me till I'd take an oath I felt them making whistles of my ribs within? *Turn toward Sara, DL*
step toward
SARA. Ask Pegeen to aid you. Her like does often change.

CHRISTY. I will not then, for there's torment in the splendour of her like, and she a girl any moon of midnight would take pride to meet, facing southwards on the heaths of Keel. But *XL* what did I want crawling forward to scorch my understanding at her flaming brow? *Lean R of table. Girls jeer.*
X in
PEGEEN (*to MAHON, vehemently, fearing she will break into tears*). Take him on from this or I'll set the young lads to destroy him here. *X up to Phil. Mahon moves on Christy. Crowd backs up in fear. ad libs. Nelly UL to shawn.*
MAHON (*going to him, shaking his stick*). Come on now if you *Honor,* wouldn't have the company to see you skelped. *Su,*
XDR

PEGEEN (*half laughing, through her tears*). That's it, now the world will see him pandied, and he an ugly liar was playing off the hero, and the fright of men. *Ed, Jo, Sara*

CHRISTY (*to MAHON, very sharply*). Leave me go! *duck UL, center*
Joe   Ed   Tom   Knot X ULC. Peg
CROWD. That's it. Now, Christy. If them two set fighting, it will *X DRC* lick the world. *others ad lib*

MAHON (*making a grab at CHRISTY*). Come here to me.

CHRISTY (*more threateningly*). Leave me go, I'm saying.
Tom
MJ ☐ Wo Su   Peg   Ma Ch   Q Ph J   N Sh ☐   Ed s Jo

Fig. 1.   Promptbook from Printed Page

① x up. Crowd murmurs: serves him right.

② Turn toward Sara, DL

③ Step toward

④ x L

⑤ Lean R of table. Girls jeer. Pegeen x in

⑥ x up to Philly. Mahon moves on Christy, shaking stick. Crowd backs up in fear. ad libs. Nelly runs to Shawn UL. Honor, Susan x DR

⑦ Ed, Joe, Sara quickly duck UL, center knot dart ULC, Pegeen to DRC

Fig. 2A.   Interleaf

QUIN
I've tried a lot, God help me, and my
share is done. ①

Looking around in
desperation

CHRISTY
And I must go back into my torment, is it,
or run off like a vagabond straying through
the Unions with the dusts of August making
mudstains in the gullet of my throat, or the
winds of March blowing on me till I'd take
an oath I felt them making whistles of my
ribs within? ②

SARA
③ Ask Pegeen to aid you. He like does often
change.

CHRISTY
I will not then, for there's torment in the
splendor of her like, and she a girl any
moon of midnight would take pride to meet,
facing southwards on the heaths of keel.
④ But what did I want crawling forward to
scorch my understanding at her flaming brow? ⑤

To Mahon, vehement-
ly, fearing she will
break into tears

PEGEEN
Take him on from this or I'll set the young
lads to destroy him here. ⑥

going to him
shaking his stick

MAHON
Come on now if you wouldn't have the company
to see you skelped.

Half laughing thru
her tears

PEGEEN
That's it, now the world will see him pandied,
and he an ugly liar was playing off the hero,
and the fright of men.

To Mahon, very
sharply

CHRISTY
Leave me go! ⑦

CROWD
That's it. Now, Christy. If them two set
fighting, it will lick the world.

Making a grab at
Christy

MAHON
Come here to me.

more threatening

CHRISTY
Leave me go, I'm saying.

Fig. 2B.   Typed Promptbook

they then put into a spring binder. To save money, a single copy may be purchased and pasted on a page the middle of which has been cut out, so that both sides of the page of script can be seen. Either of these plans gives wide margins and, if an interleaf is also used, may be satisfactory, unless the play is very difficult to interpret, or unless there is a crowd scene or a great deal of stage business.

The professional director, dealing with new plays, usually has a typed copy, which becomes very messy as the playwright revises during rehearsals, and usually has to be retyped two or three times in order to be fit to study during the road tour. Although few changes are made in the dialogue of a play after it has been professionally produced, there are many advantages to using a typed promptbook. It is especially convenient to type only the dialogue, double spaced and with wide margins, and to place between each page an interleaf on which to write stage business and technical directions. With this form, if there are many changes of stage business in a scene, it is easy to replace the untidy interleaf with a new, clearly written one, while the prompter's page remains neat.

A director who can type may find it advantageous to type the promptbook himself, because, in typing the script (1) he must read the script with complete accuracy at an early stage of his study; (2) he finds many problem passages as he types that he might hurry over in simply reading; and (3) he tends to memorize key passages at least well enough to quote from them in support of his interpretation.

The Contents of the Promptbook

By the time rehearsals start the promptbook will contain the whole plan. It begins with the title page containing the name of the play and the author, the publisher, cost of royalty, and place and date of production. The second page contains a list of the characters and scenes as they will appear in the program. Later, time will be saved if there are half a dozen copies of this page, one for the record, two or three for casting purposes, a couple for the press, and one for the printer of the program. The next pages may be notes on the history of the play and the biography of the author.

Early in the planning stage one begins to think about the setting. Since the plans for this come about as a result of studying the play, they cannot go into the promptbook at once, but, by the time rehearsals start, the book should contain a ground plan drawn to scale and, if possible, a color sketch of the set, so that the actors will be able to work with a clear notion of the space they play in. Three extra copies of the ground plan are needed, for the stage manager, the property master, and the

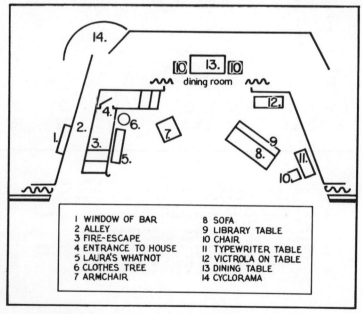

Fig. 3.   Ground Plan—The Glass Menagerie

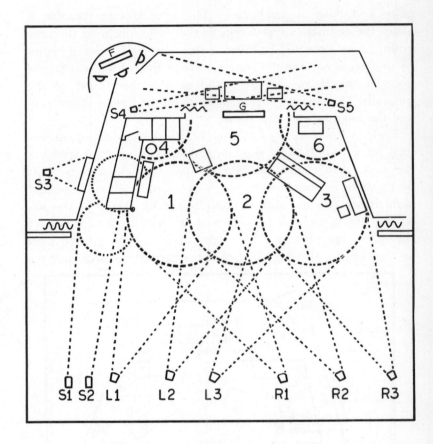

A. L and R 1,2,3 are left and right beam Lekolites, daylight
blue gelatin in left, straw in right instruments.
B. L and R 4,5,6 are left and right bridge spotlights,
daylight blue and straw as above. 400 w.
C. S1, S2 are special spots lighting fire escape and alley.
500 w. 1 daylight, 1 pink.
D. S3 is a special projection to indicate changing
colored light in bar across alley.
E. S4, S5 are special 400 w. spots to light dining room area.
F. 3 floodlights, 2 daylight, 1 dark blue and a 6 foot strip
(3 circuits; red, blue, green) to light cyclorama.
G. 6 foot strip (red, blue, green) above dining room arch
to blend S4 and S5.

Fig. 4. Light Plot—The Glass Menagerie

lighting operator. In the text, when one is sure what is needed, light cues can be underlined in colored pencil and sound cues in pencil of another color, so that the heads of these crews can go to the promptbook and find out exactly what is expected of them. If there are many cues, it is best to give the light and sound men their own full copies of the play.

The property plot grows as rehearsals progress. Usually, along with the diagram of the set, the property plot in the acting edition may be disregarded, for each production will set up property requirements of its own. By dress rehearsal time, the property plot includes a scene by scene list of all furniture and decoration on the stage and everything carried on by the actors. The plot must clearly show where each item is to be placed, and it should include a diagram of any table top, drawer, or other piece of furniture that is crowded or in any way unusually arranged, so that the actors will find their properties where they have pantomimed finding them during rehearsals. The property plot should also include a list of all articles to be struck (removed from the stage) at the end of each scene.

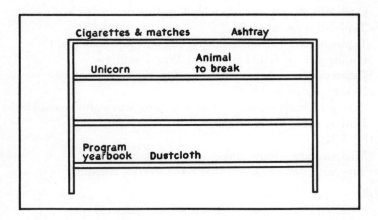

Fig. 5. Laura's Whatnot

Furniture
Whatnot DR
Armchair RC
Daybed LC
Table above daybed
Table UL
Typewriter table DL
Chair DL
Dining room table UC in alcove
3 Dining room chairs UC in alcove
Coatrack UR

1-1 and 1-2
Telephone on table above daybed
Amanda's red book and pencil R of phone
Old-fashioned phonograph, lid open, on table UL
6 old records L of phonograph
"Scores" of small glass animals glued on whatnot shelves. One, not glued, is broken each night
1 small glass unicorn (horn is broken each night)
Yearbook on bottom shelf of whatnot
Program, "Pirates of Penzance" inside (top side) of yearbook
Dustcloth inconspicuously folded upstage of yearbook
Typewriter on table DL
Typing charts upstage beside typewriter (torn each night)
Photograph of father in World War I uniform
Cigarettes, matches, ashtray on top shelf of whatnot
Newspaper on porch
Dining table set for three (plates, glasses, knives, forks, napkins)
Plate of sliced bread on table
OFF UR
Medium large empty tray — Amanda
Tray with three cups of coffee on saucers — Amanda

1-3
Strike typewriter, charts, Amanda's hat, purse, gloves.
Open portieres
Tom's coat and muffler on coatrack

THE GLASS MENAGERIE
Costume Plot

	PROLOG (EVE)	SC. 1 (EVE)	SC. 2 (NOON)	SC. 3 (NIGHT)	SC. 4 (MORN)
TOM	Coat, hat of mercht sailor navy trous.	Worn gray sleeveless sweater, lt. gray shirt		Repeat I O'coat with torn sleeve lining (Sleeve is ripped out each night)	Repeat I
AMANDA		Rose + tan figured housedress, old, frilled apron	Old beige plush coat, ratty fur collar, cloche hat, big beat purse, old gloves	Repeat I without apron THEN old (man's) bathrobe	
LAURA		Lt. gray wool, wht. collar faded blue sweater	Soft, violet housecoat	Repeat I without sweater	Nightgown, repeat housecoat

If the play calls for sound effects, the promptbook should include a list of the effects needed, with cues underlined and the effect described on the interleaf. If there are many sound effects, the sound operator must be present at a good many rehearsals because cueing in sound is difficult for both operator and actors.

Two copies of the costume plot are needed, the second copy for the use of the crew head. This plot should state what each actor wears in each scene, with a note of any change within a scene, in case quick change is needed.

A copy of the budget may go into the promptbook, later to be followed by a financial report as a check against the accuracy of the original estimates. If the play contains dialect or archaic words, a glossary may be needed. The tentative rehearsal schedule will go into the book until it is replaced by the one agreed upon by the company. The promptbook will be completed at performance time by clipping in the program.

Planning the Rehearsal Schedule

The rehearsal schedule must be tentatively planned to save the maximum time for the maximum number of actors. From tryouts to opening night there must be enough rehearsals to do the play well — twenty-four or more for an easy play, thirty or more for a difficult one. Since the companies are not professional, they must fulfill essential academic, business, and social commitments along with their rehearsals. They must also get extra sleep, for rehearsal makes terrific demands on the actors' energy, and at performance time one of the first requirements of good projection is a superabundance of vitality. It is possible to grind out a play with good college actors in three weeks, but the play will be better and the actors healthier and happier if they have five or six.

(All rehearsals at 7:15 on stage unless otherwise noted)

FIRST WEEK
1 Act I   Interp and Block
2 Act I   Interp and Block
3 Act II   Interp and Block
4 Act II   Interp and Block
5 Act III Interp and Block

SECOND WEEK
6 Whole Play, Continuity
7 Act I   Lines and Interp
8 Act II   Lines and Interp
9 Act III Lines and Interp
10 Whole Play, Continuity

THIRD WEEK
11 Act I   Detail
12 Act II   Detail
13 Act III Detail
14 Act I   Detail
15 Act II   Detail
16 Act III Detail
17 Whole Play, Continuity

FOURTH WEEK
18 Act I   Detail and Tech
19 Act II   Detail and Tech
20 Act III Detail and Tech
21 Whole Play, Pace III
22 Whole Play, Pace II
23 Whole Play, Pace I

FIFTH WEEK
24 Whole Play, Full Technical Rehearsal
25 Whole Play, Dress Rehearsal
26 Whole Play, Dress Rehearsal
27 Whole Play, Dress Rehearsal
28 Performance, Check in at 6:30

The length of the rehearsal period varies, of course, according to the time and energy of the participants. A comfortable rehearsal period for college or community theatre is three to three and one-half hours, with additional time scheduled for the development of special skills such as dancing or fencing. It is wise to schedule technical rehearsals early enough and frequently enough that they need not keep the company past midnight for three or four nights just before the play opens. Afternoon rehearsals are seldom satisfactory in the non-commercial theatre for three reasons. First, the actors arrive rushed and tired from work or classes and are not in a good psychological state to concentrate on the difficult job of commanding their emotions. Second, not enough time is available between the job or last class and supper, and hunger is a great stealer of energy. Third, it is bad for morale to sandwich rehearsals between other things instead of giving it special importance. Still, there are some situations, particularly in high schools, where afternoon rehearsals are unavoidable, and they must be utilized.

Rehearsals generally fall into four periods: an initial period of basic interpretation and blocking — that is, plotting the physical actions that reveal relationships; a period of deepening the actors' and the director's understanding of characters and relationships; a period of synthesis that brings the audience into the computations; and a final period that synchronizes the actors with the technical aspects of the production and returns the play to the actors.

Directors plan their rehearsal schedules and objectives in any number of ways. Many directors believe that rehearsals should start with a round table reading of the whole play, to give the company one consistent feeling of what the play is to do. Usually at these rehearsals the actors themselves read. Sometimes a director with a very strong feeling of the quality of the play reads to the company, running the risk of the actors imitating instead of creating. If the material is quite foreign to the actors, it may be necessary for the director to give them its flavor. Gorchakov reports, in *Stanislavsky Directs,* that even Stanislavsky had to show the Moscow Art Theatre company how to play French satire.

Some directors believe that actors gain most by studying for a long time around a table and that blocking should not be done until late in the rehearsal period. But when a company is made up largely of actors who are too young to understand the play without a great deal of help, and too inexperienced in theatre to be able to express what they do understand, time seems to be saved by teaching meaning and technique concomitantly.

There is also difference of opinion as to when the actors should memorize. This matter, too, must be settled in terms of the actors involved. Professionals usually know their lines by the end of the first week — sometimes even before the first rehearsal. For the beginner, however, it seems advisable not to memorize before he understands the play, lest he become glib, or develop speech patterns that are meaningless and hard to eradicate. As a matter of fact, if an actor rehearses with proper concentration, he will find that he has almost memorized his lines by about the third rehearsal of a scene. Since many actors have not acquired this ability to concentrate, it may be desirable to hold a series of "line" rehearsals in the second week. These should not be mere line rehearsals, for the actor should never walk through a scene without the full emotional pattern, at least as completely as he has learned it to date. At "line" rehearsals, the actor's memory usually fails when his concentration lapses or when his understanding is incomplete. The best way to help him memorize is to help him complete his understanding of and emotional involvement in the scene.

Actors should not be encouraged to learn lines by murmuring the words to themselves. They should be urged to seek their partners when they are offstage during rehearsal and to play the scene over together several times. In this way they not only save time, but they become better acquainted and stimulate each other.

There is great memorizing value in saving a little time at the end of each rehearsal to repeat what was done during the evening.

In any case, for non-professional actors a date must be set as the last moment when books are to be used, and discipline must be unswerving on this point, however badly the rehearsal may limp on this date. An actor who cannot learn his lines in ten days or two weeks will probably never be of much value to the play, and perhaps should be replaced.

Another point that bears discussion before the schedule is formulated is the number and times of continuity rehearsals. Since complete understanding of a scene comes about through ever more minute analysis, hundreds of suggestions, and drill to get each point done accurately, the actor risks thinking of the play in fragments. It is therefore necessary to give him some rehearsals in which he will play uninterruptedly, so that he can synthesize what he has learned so far. How many of these rehearsals are needed depends on how the director works as well as on the nature of the company. At least one continuity rehearsal is needed after each block of objectives is accomplished.

Thus a director adapts his method to the task at hand, and even with a plan such as that suggested here, he may in general adhere to the schedule, while at the same time dealing differently with certain scenes or certain actors.

When a play is broken into many small scenes, sometimes a few actors must work for a long time while the rest of the company waits, unless rehearsals are planned very closely. It is generally possible to group the scenes in such a way that certain actors may stay away from certain rehearsals, and thus use the actors' time more economically. One begins by making a chart of the actors needed in each scene.

SCENES IN WHICH CHARACTERS APPEAR

	I.1	I.2	I.3	I.4	I.5	II.1	II.2	II.3	II.4	II.5	III.1	III.2	III.3	III.4	III.5	IV.1	IV.2	IV.3	IV.5	V.1	V.2	V.3
pp	8+	3+	4+	4	7	1	7+	3	7	3+	6	4+	5+	1+	10	4+	1+	2+	3+	2	2	9
Prologue	x																					
Sampson	x																					
Gregory	x																					
Balthasar				x																		
Abram	x																					
Benvolio	x	x		x	x	x			x		x											
Tybalt	x				x						x											
Officers	x										x											
Paris	x	x												x		x			x			x
Capulet	x	x			x						x			x	x		x		x			x
Lady Cap.	x		x		x						x			x	x		x	x	x			x
Montague	x										x											x
Lady Mont.	x																					
Escalus, Pr.	x										x											x
Attendants	x										x											
Romeo	x	x		x	x	x	x	x	x	x	x		x		x					x		x
Nurse			x		x				x	x		x	x		x		x	x	x			
Juliet			x		x		x			x		x			x	x	x	x				x
Mercutio				x		x			x		x											
Potpan					x																	
Friar Lawrence								x		x			x			x			x		x	x
Friar John																					x	
Peter									x										x			
Apothecary																				x		
Danc., Mus.					x														x			

With this chart, the director can divide rehearsals into groups of scenes involving only certain actors. He can also tell what doubling is possible among the minor roles.

GROUP A.　Romeo, Benvolio, Mercutio, Tybalt

SCENE	NO. PAGES
I-1	4
I-2	3
I-4	4
II-1	1
II-4	7
III-1	6

Total 25 pp.

GROUP B.　Juliet, Nurse, Capulet, Lady Capulet, Paris

SCENE	NO. PAGES
I-2	$1\frac{1}{2}$
I-3	$4\frac{1}{2}$
II-5	$3\frac{1}{2}$
III-2	$4\frac{1}{2}$
III-4	$1\frac{1}{2}$
III-5	7
IV-2	$1\frac{1}{2}$
IV-3	$2\frac{1}{2}$

Total $26\frac{1}{2}$ pp.

GROUP C.　Friar Lawrence, Friar John, Romeo, Juliet, Nurse, Paris, Apothecary, Balthasar

SCENE	NO. PAGES
II-3	3
III-3	$5\frac{1}{2}$
IV-1	$4\frac{1}{2}$
V-1	$3\frac{1}{2}$
V-2	$1\frac{1}{2}$
V-3	9

Total 27 pp.

GROUP D. Romeo and Juliet

SCENE	NO. PAGES
I-5	5
II-2	7½
III-5	2½

Total 15 pp.

GROUP E. Whole Company

SCENE	NO. PAGES
I-1	8½
I-5	7
III-1	½
V-3 (Not Lady M)	½

Total 16½ pp.

This is dull work, but it pays off, for with the following schedule even Romeo gets an occasional night off.

ROMEO AND JULIET
Rehearsal Schedule

1 Group A   Interp and Block
2 Group A, D   Interp and Block
3 Group B   Interp and Block
4 Group B and D   Interp and Block
5 Group C and D   Interp and Block
6 Group C   Interp and Block
7 Group B   Interp
8 Group E and A   Interp and Block
9 Group C and E   Interp
10 Whole Play   Continuity
11 Acts I, II, and III-1   Lines and Continuity
12 Acts III, IV, V   Lines and Continuity
13 Whole Play   Continuity
14 Groups C and D   Detail (Practice costumes)
15 Groups A and D   Detail   ”   ”

16   Group B   Detail   "   "
17   Group E   Detail
18   Whole Play   Continuity
19   Group C and D   Detail
20   Group A and D   Detail
21   Group B   Detail
22   Group E   Detail
23   Whole Play   Pace
24   Acts I, II, III-1   Detail
25   Acts III, IV, V   Detail
26   Whole Play   Spot scenes
27   Whole Play   Spot scenes
28   Whole Play   Spot scenes
29   Technical Rehearsal
30   Technical Rehearsal
31   Dress Rehearsal   (Makeup, except beards)
32   Dress Rehearsal   (Only beards)
33   Dress Rehearsal   (Only beards)
34   Dress Rehearsal   (Makeup)
35, 36   Performance
37   Rehearsal
38-43   Performance

There are two or three cautions in using this procedure. First, there must be a night's work in each group. Scenes that total twenty-five pages or so are enough to keep the evening interesting, as a rule. Second, all transitions must be thoroughly rehearsed by scheduling a good many run-throughs at which the whole company must be present. And finally, every group must be thoroughly rehearsed, so that there will not be one weak against one strong scene.

When the schedule is approved by everyone who will use it, that is, at the first rehearsal or last tryout, a copy should be given to every actor and every crew head.

At last one may get to work again on the script. But by the time one has tentatively worked out all these organizational problems, he knows a great deal more about the play.

Assignments

1. Write an outline history of *The Playboy of the Western World,* using Greene and Stephen's life of Synge and either Robinson's or Fay's account of the Abbey Theatre.
2. Find quotations from reviews that could be used in publicizing *The Glass Menagerie.* Don't forget the Chicago papers.
3. Work up a bibliography of half a dozen items that would help you to design settings, costumes, and properties for *The Importance of Being Earnest.* What portrait painters would help? Does this research make the play more credible or interesting to you?
4. List all the sound effects needed in The Glass Menagerie. Where would you get them?
5. What composers would be appropriate for Algy's opening selection (offstage) in *Earnest?* What instruments would be suitable for the dance orchestra in *Romeo and Juliet,* Act I, Sc. 5?
6. Find a history of dance and a history of fencing that would help you to direct *Romeo and Juliet.*
7. Formulate a rehearsal schedule for *The Importance of Being Earnest* that solves the following problems:
    (*a*)   The actor who plays Algernon has ROTC drill every Tuesday night.
    (*b*)   The actress who plays Miss Prism belongs to a dinner club that meets on Thursdays.
    (*c*)   The actress who plays Gwendolyn must be a wedding attendant on the third Monday.
    n.b.   All of these actors agree to be present at every rehearsal during the last week of the schedule.
8. Make a tentative property plot for *The Glass Menagerie,* Scene 7.
9. Note all quick changes of costume in *The Glass Menagerie,* and finish the costume plot started in the text.
10. List all light changes between Amanda's last speech in Scene 3 of *The Glass Menagerie* and Tom's "I'll rise — but I won't shine." Underline the cues in red pencil. Underline all sound cues in this passage in blue pencil. Describe each effect in the margin.

11. List all the items for which you would expect to spend money on *The Glass Menagerie*.
12. Select a play and begin a promptbook that will be your major project for the course.

Reading List

Baker, George Pierce. *Dramatic Technique*. Boston: Houghton, Mifflin, 1919, pp. 474 ff.

Fay, William George. *The Fays of the Abbey Theatre*. New York: Harcourt, Brace, 1935.

Greene, David H. and Edward M. Stephens. *J. M. Synge*. New York: Macmillan, 1959.

Robinson, Lennox. *Ireland's Abbey Theatre*. London: Sidgwick and Jackson, 1951.

Rowe, Kenneth. *Op. cit.*, Chapter 3.

PART TWO

Absorbing the Play

Chapter 5

Analyzing the Play

With most of the superficial problems evident and to some extent solved, the director undertakes to master the inner content of the play, so that his aesthetic intent may become as nearly as possible identical with that of the playwright. This is the most difficult and also the most essential part of the director's work.

No one would try to conduct a symphony orchestra without knowing not only what the various instruments could do, but also a great deal about the symphony as a musical form, the relation of its parts, and the effect of the whole. A play, because of its verbal nature, is even more difficult, for words have specific values only in terms of when and how they are said, and by whom. Often they stand for thoughts or feelings that the dictionary does not note, or for the very opposite of the dictionary meaning. Besides, the words of a play, while revealing the speaker, also have a two-way effect, one upon the listener on the stage and quite another on the listener in the auditorium.

A clear, complete understanding of a play takes time. It is arrived at by a variety of means. Sometimes the director's own experience illuminates the play. Sometimes by a process of as-

similation he wakes up one morning with understanding. But
. if these fail and he needs help, he settles down to analysis. However sluggard the spirit, it is always possible to force the mind
to concentrate.

The more definite the questions he can ask from the start,
the more quickly he can arrive at the playwright's intent and
muster his particular skills to complete the externalization. It
is pointless to attempt to put something on the stage until one
can do so purposefully.

One learns about the script by learning the words that the
playwright has written. But the audience in the theatre are not
reading words at all. True, they are sometimes *hearing* words,
but they are also hearing tones of the actors' voices, and seeing,
and inferring, and, at a well-produced play, they are often waiting, with muscles, breath, and pulse behaving as the actors
induce them to behave in empathy. They are waiting, not for
the next words, but for something to happen, some significant
change in the relationships of the characters. When the audience
actively waits, with mounting tension, we are creating crisis
through suspense. When the awaited event occurs, the released
breath of the audience indicates that there has been a climax.
It is the anticipation of this experience of tension and release,
suspense, crisis and climax, that draws the audience into the
theatre.

This chapter is designed to show how the content of the
play helps to bring about this experience.

The Dramatic Event

A play is like life, in that it is full of uncertainties. A tiny
happening can produce enormous changes, because of the complexity of human life. A relatively simple machine like a typewriter can make this clear. Day after day everything seems to
be working well, but, under the carriage a tape frays, a tiny

screw works loose, until suddenly a vital contact is broken and the machine is useless until action is taken to repair it. Human life is, of course, much more complex than this. Not only must the physical mechanism of a human being function in almost perfect relationship between its parts, but a man must exist in a complex and changing milieu of things and relationships, all of which affect him and what he does. A broken leg, a thunderstorm, a scruple, a hard word from someone he cares about can change him, make him behave differently, and thus cause differences in the behavior of people around him. Moreover, thinking ahead of all one means to do and all the people who may be involved in one's actions, it is evident that the human machine, physical and psychological, is charged with potentialities of change which bring about other changes in an endless pattern of cause and effect, like the overlapping ripples of pebbles thrown into water.

The playwright and the director have the faculty of being alert to the driving, eruptive nature of man's needs, and to the potentialities of change that lurk in every human action. This sense of the mutability of human life is essentially the dramatic point of view. It is not based on any rules of dramaturgy; on the contrary, dramaturgy finds its rules in the ephemeral conditions of human life.

A *dramatic event,* then, is any action which threatens or promises change in the relationships of human beings to each other, to a situation, or to themselves. It has a cause or causes — change, growth, deterioration — and it produces some results. The action is exciting in proportion to the quality or magnitude of the change it promises or threatens. The American stock market crashes; a great leader dies on the eve of a peace conference; an aviator makes a forced landing and is arrested before he can dispose of the evidence that he is a spy. These events are obviously dramatic, because they create clear and world-shaking possibilities; they are also touching in terms of individual human feelings.

It seems of no importance at all if a student decides to turn the radio off or on when he begins to study; or to do his studying at five in the morning instead of at night; or to sleep every afternoon and stay up late to study. Yet any one of these decisions might affect his work and ultimately his career; and any one of them might annoy his roommate and disrupt their established system of relationships. Because of its possibility of effecting change, a simple, apparently commonplace decision can be exciting, dramatic. Any number of such pregnant events can be found in even the quietest life.

Much confusion has arisen because long ago Aristotle distinguished between character and plot. Even in the Greek tragedies, one feels pity at the spectacle of the character, Oedipus, a fundamentally just man, bringing about his own ruin in the attempt to avert a plague from his city. One weeps for the character, Andromache, the virtuous wife, parting from her child. The event is not really separable from the character in the event, for it is the character who brings about the event and who endures it.

Contemporary thought has swung very far from Aristotle. Instead of regarding the action as the most important element of a play, we go to the opposite extreme. We have popularized psychology to the point that the revelation of character is almost sufficient *raison d'être* for a play. Yet, however plotless a play may be, the characters must necessarily be revealed through action of some kind. Depending on the usage of the period and the interest of the playwright, there is a little more emphasis on the action or a little more emphasis on the motives; but in every play, as in every manifestation of human life, the motive — the inmost truth of the character — causes and is revealed in whatever action the individual takes.

The plot of a play is, then, a dramatic event which comes about through the motivation of characters.

The Character-Situation

In a play, as in life, the dramatic event is brought about through the emergence of some need. It seems fair to say that no life is complete; that each of us, however tranquilly we seem to sit in class or go about our work, has some personal wish that must be satisfied, or some personal satisfaction which, if destroyed, would leave his life unendurable. We want affection, prestige, possessions, excitement. We find it difficult to live under certain conditions of our environment or in association with certain people. Some of us even find certain aspects of our own personalities intolerable. As the Greek dramatists say repeatedly, only the dead are free from pain.

One understands people most clearly through learning what kinds of things they want and need — not what they say they want, but what they actually expend effort to achieve. A teacher, for example, may seem pompous. The adjective is a tag which enables one to dismiss the man as static, uninteresting, a stereotype. But if he is described by saying, "He needs the captive audience in order to feel a little authority," a whole inner life unfolds, involving the survival of his ego in a world which perhaps has no other use for him. As the static objective becomes translated into dynamic terms of need, the man himself emerges from his shell of pomposity. He becomes less repellent, even evokes a touch of sympathy. Who does not need some food for his ego? Thus, in naming a person's objective, one deeply characterizes him. The same is true of the characters in a play. Adjectives imprison and crush; it is the motivated action, the expression of a need, that makes a character seem real and alive. Moreover, since need is universal, people respond sympathetically to need *per se,* even though the particular need of a character in a play may not have been experienced by the audience.

When something goes wrong in a human being's life, creating a need, a real need and not a mere whim, he will try to take some action to bring the disturbing element into line. He may even focus all his attention for a time toward the action that is to set things right. This is exactly what happens in a play.

A human being may take years, a lifetime, to achieve his most important desires. As his life and relationships are complex, his conscious purpose bends one way and another and is sometimes lost in the purposes of other people and in necessity. Yet in the very swaying and shifting of purposes, and in the simple pursuit of a minor objective, the basic life wish of a person is perpetually revealed.

An audience in a theatre must see a whole personality revealed through the pursuit of a single objective in the "two hours traffic" of the stage. A play, therefore takes advantage of the revelation of the universal through the particular, telescoping the whole life wish in the need for a particular objective by one or a few characters. The core of a play, then, is somebody who wants something badly enough to struggle for it. That is, some element of his life is deeply disturbing, out of harmony, at odds with other aspects of his world, and must be set right.

One earmark of the protagonist is that he is in some way sympathetic. He may be as ugly as Quasimodo, but he will have some beauty of spirit, some gallant or delightful characteristic that will enable the onlooker to support him in his struggle, to wish with him. Even Macbeth, a murderer, commends himself by his scruples; even Volpone, a selfish cheat, delights us by cheating shameless hypocrites. There will be specific moments early in the play when the audience perceives his "good" qualities. The director must be alert for these moments.

Usually in a play this touching individual says clearly and passionately what he wants. The statement of the objective is one of the most important moments of the play, for it tells what the whole play is about. Even though in some plays as in some lives, the protagonist himself is not entirely aware what will restore his world to order, the audience must know, for it is out of this need that the action of the play evolves. The play begins when some aspect of the protagonist's life breaks down, revealing the need; it moves ahead as a quest for the objective, and it ends when some means is found either to fulfil the need or to eradicate it.

The director's business is to find in the words of the playwright the living, changing relationships which the words express. He seeks in each scene what *happens,* what changes occur to bring the protagonist nearer, or to make his way more difficult toward the fulfilment of his need.

The need does not exist without the circumstances that prolong it. There would be nothing dramatic in changing one's study hour or turning on the radio if one's roommate did not object. Not until one knows what the obstacle is can one plan a course of action. The more difficult the obstacle is, the harder one has to work, the more tension develops, the more people may become involved, and the more risk there is that even very slight events will affect the solution. Obstacle and complication are part of a play because they are inherent in life.

Thus the structure of a play derives from the way life actually is: a live individual, not completely satisfied, tries to find a way to make his life more satisfactory. He selects or is driven toward a specific goal, with some odds against him, and ultimately he succeeds, or abandons his goal. The preliminary analysis of a play should therefore reveal concrete answers to four questions:

1. Who is the protagonist?
2. What does he want throughout the play?
3. What stands in his way?
4. Does he achieve his wish?

This tells nothing about the quality of the play, but it defines the through line of action, shows the main points to be emphasized, the lines of suspense, main crisis, and climax. There is a fifth question that must also be answered, "How does he arrive at the ending?" But this requires more study.

The Course of Action

Aristotle wrote that the story "as an imitation of an action," must represent one action, a complete whole. He described a whole as "that which has beginning, middle and end." This may sound fatuously simple, until we consider what the terms mean. The beginning. The middle. The end.

Since a drama is about someone seeking closer harmony within his world, we shall see in "the beginning" the world he inhabits, with its inharmonious element. We must understand what will restore harmony, and why he, in particular, needs this objective. Our sympathies must be established, so that we will care about his success or failure. We also will have attitudes toward other personages in the play, and we will know in part how their objectives relate to that of the protagonist, for they, too, are living, desiring individuals. We must know the forces that deter him, so that we can empathize (that is, share his strain, wish with him) in the quest. Sometimes we need to know what Hegel calls the "collision factor," what happened to bring the need into focus. Whether this material is presented by the playwright as narrative or as effect-producing event, it is exposition, and it is part of "the beginning." Usually before "the beginning" is complete there is a passionate speech by the protagonist revealing exactly what it is he needs— the statement of the objective. Exposition leading to this statement is one of the main functions of "the beginning."

We must also glimpse the path ahead at least a little, so that we may foresee the pitfalls the protagonist may incur in the pursuit of the objective. The devices that enable us to foresee what may happen may be called pointers. They begin the suspense.

To both playwright and director, "the beginning" is often the most difficult part of the play, for it must be both clear and interesting. To miss any of the pointers may make the difference between an alert and eager audience and a sleepy and inattentive one.

A play is usually divided into acts, mainly to let the audience rest. The divisions usually occur at points where something is complete and something important is incomplete, so that during the intermission the audience both feels that the pause was right and also wants to go back and see the rest. Most of "the beginning" and some of "the middle" occur before the first intermission.

"The middle" contains the course of action, the route by which the ending is reached. Since this course is never pursued *in vacuo,* but in a larger world, there may be complications. A complication is a twist in the story that aids or threatens the protagonist. It can be detected by the fact that it causes something. Usually it comes about through a character whose pursuit of his own objective impinges on that of the protagonist or the obstacle, or through an incident that causes a change in the straight progress of the story. Usually there are from two to four important complications in a full-length play, but some one-act plays get along with none at all.

As the complications affect the struggle, making it seem alternately easier or more difficult, the objective becomes increasingly important. The protagonist approaches his maximum effort, and his increasing tension is felt in the audience. This is the second step in suspense. The showdown is becoming obligatory.

The showdown between the protagonist and his obstacle is the main crisis, but there are also many other crises in a play. Crisis is a moment of instability, indecision, clash, danger, sharp dissatisfaction of one of the characters, accompanied — and this is important — by tension in the audience. Crisis may be of any degree of excitement, from a threatened death blow to a mild intellectual shock, depending on the characters involved, their objectives, their milieu, and the extent of change threatened. The important thing is that crisis focuses the instability of a situation and repeatedly brings into prominence the need for some kind of change. Crisis is the peak of suspense.

A list of the main crises of a play is always an outline of "the middle," for the play is actually an interlocking system of critical events increasing in tension as it progresses. Some scenes are, of course, more tension-filled than others. Some scenes contain only two or three moments that could be called critical, while others are built in a series of small crises to one intense moment, a major crisis. When the protagonist and the obstacle come to final grips, with the full passion of both participants aroused and the audience waiting eagerly to see what will happen, the play has reached its main crisis and the scene is the obligatory scene of the play. Sometimes in a single play as many as a hundred crises can be found leading to this main event.

It is important that the audience share the tension, for unless it does, the so-called crisis is a mere dramaturgist's term, a label of nothing. The playwright has laid the ground for this audience involvement in the beginning by establishing sympathies, making objective and obstacle clear, and establishing alternatives. It is not the least part of the director's function to keep these points emphatic during "the middle."

"The middle," then, contains the main action of the play, presented as a system of complications and crises, with all those pointers that allow the audience to anticipate the main crisis and solution. "The middle" in a three-act play, usually begins in Act I, often before the exposition is complete, and ends as late in Act III as the playwright can manage to defer it. Obviously, the terms "beginning," "middle," and "end" do not refer to formal divisions of the play, but to content.

"The end" begins when all the elements of the play have come together into a showdown, the main crisis, involving the maximum effort of the protagonist and the greatest tension in the audience. The showdown eventuates in the solution, the protagonist getting what he needed to restore his equilibrium, or not getting it. This is the moment for which the audience has been waiting, the main climax of the play. If there is a theme, the final action makes it clear, and the audience feels it has glimpsed a universal truth. From the point of view of both form and content, of course, there are endless ways of handling the end of the story, but these elements are always in it, however disguised by the art that conceals art.

"The end" lets the audience know when the play is over by concluding the protagonist's struggle for his objective. No modern playwright, barring perhaps certain eccentrics, will expect the audience to remain interested when, from every angle, the protagonist no longer needs his objective, or has no further chance of achieving it. Thus, in analyzing a play one can expect the complete solution of the main problem within the last few pages of the play. Even if the main crisis begins, as it sometimes does, within Act II, the tying up of the complications will usually take place in a series of crises before the main solution can be completed. Once the main solution is reached, the curtain may as well be rung down, for the audience is thinking of home.

"The end" is important in the director's analysis, therefore, because it is the test of his interpretation of the play. The protagonist's objective is clear at this point, usually even to him, and the theme is fully revealed in the final action. Thus, in terms of the ending one can tell what must be emphasized in order to create audience tension in a straight line from opening to final curtain.

Now the play is no longer so many lines to be memorized by the actors. It is, first, two hours' worth of rising tension for the audience, rewarded by the relaxing moment of climax. Certain specific elements of the play bring this about: a protagonist the audience can like *in some way,* an individual who wants something enough to struggle against odds for it; a beginning that helps the audience to understand his need and to care about him; a middle that involves the audience in the growing difficulty of the struggle, and comes to a focus in an obligatory scene which has been foreshadowed; and an ending that rewards their concern and pulls the curtain down as soon as possible after they are satisfied. These are the elements out of which plays have been made from Aeschylus to Arthur Miller. They do not constitute a pattern, any more than the steel and stone of the architect constitute his pattern. Rather, because these elements can be almost infinitely varied, they enable the playwright to create the pattern which communicates his personal view of his material to the audience of his particular time.

It is inevitable that the content of drama varies with varying conditions and attitudes and that forms will be modified to express new content. Hero becomes hop-head (*The Connection*); the dynamic objective gives place to half-hearted waiting (*Waiting for Godot*) or to regret (*Krapp's Last Tape*); violent suspense gives way to other kinds of shock (*The Balcony*); and even incomprehensibility becomes a virtue when it is deliberately and impertinently theatrical (*The Bald Soprano*). Yet any plays that are not frankly anarchistic deal with human needs and anyone who writes for the theatre wants an audience to be moved to some kind of feeling about his characters and measures his success in terms of how the audience responds. Whatever the playwright may wish to say, he must utilize the fundamental dynamic elements, modified according to his material, his point of view, and his intent with regard to the audience. And any director, however he may phrase his inquiry into the nature of the play, will have to help his actors and his audience by some such analysis as this.

Assignments

1. Think of five people you know, and for each name one need that, if satisfied, would make them happier; or one possession (physical or spiritual) that, if taken away, would make their lives unendurable. List your evidence in each case.
    What, in each case, is or might be the obstacle?
2. Find ten dramatic actions that you have experienced or witnessed in the past week. List some of the changes that might have resulted from each action.
3. Define *empathy; universality.* Give an example of each in your personal experience; in your play-going experience.
4. What is the objective of Tybalt? Of Mercutio? Of the Nurse? The apothecary? Who is the protagonist of *Romeo and Juliet?* What is his (her, their) objective?
5. Show how Tybalt's objective is revealed in his opening scene with Benvolio. In the "goodman boy" scene with Capulet. In his dealing with Mercutio.
6. See if you can name Capulet's objective, in the light of all of his scenes.
7. Who is the protagonist in *The Glass Menagerie?* What is his (her) objective? What makes you wish with him (her)? In what speech is the objective clearly and passionately stated? At what point is it gained (or lost)? Name the obstacle.
8. Answer the same questions for *The Importance of Being Earnest.*
9. List all the items in *The Glass Menagerie* that are properly a part of "the beginning."
10. List all complications in *Romeo and Juliet.* In *The Glass Menagerie.* In *The Importance of Being Earnest.*

11. List the obligatory scenes of each of the four plays we have been studying. What moment is the main crisis of each?
12. Outline "the middle" of *The Glass Menagerie*. Of *The Importance of Being Earnest*.
13. Try this kind of analysis on an *avant-garde* play, such as those mentioned on page 87. Which of the elements is disregarded or distorted?

Reading List

Aristotle. *Poetics*. Modern Readers Series. New York: Macmillan, 1930, pp. 11-35.

Baker, George Pierce. *Dramatic Technique*. Boston: Houghton, Mifflin, 1919, Chapter 2.

Brunetiere, Ferdinand. "The Law of the Drama." In Barrett H. Clark. *European Theories of the Drama*. New York: Appleton-Century, 1936, pp. 404 f.

Dolman, John. *The Art of Play Production*. New York: Harper and Bros., 1946, Chapters 2 and 3.

Gallaway, Marian. *Constructing a Play*. Englewood Cliffs, N. J.: Prentice, Hall, 1950, Chapters 2, 12, and 17.

Langfeld, Herbert Sidney. *The Aesthetic Attitude*. New York: Harcourt, Brace, 1920, Chapter 5.

Lawson, John Howard. *Theory and Technique of Playwriting and Screen Writing*. New York: G. P. Putnam, 1936, Part III, Chapter 3.

Rowe, Kenneth. *A Theatre in Your Head*. New York: Funk and Wagnalls, 1960, Chapters 6, 7, and 8.

Chapter 6

A Sample Analysis

Obviously the analysis of a play is highly subjective, full of judgments which one makes in the light of his own experience. It is exactly here, in the analysis, that the creative part of a director's work lies, for all the delightful bits of business and technical devices he can think of are merely decorative frills, quite pointless, unless they stem from a sincere, creative analysis of the play.

The Playboy of the Western World has been selected for exhaustive analysis for several reasons. It presents moderate difficulties in defining the main elements of the plot; it contains both serious and comic elements; it contains several technical problems — offstage action, crowd scenes, a fight — that will be discussed later; it has a theme, which depends on how one analyzes the play, and which determines the quality or kind of effect to be attempted.

The Character-Situation

In analyzing a play, a director seeks first the core, the "spine," the dramatic event upon which the whole play hinges. Is *The*

Playboy the story of Pegeen Mike's failure to get Christy? Is it Christy's failure to get Pegeen Mike? Is it something else? Exactly what happens that unifies all of the elements of the play? The answer cannot be found until the elements of the character-situation are established — protagonist, objective, obstacle, and ending, according to the director's personal reaction to the script. The solutions reached here are not necessarily final and absolute. They are given merely as an example of how the director studies a play; the reader should be ready at every point to refer to the text in rebuttal and to undertake sincerely the exercises which indicate disagreement.

It is usually easy to tell who the protagonist is; he is the one whose fate the director cared most about as he read the play the first time, the one whose story is the substance of the play. Yet, the richer the play in characterizations, the harder it may be to find the main character. Sometimes one has to jump to a second question, what objective is the core of the play and to whom does it belong? Sometimes it is only by reference to the ending that one can tell what story line to emphasize in directing the play. What happens at the end? To whom does it happen? In *The Playboy* one must consider all of these points in order to discover the main event.

Is Christy the protagonist, or is it Pegeen Mike? We care about them both, in spite of their selfish and ugly traits, and we tend to hope that each will get what he wants. But what do they want?

Pegeen is ordering her wedding finery as the curtain rises, and, immediately after, we see that she is rather scornful of her fiancé, Shawn Keogh. She is possessive about Christy, securing him as her potboy and defending him against the Widow Quin. She has already expressed her hunger for adventurous men, possibly a statement of her objective. She speaks to Christy of the great people in his family and praises him as a powerful and fearless person and as a poet, always assuming superlative

qualities and luring him to build himself a false aura of gran-
deur. In the end, Christy actually becomes a "gallant captain,"
but Pegeen's house of cards collapses and she does not get
Christy. Since this is a comedy, the audience should feel a certain justice in this ending. Was Pegeen in love with Christy?
Is she the protagonist, with Christy as her objective? Or is she
after some other objective?

Christy comes in looking for a safe place to hide. He evades
the curiosity of the men, but resents Pegeen's taunt that he is
not a criminal. His confession of the "murder" pops out of him
when she threatens to strike him with the broom handle. There
is a change: he seems to expand to the compliments of the men.
With the Widow Quin, he is tacit, preferring Pegeen. He is
glad to learn that Pegeen is not engaged to Shawn. But his final
speech in Act I does not suggest a sentimental feeling for
Pegeen:

> . . . . its great luck and company I've won me in the end of
> time — two fine women fighting for the likes of me — till I'm
> thinking this night wasn't I a foolish fellow not to kill my
> father in the years gone by.

What does he want? At the end of the play, his father returns and tries to beat him, and Pegeen turns on Christy —
for lying to her? Or was she the one who manufactured the
lie? But Christy throws off his father's domination, and his last
speech is:

> Ten thousand blessings on all that's here, for you've turned
> me a likely fellow in the end of all, the way I'll go romancing
> through a romping lifetime from this hour to the dawning of
> the judgment day.

He leaves without, apparently, a second thought for Pegeen.
From the happenings of the play, Christy's objective has something to do with the change in his character from the frightened
mouse of Act I to the "gallant captain" of the last scene. What
does he want? Does the play hinge on his objective or on Pe-

geen's? The answer to this question will determine what, in this particular production, will be the through line of action, what will create suspense, what is to be played seriously and what must get laughs, and how to cast the two parts.

Of course one cannot name the obstacle, and hence cannot know what the course of action is, until the protagonist and objective have been defined, though there may be some idea of who is struggling against whom.

If Pegeen is the protagonist and her objective is to marry a hero, could Shawn be the obstacle? Or is it Pegeen's pride? Or is it that Christy is a fraud? If Christy is the protagonist and his object independence, is his father the obstacle, or is it, perhaps, his ingrained habit of cringing? Or is it something else?

Since the main crisis is always the moment when protagonist and obstacle come to final grips, this moment may give a clue about protagonist, obstacle, and objective. The main crisis may be the meeting between Christy and his father, or the scene in which Pegeen ropes Christy to take him to justice. These seem to be the most dramatic scenes in the play, that is, most pregnant of change. The selection of one or the other scene as the main crisis will lead to answers during the first few readings of the play.

Questions are also being raised about the less prominent characters. How do Jimmy and Philly fit into the play? Why are both of them included, when one might have provided the exposition or dealt with Old Mahon or led the mob in? Why two? How do four young girls move the story along? And again, why so many?

In the first readings, a feeling emerges that there is a theme, that the play states a proposition, and universal truth. The theme of *The Playboy* might be any of the following statements:

> The course of true love never did run smooth.
> As a man thinks, so shall he be.
> Pride goeth before a fall.

Is there a better statement of the theme? Is there really a theme?

After several readings and much thought, an answer comes. This may not be everybody's answer, but if in the direction of the play all of the details fit into this interpretation of protagonist, objective, obstacle, main crisis, and theme, the interpretation is legitimate and the play will have clarity for the audience. If, on the other hand, the answers leave loose threads, if some scenes are hard to tie in, if the story is over before the last curtain, then the interpretation is probably wrong.

In order to proceed with the analysis, it will be necessary to adopt some conclusions. Let us accept Christy as the protagonist, on the ground that most interesting action of the play centers around his change from the frightened boy of Act I to the "gallant captain" who blesses the company for making a man of him and who walks out without a backward glance at Pegeen.

Now we can seek the statement of the objective, which is the climax of "the beginning." Since Christy is immature and confused by Pegeen's charms through much of the play, we cannot expect a perfectly clear statement very early, but, in his opening soliloquy of Act II, he comes near it:

> This'd be a fine place to be my whole life talking out with swearing Christians, in place of my old dogs and cat, and I stalking around, smoking my pipe and drinking my fill and never a day's work but drawing a cork an odd time, or wiping a glass or rinsing out a shiny tumbler for a decent man.

A little later he touches the negative of his wish:

> And isn't it the poor thing to be starting again, and I a lonesome fellow will be looking out on women and girls the way the needy fallen spirits do be looking on the lord.

These speeches indicate that he wants to do as he has seen other men do — in other words, to be a man. This interpretation is reinforced by the way he warms to admiration in Act I and clings to his newly won reputation in Act III:

> I'm after hearing my voice this day say words would raise the topknot on a poet in a merchant's town. I've won your racing and your lepping . . .

His new status is so necessary to him that he even "kills" his father, quite deliberately, the second time.

If this is the objective — a little status — then the obstacle is his long habit of cringing, which we see when Pegeen threatens him in Act I, when he flees from the stranger girls at the opening of Act II, when he trembles at Pegeen's fabrication about the hanging, and when he clings in panic to the Widow Quin as he sees his father coming. The change in his character is marked at the main crisis, when Mahon beats him and Pegeen reveals her scorn, as he finds the resistance to "stretch" his father a second time. This, of course, creates a real crime, or seems to, after which Pegeen is hardened against him to the point of roping him and burning his leg to make him go to the police. Will his courage now hold, when the object of his conscious search turns against him? He finds the strength to laugh and gibe as he tries to free himself. His change is complete. He is now exactly the sort of devil-may-care fellow that Pegeen praised to Shawn in Act I.

If we accept this interpretation the end of the story is that Christy gets what he wanted — a proper ending for a comedy. The theme, then, would be, "As a man thinks, so shall he be," for with an appreciation of his own capacities, Christy is able to conquer his fear even of his father and to anticipate a good life ahead. It is consoling that Pegeen, who started Christy off on his fabric of lies, gets spanked for her selfishness and false values; yet we are rather pleased that she has a steady, commonplace Shawn to fall back on "when his vicious bite is healed."

The Course of Action

Having satisfied himself in answer to four of the basic questions, the director can begin to study the fifth, "How is the conclusion reached?" He finds this answer through Aristotle's terms, beginning, middle, and end.

The beginning tells what is wrong in the protagonist's world, what he wants, and why he wants it.

Christy's inadequate world is conveyed in four scenes in the first and second acts. Briefly, his father was driving him too hard and was intolerable when drunk, as he usually was. Christy's life had been spent in working in the fields all day and poaching alone at night. He refers several times to his loneliness, including the optimistic curtain speech of Act I. His only friends seem to have been his "old dogs and cat." Although he has watched girls with their boys, he admits never having had a girl, and he seems hardly to have thought he ever would have one of his own. His father reports that the girls called him "the looney of Mahon's." The collision factor, reported by Christy in the scene with the girls in Act II, was Mahon's insistence that Christy marry his old wet nurse in order to get her property. Upon this, Christy "killed" his father and fled.

The beginning thus helps us to understand Christy. It also gives us some reason to like him. First, we vaguely dislike Shawn, who is a sort of foil to Christy. He is scared of a chimera, while Christy's hide attests his reason to be scared. Then, Christy's entrance, an anticlimax, makes us laugh, not at Christy, but at the men who were afraid of him. We like people who make us laugh. We are touched by his misery, his bashfulness, his flash of pride ("And I the son of a strong farmer"). We share the men's fascination for learning his crime. His surprise at their interest endears him. His comic confession and his several declarations of virtue reveal his complete naïveté, for which we also laugh and like him. He swells with surprise as the men declare him brave, and when Pegeen declares him handsome he cries,

"Is it me?" After his tension in the first part of Act I, he relaxes with Pegeen in his first quiet talk with a girl, — and he does it rather well, in his new security.

The beginning also tells us about the world into which Christy wishes to enter. We learn at once that Pegeen is to be married, and we sense that the Flahertys are reasonably well to do. Pegeen ridicules Shawn, admitting her love of adventurous men. We see that not only Shawn, but Michael James and the others are utter cowards. We also see that they are at ease in the material world, and their well-being externalizes Christy's idea of the good life.

Pegeen, Christy's pseudo-objective, appeals to the audience, because she is young, pretty, dissatisfied with her poltroon of a fiancé, talks of adventure, and has justice on her side in her argument with Michael James:

> If I am a queer daughter, it's a queer father 'd be leaving me lonesome these twelve hours of dark, and I piling the turf with the dogs barking and the calves mooing and my own teeth rattling with the fear.

We like her most in Act I when she stands up for Shawn against her father and when she makes Christy comfortable for the night.

As preparation for the break with Christy in the end, we also have reason to dislike her. Although she flirts with Shawn in Act I, she is really quite mean to him, actually driving him out in the end of the act. She has an ugly temper, threatening Christy with the broom handle when he will not reveal his crime. In the brawl with the Widow, we see clearly her biting tongue in a speech that was excised from the opening production:

> Doesn't the world know you reared a black lamb at your own breast, so that the Lord Bishop of Connaught felt the elements of a Christian and he eating it after in a kidney stew? Doesn't the world know you've been shaving a foxy skipper from France

for a threepenny bit and a sop of grass tobacco would wring the liver from a mountain goat you'd meet lepping the hills?

And early in Act II, she has the cruelty to scare Christy about the "hanging of a man." One other shrewd bit scores against Pegeen: the Widow, even though Christy rejects her, befriends and takes care of him. The Widow has a kind heart.

The middle is the story: how Christy changed from a cringing mouse to a "gallant captain." Six major events occur in Act I that belong to the middle.

1. The glimmer of change occurs when the men take an interest in his crime and he prolongs the mystery in sly enjoyment of "holding center" for the first time in his life.

2. Pegeen's first important action toward him is to threaten him with the broom handle, a crisis which reveals his intense terror of beatings and precipitates his confession.

3. The men's recognition of his outstanding bravery is emphasized by his astonished, "Well, glory be to God!" and is productive of another step toward self-respect.

4. His getting the job of potboy enables him to stay in the shebeen, so that his progress may continue.

5. In his first talk with Pegeen, he is lured to the false position that builds him up and almost leads to his downfall. It should be noted that Pegeen claims more for him than he ever claims for himself, a fact which is pointed during the main crisis by Christy himself: "If you're after making a mighty man of me this day by the power of a lie . . . ."

6. In the brawl between Pegeen and the Widow, who supplies one of the main complications, he remains quiet until Pegeen forces him to express a preference. Has he made an enemy of the Widow Quin?

The end of the act is a climax that seems to summarize Christy's progress to that moment, "It's great luck and company I've won me in the end of time."

Act II is a series of events which alternately help and hinder Christy in his progress toward self-respect:

1. The stranger girls bring him gifts, building his ego.
2. Pegeen terrifies him with the threat of hanging, so that he backslides, cringing in fear.
3. Shawn's attempt to bribe him only increases his confidence. In Shawn's clothes he has the courage to think of winning Pegeen.
4. His panic returns when he sees Mahon arriving and continues through the ensuing scene with the Widow, in which he begs her to help him win Pegeen.
5. He enters the races, a complication induced by the Widow, which reveals to him that he can excel.

The middle continues into Act III with three events leading to the main crisis:

1. Parallel with Christy's progress toward self-confidence, the other main complication develops. Mahon returns, sees the race, recognizes the winner as Christy, and wants to beat him, but the Widow outwits him and sends him on his way. But Jimmy and Philly, suspecting her honesty, follow Mahon and bring him back.
2. Christy wins the crowning prize, Pegeen's promise to marry him, almost a main climax.
3. Christy drives out Shawn and forces Michael James to accept him as a son-in-law, another major climax. Now Christy is on the crest of the tide.

The end begins with Mahon's return for the obligatory scene, and the dénouement is completed in three events:

1. Mahon returns and beats Christy, who almost yields to his old habit of cringing, in the main crisis of the play. But as Pegeen turns against him, he summons strength to drive the

old man out to his "second murder," a main climax and also a crisis.

2. Now the townspeople flock to the side of the law, and Pegeen herself ropes and burns Christy in her effort to drag him to the police — partly because she is frustrated in her wish for a hero but partly too to save face after having backed a loser. As she applies the fire, Christy finds in himself the strength to taunt and laugh at the cowardly villagers. He has found his real self-respect. The main climax is building.

3. Mahon returns "to be murdered a third time." He unties Christy's bonds, and, as the main climax rises to its height, they leave, to "go romancing through a romping lifetime." Mahon grins with delight, showing that he was not the real obstacle, for he apparently got what he wanted. Pegeen howls in defeat, while patient Shawn stands by to return her to the *status quo ante*.

In this telling of the story there are three main complications. (1) In luring Christy to a false position, Pegeen gives him the push which eventually gains him his self-esteem. In the process, she, like the psychiatrist, temporarily becomes his love object. (2) The Widow Quin, in her antagonism toward Pegeen, becomes a friend of Christy and puts him in the races, where he gains real evidence of his capacity to excel. (3) Mahon's return, as evidence that his present position is built on a lie, complicates by forcing a showdown.

The crises which must be emphasized here are the ones in which Christy is in danger of being craven again. In Act I, when Pegeen threatens him, his terror must be real enough to make the obstacle clear to the audience. When he waits as Pegeen and the Widow brawl, one must feel that he is expecting blows on his own head. In Act II when he flees from the stranger girls, we must see "the looney of Mahon's." When Pegeen threatens him with hanging, his terror and loneliness are evident. He is in utter panic when he sees his father approaching, and this big crisis comes to a focus in:

> May I meet him with one tooth and it aching, and one eye to be seeing seven and seventy divils in the twists of the road, and one old timber leg on him to limp into the scalding grave . . . and that the Lord God would send a high wave to wash him from the world.

The scene in which he returns from the "second murder" has a peculiar quality, for in it he realizes fully that he may have forfeited his newly found independence. He knows that unless he can maintain this, life is not worth living. Even Sara's comic business of trying to put a skirt on him to aid his escape is not funny.

Another special moment is the one in which he says, "You're blowing for to burn me. That's your kind, is it?" In this final crisis, with no words to tell it, he realizes that he does not really want Pegeen, for in the next instant he jibes gaily at the cowardly crowd. The actor is left with the problem of making this enormous transition.

If Pegeen is the protagonist, as she will surely seem to be when a famous and charming actress like Sioban McKenna plays her, or, if the love story seems paramount and Pegeen is regarded as the objective, the whole story must be told differently.

Functions of the Supporting Characters

It remains to consider the functions of the other characters. If Christy is the protagonist, Pegeen is the main complication. The Widow Quin not only complicates, but is also a foil to Pegeen. Shawn complicates by getting the Widow into the story and by giving Christy the clothes that give him the courage to aspire to Pegeen. He also serves as a foil to Christy, for Christy is afraid for good reason while Shawn is afraid of a chimera.

The greatest use for Shawn is as a solution for Pegeen. She will marry him and brag of his wealth, if not of his courage.

Michael James seems to have one main function, that of authorizing Christy's stay in the shebeen. He also has a moment in Act III that puts the period on the "rising action."

Old Mahon, of course, provides the other main complication that destroys the lie and forces Christy to triumph over his weaker self. In a sense, Mahon might be regarded as the obstacle, since he has been the cause of Christy's cringing. Yet, in his defeat, he smiles broadly, showing that all along he wanted his son to show a spark of manhood. He has a speech which makes this clear:

> My son and myself will be going our own way, and we'll have great times from this out telling stories of the villainy of Mayo and the fools is here.

Jimmy and Philly help to exposit the well-being Christy desires. They are complications in bringing Mahon back to confront Christy. They also serve to remind us that Michael James is coming back from the wake, so that his interruption of the love scene does not seem contrived. They are two instead of one, to avoid emphasis. If only one character served all these purposes, he would be a major character in the play. By dividing their functions, Synge divides their importance and thus avoids the necessity of punishing them as well as Pegeen in the fast-moving end of the play.

The girls complicate a little by bringing gifts and raising Christy's opinion of himself and clinching his decision to remain where he is. They are four instead of one, to avoid anything like a rivalry with Pegeen, which would emphasize the love story and confuse the main issue, Christy's struggle for self-esteem. Sara is a foil to Pegeen and could easily become a main character, if the playwright had not been so shrewd.

The test of the interpretation will come in rehearsal when the actors ask more specific questions and in performance when the audience receives its impression. If the actors' questions can be answered in relation to the central proposition that Christy is striving for self-esteem, and if the audience feels that he got what he wanted and Pegeen what she deserved, the interpretation can be presumed valid.

Assignments

1. State the objective, obstacle, and ending of *The Playboy of the Western World* with Pegeen Mike as the protagonist.
2. Answer the four basic questions for *Romeo and Juliet, The Glass Menagerie,* and *The Importance of Being Earnest.*
3. Tell the beginning, middle, and end — major events, complications, main crises, and climax of all four plays in terms of your answers to the basic questions.
4. List *evidence* for liking each protagonist that you have chosen.
5. Quote the statement of objective in each play.
6. List the functions of the subordinate characters in *The Glass Menagerie* and *The Importance of Being Earnest.*

Reading List

Wilde, Percival. *The Craftsmanship of the One-Act Play.* Boston: Little, Brown, 1938, Chapter XXIII.

Stanislavsky, Constantin. *An Actor Prepares.* New York: Theatre Arts, Inc., 1936, Chapter XIII.

Gallaway, Marian. *Constructing a Play.* Englewood Cliffs, N. J.: Prentice-Hall, 1950, pp. 153-160.

Lawson, John Howard. *Theory and Technique of Playwriting and Screenwriting.* New York: G. P. Putnam, 1949, Part IV, Chapter 4.

Rowe, Kenneth. *A Theatre in Your Head.* New York: Funk and Wagnalls, 1960, Chapter 3.

Chapter 7

The Scene as the
Dynamic Unit

Once the director knows the main line of the play, he studies
the function and the individual structure of each scene. In this
work, he seeks the underlying rhythm and at the same time finds
nuances of rhythm that make for diversity within the dynamic
unity of the play. Though still at his desk, he is also doing his
most basic work for the actors; for, in discovering what they are
to do in each scene, he takes the first step toward releasing them
from the physical tensions of self-consciousness and gives them
the motives upon which their childhood tendencies to make-
believe can begin to operate in the interpretation of their roles.

Definition of a Scene

The smaller divisions of a play are called scenes. A "scene"
used to mean all the speeches from the entrance of a character
to his exit or to the entrance or exit of another character. Because the term was thus used in France in the seventeenth century, it is called a "French scene." This definition is not much
help to the actors and actually confuses the director in his analy-

sis. A more useful definition is: a sequence of material about one specific objective of a specific character. In this sense a scene often builds to one event, the conclusion of the effort toward the objective, a small climax; but, sometimes, as in the second scene of *The Playboy,* the end of the scene leaves the objective uncompleted and the situation more or less critical.

If we refer to a scene as a whole sequence about one objective, the first scene in *The Playboy* is: Pegeen writes a letter ordering her wedding finery, while Shawn gets up enough courage to come in (the event). It is interesting that, while Pegeen has all the lines, the scene is Shawn's, because he has a struggle before gaining his objective. His entrance is climactic, if he has managed to make the audience hope he will enter.

In Scene 2, Pegeen tries to get Shawn to stay with her overnight for protection (the objective), while her father attends a wake. Shawn clings to his scruples (the obstacle in both scenes). Michael James and his friends pursue the same objective, until Shawn flees (the climactic event). Pegeen does not achieve her objective, which she restates after Shawn leaves.

Functional Nature of a Scene

When a play goes through rehearsals with a professional company, one of the most important jobs of both director and cast is to get the play easily into two hours' playing time. All nonessentials have to be eliminated, and essentials have to be accomplished in minimum time. What is left is all functional. There is hardly a word in the play, when it reaches its professional opening, that could be omitted without destroying something important. A study of the apparently leisurely opening of *The Playboy* will show how packed with significance these first two scenes are.

Scene 1 exposits that Pegeen loves finery, is about to be married, and is innately practical (if the three barrels of porter are

for the shebeen, not for the wedding); and that Shawn is fond
of her and overshy. Since they are young people thinking of
love and weddings, we like them, even though we know very
little about them as Shawn comes in.

Scene 2 tells us that Shawn is not the adventurous hero Pegeen would like to marry, but practical, constant, and hag-
ridden by Father Reilly. The scene shows that Pegeen can be
heartlessly cruel (I'll maybe tell them and I'll maybe not) as
well as desirable. It prepares for Pegeen's fastening upon Christy
as potboy and for her making a hero of him. It shows Pegeen
standing up to her father and contains a reference to the dispensation, the arrival of which triggers her defiant announce-
ment in Act III that she will marry Christy. It prepares for
Michael James's drunken return from the wake and the interrupted love scene. In the comic sequence between Michael
James and Shawn, it reveals the jibing cruelty that comes to a
focus in the tying and burning of Christy. It prepares for the
ending and makes us like Pegeen, in that she stands up for Shawn
after his departure. And it supplies three pointers to Christy's
entrance.

Thus the primary function of these two scenes is exposition of
the world which Christy enters. It gives him a pretext to stay
and lets us understand why he found it attractive and why he
gave it up. Now the director may examine the motives of the
characters in each scene, making sure that they serve the function of the scene in the play as a whole.

The Structure of a Scene: Built-in Rhythm

Structurally, every scene is a unit of action toward a character's objective.[1] Some character wants something and is trying

[1] In transitional scenes and a few others, often the motive is not apparent,
as in Pegeen's scene of locking the door and covering the window after
the Widow Quin's exit in Act I. In such scenes, the actor must find or
invent a suitable motive.

to get it in whatever way his nature and milieu permit. A long scene usually follows a more or less obvious pattern of several increasingly insistent attempts to achieve whatever the main character in the scene wants. The scene is unified around his objective and varied in terms of the number and kinds of attacks. There is at least a minor crisis just before the conclusion of each attack, and the new attack is based upon the reaction of the other character or characters in the scene.

Anyone can recall in his own experience that this is everyday human practice. Suppose, for example, a young man is trying to get his father to let him use the family car for an important date. He might begin by bringing his father the paper and making him comfortable when he comes home, *softening him up* for the big question. He might sit with his father a while and tell him some of the good things that have happened during the day, including the plan for the very special date, *to make him feel proud* of his son. He might brag a little about watering the lawn and washing the car, *obligating* his father to do something in return. He might even *avoid the subject* of borrowing the car until after his father has had supper. He could "work on him" in any number of ways, but they all lead to the critical question. This is exactly the way a scene builds, in a series of attempts to secure the objective. These attempts or attacks, sometimes called beats, keep the scene dynamic, keep it from being mere verbiage. They supply a basic built-in rhythm of renewed desire.

The Pattern of Attack and Response

An analysis of the second scene of *The Playboy* clearly illustrates what we have been talking about.

Shawn's objective: to court Pegeen and to keep on the good side of Father Reilly	(SHAWN enters)	Pegeen wants someone to stay with her while her father goes to an all-night wake

He seeks a chaperone

SHAWN
Where's himself?

PEGEEN
He's coming. (Addressing the letter) To Mr. Sheamus Mulroy, Wine and Spirit Dealer, Castlebar.

SHAWN
I didn't see him on the road.

PEGEEN
How would you see him and it dark night this half hour gone by?

He permits himself a little romance

SHAWN
I stood a while outside wondering would I have a right to pass on or walk in and see you, Pegeen Mike, and I could hear the cows breathing and sighing in the stillness of the air and not a step moving any place from this gate to the bridge.

PEGEEN
It's above at the crossroads he is meeting Philly Cullen and a couple more are going with him to Kate Cassidy's wake.

But it doesn't last long

SHAWN
And he's going that length in the dark night?

PEGEEN
He is surely, and leaving me lonesome on the scruff of the hill.

Attack I. She flirts.
a. Playing blasé, a "come-on"

b. Trying to rouse his protectiveness

Isn't it long the nights are, Shawn Keogh, to be leaving a poor girl with her own self, counting the hours to the dawn of day?

c. Making him want her

SHAWN

Caught

If it is, when we're wedded in a short while you'll have no call to complain,

But not letting himself go

for I've little will to be walking off to wakes or weddings in the darkness of the night.

PEGEEN

You're making mighty certain that I'll wed you now, Shaneen.

d. Coquetting to lead him on

CRISIS
She has scared him a little

SHAWN

Aren't we after making a good bargain, the way we're waiting only these days on Father Reilly's dispensation from the bishops or the courts of Rome?

SHE FAILS

PEGEEN

It's a wonder, Shaneen, the Holy Father'd be taking notice of the likes of you; for if I was him I wouldn't bother with this place where you'll meet none but Red Lanahan has a squint in his eye, and Patcheen is lame in his heel, or the mad Mulrannies were driven from California and they lost

Attack II. She tries to make him assert his masculinity
a. Jeering

in their wits. We're a queer lot these times to go troubling the Holy Father on his sacred seat.

He ducks and hedges

SHAWN

If we are, we're as good this place as another, maybe, and as good these times as we were forever.

PEGEEN

As good is it? Where now will you meet the like of Daneen Sullivan knocked the eye from a peeler, or Marcus Quin, God rest him, got six months for maiming ewes, and he a great warrant to tell stories of holy Ireland till he'd have the old women shedding down tears about their feet. Where will you find the like of them, I'm saying?

b. Tries to make him jealous of the roughneck heroes

SHAWN

Doesn't bite

If you don't, it's a good job, maybe, for Father Reilly'd have small conceit to have that kind walking around and talking to the girls.

CRISIS

PEGEEN

Stop tormenting me with Father Reilly, when I'm asking only what way I'll pass these twelve hours of dark and not take my death of the fear.

SHE FAILS
She naps in irritation

c. She works on his protectiveness

He tries to help

SHAWN
Would I fetch you the
Widow Quin, maybe?

PEGEEN
Is it the like of that   **She snaps again and**
murderer? You'll not   **gives up**
surely.

He ends the argument   SHAWN
by agreeing   Then I'm thinking
himself will stop along
with you when he sees
you taking on, for it'll
be a long night time
with great darkness.

and changes the   And I'm after feeling
subject   a kind of fellow above
in the furzy ditch,
groaning wicked like
a maddening dog, the
way it's good cause
you have, maybe, to
be fearing now.   **CRISIS**
                             Attack III. She slaps
PEGEEN   **in retaliation**
What's that? Is it a
man you seen?

SHAWN
I couldn't see him at
all, but I heard him
groaning out and
breaking his heart. It
should have been a
young man from his
words speaking.

PEGEEN
And you never went
near him to see was
he hurted or what
CRISIS   ailed him at all?

SHAWN
He hangs on to his   I did not, Pegeen
dignity   Mike. It was a dark,
lonesome place to be
hearing the like of
him.

CRISIS

PEGEEN
Well, you're the daring fellow, and if they find his corpse stretched out in the dews of dawn, what'll you say then to the peelers or the justice of the peace?

Now he wants protection — The tables are turned — a minor climax

SHAWN
I wasn't thinking of that. For the love of God, Pegeen Mike, don't let on I was speaking of him. Don't tell your father and the men is coming above, for if they heard that story they'd have great blabbing this night at the wake.

She watches him squirm

PEGEEN
I'll maybe tell them and I'll maybe not.

CRISIS

SHAWN
They're coming at the door. Will you whisht, I'm saying?

PEGEEN
Whisht yourself.
(**MICHAEL JAMES, JIMMY, PHILLY** enter)

MEN
God bless you. The blessing of God on this place.

PEGEEN
God bless you kindly.

Shawn is trying to say good night

MICHAEL
Sit down now and take your rest. And how is it you are, Shawn Keogh? Are you coming over the

Attack IV. She works on her father, drawing drinks as they make themselves comfortable

sands to Kate Cassi-
dy's wake?

SHAWN

Hardly condescending   I am not, Michael
James. I'm going
home the short cut to
my bed.

PEGEEN
He's right, too. And   Attack V. She jabs
have you no shame,   her father
Michael James, to be
quitting off for the
whole night and leav-
ing myself lonesome
in the shop?

MICHAEL
Isn't it the same
whether I go for the
whole night or a part
only? And I'm think-
ing it's a queer daugh-
ter you are if you'd
have me crossing
backward through the
Stooks of the Dead
Woman with a drop
taken.

PEGEEN
If I am a queer   Stabs him with an
daughter, it's a queer   icicle
father'd be leaving me
lonesome these twelve
hours of dark, and I
piling the turf with
the dogs barking and
the calves mooing and
my own teeth rattling
with the fear.

JIMMY
What is there to hurt
you, and you a fine
hardy girl would
knock the head of any
two men on the place?

PEGEEN
Isn't there the harvest boys with their tongues red for drink, and the ten tinkers is camped in the east glen, and the thousand militia, bad cess to them, walking idle through the land. There's lots surely to hurt me, and I wont stop alone in it, let himself do what he will.

She pushes Jimmy out of the family fight

and throws down the gauntlet

MICHAEL
If you're that afeard, let Shawn Keogh stop along with you. It's the will of God, I'm thinking, himself should be seeing to you now.

Attack VI. She lets Michael James take over

SHAWN
I would and welcome, Michael James, but I'm afeard of Father Reilly. And what at all would the Holy Father and the Cardinals of Rome be saying if they heard I done the like of that?

Tries to back out with dignity

MICHAEL
God help you, can't you sit in by the hearth with the light lit and herself beyond in the room? You'll do that surely, for I've heard there's a queer fellow above, going mad or getting his death, maybe, in the

He jeers

then wheedles

then urges

gripe of the ditch. So she'd be safer here this night with a person here.

CRISIS

SHAWN

His dignity ebbs with his courage

I'm afeard of Father Reilly, I'm saying. Let you not be tempting me and we near married itself.

Pegeen snorts

PHILLY

Lock him in the west room. He'll stay then and have no sin to be telling the priest.

MICHAEL

CRISIS

Go up, now.

Starting to use force, blocking the exit

SHAWN

He panics, screaming, tries to dodge to the door

Don't stop me, Michael James. Let me out of the door, I'm saying, for the love of the Almighty God. Let me out.

Pleading

Let me out of it and may God grant you his indulgence in the hour of need.

Pegeen and the men laugh as Michael hops from side to side, barring Shawn

MICHAEL

Stop your noising and sit down by the hearth.

Laughing, good-natured

CRISIS
Gibbering

SHAWN

Oh, Father Reilly and the saints of God, where will I hide myself today? Oh, St.

He gives up

Joseph and St. Patrick and St. Brigid and St. James, have mercy on me now.

but sees the door clear and makes a dive for it
CRISIS

MICHAEL

You'd be going, is it?

The men seize his coattails

SHAWN

He struggles, a
trapped rat

Leave me go, Michael
James. Leave me go,
you old pagan or I'll
get the curse of the
priests on you and
of the scarlet-coated
bishops of the courts

CRISIS

of Rome.

(With a sudden movement he pulls himself out of
his coat and disappears out of the door, leaving the
coat in Michael's hands.)

CLIMAX

MICHAEL

Well, there's the coat
of a Christian man.
Oh, there's sainted
glory this day in the
lonesome west; and
by the will of God
I've got you a decent
man, Pegeen, you'll
have no call to be spy-
ing after if you've a
score of young girls,
maybe, weeding in
your fields.

Pegeen Fails

PEGEEN

What right have you
to be making sport of
a poor fellow for
minding the priest
when it's your own
the fault is, not pay-
ing a penny potboy to
stand along with me
and give me courage
in the doing of my
work?

Attack VII. She
brawls, demanding
protection

MICHAEL

Where would I get a
potboy? Would you
have me send the bell-
man screaming in the
streets of Castlebar?

OBJECTIVE NOT
ACCOMPLISHED

(Shawn enters in terror of the queer dying fellow)

Summarizing the action of the scene, Pegeen wants someone to stay with her and protect her while her father goes to the wake. She uses three attacks on Shawn before her father comes in, two while her father is there, and one more after Shawn leaves. The objective has not been achieved, but we are well prepared for, "That'd be a lad with the sense of Solomon to have for a potboy . . . ." The whole scene, up to Shawn's second entrance, prepares for the hiring of Christy.

In the scene with Shawn, Pegeen tries first to take advantage of Shawn's romantic mood, then to put some spine into him, and finally, having failed, she slaps at him for his unromantic behavior. This part of the scene reverses the positions of the couple; now Shawn is trying to get Pegeen's protection and she is holding out, in revenge.

The fourth attack, not written, is devised by the actress, perhaps making her father feel good in order to get his help, perhaps showing off to Shawn how sweet she can be, in order to make him stay. This does not last long.

The next two attacks she leaves to Michael James, but she is not out of the picture, for it is her objective that the men pursue. When Shawn leaves, she is still demanding protection, and by this time, presumably, the audience is wishing with Pegeen.

One of the most important reasons for studying a scene this closely is that the method reveals how each attack induces a response from the playing partner, which in turn creates a new attack. The responses are not merely the words written by the playwright, but they are the thoughts and feelings and bits of behavior of human beings reacting to each other in terms of what each wants. The actors who play the scene will think of many more such responses.

Of course the interpretation of a given scene depends on the analysis of the play as a whole. The better the play, and the more it reveals the complexity of human nature, the harder it is to make firm decisions about the motives of the characters.

But sooner or later the director must decide, for only in this way can the play be carried along in a straight line of suspense to the main crisis and climax. At this stage, the only test of the interpretation is its consistency, its relation to the whole, and to the logic of human behavior.

The All-Inclusive Objective

Crucial in analyzing a scene is the definition of objectives. Sometimes it is quite difficult to find an objective that motivates the whole scene. The "love scene" between Christy and Pegeen appears easy, with the audience empathizing (wishing with both characters) and anticipating a romantic love passage. But there are several important problems. First, if one takes as the statement of the objective Christy's first speech (". . . your promise that you'll wed me"), the objective is accomplished one-third of the way through the scene, with Pegeen swooning away as she says, "I'd be nice so, is it?" The rest of the scene, then, is mere lyrism, unless the objective is defined more comprehensively. Also, Pegeen and the audience know that the end of a love scene is an embrace, but Synge gives no direction for the lovers to kiss. If the main objective is "to win Pegeen," Christy looks like a lame lover. On the other hand, if he does kiss her, the meaning becomes twisted.

The objective must be defined in the light of the ending of the play. In this scene, the lovers agree to marry, but, before the play is over, Pegeen has turned against Christy with actual physical cruelty, and Christy leaves the house in triumph without a backward thought of Pegeen. Since the audience must feel satisfied in the ending, it would be a mistake to let anything happen in this scene that would make the ending disappointing. Although the language is ecstatically poetic, the scene has to be kept essentially comic. It must be clear through the definition of the objectives that the two young people are not really in love.

Since they think they are, however, a valid explanation must be found for the absence of a romantic kiss.

The scene begins with a short, positive attack. As Pegeen wipes Christy's face with her shawl, he instinctively grabs for her as "the crowning prize." The key to the scene is in these words. Christy thinks of Pegeen not as a woman to cherish and possess, but as the final proof of his power, another prize in a day of winning. It is interesting that all of the lyrical speeches are possessive, reveling in the envy of the "mitred bishops" and the Lord God. He struts and crows, carried away by his sense of power. He is still a long way from emotional adulthood.

Pegeen's objective is to be taken by storm by a hero lover who will be the envy of seven townships. To her, a husband is something to flaunt before Sara and the Widow Quin as a symbol of power. At the end of the scene, each of the lovers is carried away not by the sweeping attractiveness of the other, but by admiration for his own success. Apparently, each is seeking in love confirmation of his own worth.

By this definition of objectives, the scene is kept fundamentally comic, through the inflexibility of the lovers; they see in each other not what is there, but the mirror of themselves. The audience suspense can be phrased in the question, "Will they ever notice each other and behave like lovers?"

ANALYSIS OF CHRISTY'S ATTACKS IN LOVE SCENE,
Playboy, ACT II

His Objective is to fulfil his manhood.

Attack I. Seize her as his right

PEGEEN: Well, you're the lad, and you'll have great times from this out, when you could win that wealth of prizes, and you sweating in the heat of noon.

CHRISTY: I'll have great times if I win the crowning prize I'm seeking now, and that's your promise that you'll wed me in a fortnight when our banns is called.

His assurance motivates her to move away — She must be properly courted

Attack II. Ensnare her carefully. Since Christy has never actually courted before, she probably seems to him harder to get than she is — He must move carefully, keep a safe distance, avoid startling her, finally close in — He has caught rabbits this way

This is soft talk to lure his rabbit

He sees she's willing, wants to shout aloud

He should have kissed her. Disappointed, she teases.

At last he pounces — Why doesn't he kiss? The reason is in his experience — He has watched lovers, feeling his own loneliness — The fun of contact with a living creature has been in daytime romps with his dogs — This is what his body remembers as he leans over Pegeen — There is a feeling of triumphant laughter, and then he becomes aware it is a girl he is holding

PEGEEN: You've right daring to go ask me that, when all knows you'll be starting to some girl in your own townland when your father's rotten in four months or five.

CHRISTY: Starting from you is it? I will not then. And when the airs is warming in four months or five, it's then yourself and me should be pacing the Neifin in the dews of night, the time sweet smells do be rising and you'd see a little shiny new moon, maybe, sinking on the hills.

PEGEEN: And it's that kind of poacher's love you'd make, Christy Mahon, on the sides of Neifin when the night is down?

CHRISTY: It's little you'll think if my love's a poacher's or an earl's itself, when you'll feel my two hands stretched around you, and I squeezing kisses on your puckered lips,
    till I'd feel a kind of pity for the Lord God is all ages sitting lonesome in his golden chair.

PEGEEN: That'll be right fun, Christy Mahon, and any girl'd walk her heart out before she'd meet a young man was your like for eloquence or talk at all.

CHRISTY: Let you wait to hear me talking till we're astray in Erris when Good Friday's by, drinking a sup from a well and making mighty kisses with our wetted mouths,

                                        or
gaming in a gap of sunshine with

Pegeen accepts — She and the audience await the kiss — But now the significance of the moment hits him: he has won — He thinks himself the envy of the saints on high The expressive move here is away from Pegeen to embrace the biggest thing in the universe, himself

> yourself stretched back unto your necklace in the flowers of the earth.
> PEGEEN: I'd be nice so, is it?
> CHRISTY: If the mitred bishops seen you that time they'd be the like of the holy prophets, I'm thinking, do be straining the bars of Paradise to lay eyes on the Lady Helen of Troy, and she abroad pacing back and forward with a nosegay in her golden shawl.

The third attack is Pegeen's: She tries to get him to make love properly

Pegeen is disappointed and so is the audience — though they feel sure he will kiss in time — She sets about to lure him, first by pretending to belittle herself
He vigorously champions her

> PEGEEN: And what is it I have, Christy Mahon, to make me fitting entertainment for the like of you, that has such talking and such bravery of heart?
> CHRISTY: Isn't there the light of seven heavens in your heart alone, the way you'll be an angel's lamp to me from this out, and I abroad

but he is making images of a life in which he does not see her
She tries allure,

> in the darkness spearing salmon in the Owen or the Carramore.
> PEGEEN: If I was your wife I'd be along with you those nights, Christy Mahon,
>   the way you'd see I

but rapidly shifts to a comradely approach to edge into his secret life

> was a great hand at coaxing bailiffs or coining funny nicknames for the stars of night.
> CHRISTY: You, is it? Taking your

He takes a bragging, male, protective attitude — encouraging to Pegeen
Now she is openly suggestive

> death in the hailstones or the fogs of dawn.
> PEGEEN: Yourself and me would shelter easy in a narrow bush.

But she sees this is overstepping — He knows that night fishing must be done quietly without girls — She has to try belittling herself again

> But we're only talking, maybe,
>
> for this would be a poor thatched place to hold a fine lad is the like of you.

He reassures her, not wanting her to feel badly

> CHRISTY: If I wasn't a good Christian, it's on my naked knees

I'd be saying my prayers and paters to every jackstraw you have roofing your head and every stony pebble is paving the way to your door.

She plays her last card, holding her face near and speaking low

PEGEEN: If that's the truth I'll be burning candles from this out to the miracles of God that have brought you from the south today.

But he is off by himself — There is nothing to do but take him as he is — Like Christy, having won in a sort of way, she moves away in a delighted embrace of the biggest thing in the world, herself

And I with my gowns ready, the way I can wed you and not wait at all.

Fourth Attack: They try to fit each other into the new image of self. Not until they become adjusted to the new sense of power can they return to the magic moment they missed in Attack II. Now each is cuddling his new self and trying to fit the other into his world.

CHRISTY: It's miracles and that's the truth. Me there, toiling a long while and walking a long while, not knowing at all I was drawing all times nearer this holy day.

Is there an attempt to get his attention by jealousy? If so, it fails

PEGEEN: And myself a girl was tempted often to go sailing the seas till I'd marry a Jew man with ten kegs of gold, and I not knowing at all there was the like of you drawing nearer like the stars of God.

CHRISTY: And to think I'm long years hearing women talk that talk to all bloody fools and this is the first time I've heard the like of your voice talking sweetly for my own delight.

PEGEEN: And to think it's me talking sweetly, Christy Mahon, and I the fright of seven townships for my biting tongue. Well, the heart's a wonder.

He turns to her, sees her — As she goes into his arms, he savors the moment

And I'm thinking there won't be our like in Mayo for gallant lovers from this hour today.

Now he would take his kiss but

(MICHAEL JAMES is heard singing drunkenly offstage. The lovers
scramble apart.)

NO CLIMAX

The pattern of objectives and attacks, which the foregoing analyses are designed to illustrate, can be found in any scene that one studies. The less obvious it is, the more necessary for the director to find and utilize it, because without it the scene is mere talk, and nothing happens.

Characterizing Minor Characters

Through the Pattern

A third and final example will show how a very few speeches and some imagination will suggest an objective and help to characterize a thinly written minor character. In the scene be-tween Christy and the girls in Act II, the four girls seem very much alike on the first reading. They are all sixteen or seventeen, all have come up out of curiosity to see the man who killed his father, and all have brought gifts. Almost certainly the play-wright used four instead of one in order to diffuse interest, so that none of them could be thought of as potential rivals of Pegeen. Almost certainly, too, he wanted them to be quite dif-ferent types, and he has given the actors some clues.

Sara is easiest to characterize because she has the most lines, and she also has another scene that helps to reveal her. Al-though she does not enter first, she seems to be a ringleader. She is the one who examines Christy's boots and finds the traces of his wanderings on them. She tries them on and decides to keep them for going to the priest, "when you'd be ashamed this place . . . with nothing worth while to confess at all." Susan recalls how Sara drove ten miles to see another curiosity. It is Sara who calls Christy, using Pegeen as a pretext; who first speaks to him; and who first presents her gift, duck eggs (snitched from her brother's roost?), getting in a dig at Pegeen as she gives them. Though she gives the other girls their innings, she is interested in Christy's reactions and thus discovers that he does not use his right hand, because he is holding a mirror behind his back. This might change the course of the scene except that the Widow Quin joins them. When the Widow reports that she has entered Christy in the races, Sara bets her dowry that he will win. She listens to the story of the murder without comment except to shush the others and urge Christy on, and she toasts Christy and the Widow "to the wonders of the Western World." She has a quick excuse when Pegeen catches them entertaining Christy. She goes off and finds a jockey suit so that Christy can ride in the mule races, and she has a dig for Pegeen as she hurries Christy off to the races. In the scene in which the mob turns against Christy, Sara's line, "Ask Pegeen to help," is another jeer at Pegeen. Finally, Sara tries to put her petticoat and shawl on Christy to help him escape.

Sara clearly delights in adventure. She is like a child, wanting to roll in her adventure as a puppy does in grass. Perhaps she has a second objective, to get the better of Pegeen, for these are two of a kind, and Sara could easily become a rival.

Susan, who enters first, is also the first to give up, suggesting that she may have been pushed into the house by the others. She is aghast at the thought of blood on Christy's boots and seems to urge Sara to follow Christy's supposed flight. Susan's gift is a pat of butter. There is a motherly concern that his food taste good. She rather stupidly interrupts Christy's story with a pointless comment. She flat-footedly gives Christy to the Widow, with a coarse, "Lift him on her knee." When she returns later to get Christy to the races, she catches him with "Pegeen says." This is a girl who has not thought of herself as particularly attractive to men, a commonplace girl, probably a little too plump. She is Sara's satellite and would like to be as vital as

Sara, but lacks the qualifications. She tries to do what she thinks Sara would like her to do.

Honor is the second to give up when they do not find Christy at once, and, in doing so, she is sorry for herself: "and we after rising early and destroying ourselves running fast on the hill." She listens at the inner door, and first sees Christy through a crack, becoming wildly excited as she sees, "It's a man." She probably did not make the cake she brings him, for if she had, she would have mentioned the fact. She seconds Susan in the stupid interruption of the story. In hurrying Christy to the races, she betrays impatience in, "Come on, will you." Honor is pretty enough to get a husband, but she will become a typical dissatisfied wife if her husband does not adore her. She wants attention.

Nelly has the fewest lines, but they indicate that she gets the highest marks in school. Faced with disappointment, she reasons "It'd be early for them both to be out walking the hill." It is she who finds Christy's boots, the evidence that he is there, though she leaves Sara to jump to conclusions. Nelly's gift is a little laying pullet salvaged from a roadside accident and quickly popped into the pot. Nelly is smart and practical. She wants some of whatever is being passed around, including information. She may wear glasses.

From the point of view of the girls the scene breaks into seven units, in each of which the group objective is pursued, while each girl has something specific to do or some characteristic response to the situation in the light of what she wanted herself in coming to see the murderer. And each gets just what she wanted — if we are careful to give Honor a seductive exit that catches Christy's eye and prompts Pegeen to the story of the hanging.

When characters are written as scantily as these four girls, the director's interpretation is limited only by the function of the character in the play as a whole, the actual lines and business given by the playwright, and the combined imagination of director and actors. It may be indeed that some other objectives could be indicated by the lines of these characters. But until the girls have clear objectives they are little better than sticks, and there are no criteria for casting them.

ANALYSIS OF OBJECTIVES OF MINOR CHARACTERS,

Playboy, ACT II

All the girls want the thrill of meeting a real murderer. Sara wants adventure, Susan wants to please Sara, Honor wants a boy, Nelly wants to know what is going on.

Attack I. They face their disappointment in not finding Christy — Susan is ready to leave, Nelly studies the situation, Honor cries for herself, Sara salvages an adventure

SUSAN: There's nobody in it.

NELLY: It'd be early for them both to be out walking the hill.

SUSAN: I'm thinking Shawn Keogh was making game of us and there's no such man in it at all.

HONOR: Look at that. He's been sleeping there in the night. Well, it'll be a hard case if he's gone off now, the way we'll never set our eyes on a man killed his father, and we after rising early and destroying ourselves running fast on the hills.

NELLY: Are you thinking them's his boots?

SARA: If they are, there should be his father's tracks on them. Did you never read in the papers the way murdered men do drip and bleed?

SUSAN: Is that blood there, Sara Tansey?

SARA: That's bog water, I'm thinking. But it's his own they are surely, for never have I seen the like of them for whitey mud and red mud and turf on them, and the fine sands of the sea. That man's been walking, I'm telling you.

SUSAN: Maybe he's stolen off to Belmullet with the boots of Michael James. And you'd have a right to follow after him, Sara Tansey, and you the one yoked the ass-cart and drove ten miles to set your eyes on the man bit the yellow lady's nostril on the northern shore.

She puts on the boots.

SARA: Don't be talking, and we fooled today. There's a pair that do fit me well, and I'll be keeping them for walking to the priest, when you'd be ashamed this place, going up winter and summer with nothing worth while to confess at all.

Attack II. They adjust to meeting Christy — Honor flees with thrills of excitement, Sara grabs the adventure — Nellie watches — Susan stands ready to deliver her gift

HONOR: Whisht! There's someone inside the room. It's a man!

SARA: I'll call him. Mister. Mister. Is Pegeen within?

(CHRISTY enters)

CHRISTY: She's above on the cnuceen, seeking the nannygoats, the way she'd have a sup of goats' milk for to color my tea.

SARA: And asking your pardon, is it you's the man killed his father?

CHRISTY: I am, God help me.

SARA: Then my thousand welcomes to you, and I've run up with a brace of duck's eggs for your food today. Pegeen's ducks is no use, but these are the real rich sort. Hold out your hands and you'll see it's no lie I'm telling you.

Attack III. They present their gifts — Sara swaggers, slashing at her rival — Susan mothers him — Honor giggles, aware she's pretty and he's a boy — Nelly knows her gift has the most value, brags a little, complacently

CHRISTY: They're a great and weighty size.

SUSAN: And I run up with a pat of butter, for it'd be a poor thing to have you eating your spuds dry, and you after running a great way since you did destroy your da.

CHRISTY: Thank you kindly.

HONOR: And I brought you a little cut of cake, for you should have a thin stomach on you, and you that length walking the world.

NELLY: And I brought you a little laying pullet — boiled and all she is — was crushed at the fall of night by the curate's car. Feel the fat of that breast, mister.

CHRISTY: It's bursting, surely.

Attack IV. Sara finds the mirror — Sara hoots, Honor and Susan giggle, Nelly tries to make sense of it

SARA: Will you pinch it? Is your right hand too sacred for to use at all? It's a glass he has! Well, I never seen to this day a man with a looking glass held to his back. Them that kills their fathers is a vain lot, surely.

CHRISTY: I'm very thankful to you all today.

(WIDOW QUIN enters)

Attack V. They take the Widow into the group — Sara has made several visits to her house and has gained prestige from knowing the sophisticated Widow — Susan is afraid of finding out what sophistication is — Honor and Nelly disapprove of her

WIDOW: Sara Tansey! Susan Brady! Nelly Donovan! Honor Blake! What in glory has you here at this hour of the day?

GIRLS: That's the man killed his father.

WIDOW: I know well it's the man; and I'm after putting him down in the sports below for racing, lepping, pitching and the Lord knows what.

SARA: That's right, Widow Quin. I'll bet my dowry that he'll lick the world.

WIDOW: If you will, you'd have a right to have him fresh and nourished in place of nursing a feast. Are you fasting or fed, young fellow?

CHRISTY: Fasting, if you please.

Attack VI. They make him tea while listening — Susan and Nelly do most of the work

WIDOW: Well, you're the lot. Stir up now and give him his breakfast. Come here to me and let you tell us your story before Pegeen will come, in place of grinning your ears off like the moon of May.

CHRISTY: It's a long story, and you'd be destroyed listening.

WIDOW: Don't be letting on to be shy, a fine gamey treacherous lad the like of you. Was it in your house beyond you cracked his skull?

Sara laughs with her

CHRISTY: It was not. We were digging spuds in his cold, sloping stony divil's patch of a field.

Honor arranges herself prettily to catch his eye

WIDOW: And you went asking money of him, or making talk of getting a wife would drive him from his farm.

CHRISTY: I did not then. But there I was digging and digging and, "You squinting idiot," says he, "let you walk down now and tell the priest you'll wed the Widow Casey in a score of days."

WIDOW: What kind was she?

CHRISTY: A walking terror from beyond the hills, and she two score and five years, two hundred-weights and five pounds in the weighing scales, with a limping leg on her and a blinded eye, and she a woman of noted misbehavior with the young and old.

Susan is struck by this

Honor gasps, shocked

GIRLS: Glory be!

WIDOW: And what did he want driving you to wed with her?

Nelly quietly sets his cup and saucer, all ears

CHRISTY: He was letting on I was wanting a protector from the harshness of the world, and he without a thought the whole while but how he'd have her hut to live in and her gold to drink.

WIDOW: There's maybe worse than a dry hearth and a widow woman and your glass at night. So you hit him then?

Sara and Susan exchange glances as the Widow flirts — Honor tries a more interesting position

**Attack VII. To gobble his story —
Honor covers her blushes, Susan
and Nelly shift uncomfortably, but
Sara laps it up**

CHRISTY: I did not. "I won't
wed her," says I, "when all know
she did suckle me for six weeks
when I came into the world," and
she a hag this day with a tongue
on her has the crows and seabirds
scattered, the way they wouldn't
cast a shadow on her garden with
the dread of her curse.

WIDOW: That one should be right
company.

SARA: Don't mind her. Did you
kill him then?

CHRISTY: "She's too good for the
likes of you," says he, "and go on
now, or I'll flatten you out like a

**All listen wide-eyed — Sara empa-
thizes**

crawling beast has passed under a
dray." "You will not if I can help
it," says I. "Go on," says he "or
I'll have the divil making garters of
your limbs tonight." "You will not
if I can help it," says I.

SARA: You were right, surely.

CHRISTY: With that the sun
came out between the cloud and the
hill, and it shining green in my face.
"God have mercy on your soul,"
says he, lifting a scythe. "Or on
your own," says I, raising the loy.

SUSAN: That's a grand story.

HONOR: He tells it lovely.

**Nelly inadvertently screams — This
is too much information, too real**

CHRISTY: He gave a drive with
the scythe, and I gave a lep to the
east. Then I turned around with
my back to the north, and I hit him
a blow on the ridge of his skull laid
him stretched out, and he split to
the nob of his gullet.

**CLIMAX. Nelly has learned; this
is life! Honor fans herself out of
her ecstatic swoon, Susan gushes in
delight, Sara pushes more food at
him**

GIRLS: Well, you're a marvel.
Oh, God bless you. You're the lad,
surely.

SUSAN: I'm thinking the Lord
God sent him this road to make a

second   husband   to   the   Widow
Quin, and she with a great yearning
to be wedded, though all dread her
here. Lift him on her knee, Sara
Tansey.

Sara pours tea for the Widow —   WIDOW: Don't tease him.
The girls jump to the toast, except   SARA: You're heroes surely, and
Honor, who is still trying in vain to   let you drink a supeen with your
interest him in her charms   arms linked like the outlandish lovers in the sailors' song. There now.
Drink a health to the wonders of
the   Western   world,   the   pirates,
preachers, poteen makers, with the
jobbing   jockies,   parching   peelers
and   the   juries   fill   their   stomachs
selling judgments of the English
law.

This may seem unnecessarily minute *study* — until the actors
start asking questions, or fail to create anything of their own,
or until, however experienced the director may be, he bogs down
in a "talky" or static scene. When this happens, there is no use
putting in more stage business and keeping the actors moving,
for these tricks are confusing as well as boring. The thing to do
is to get down to bedrock, to ask what happens, who wants
what in the scene and how does he try to get it. Director and
actors try to find more varied and more vivid attacks. Stage
business that develops from this process clarifies and is therefore
legitimately interesting.

Although analysis as detailed as that through which the reader
has been led in the last two chapters is difficult and time-
consuming, its value to the play is proportionately great.

First, the director has taken the first broad steps toward
clarity for the audience. He has found the changes in idea and
feeling that would be marked, in a novel, by chapter and paragraph breaks. He must now seek means of letting the audience
know by visual and auditory changes where a new scene and a
new attack begins, seeking the largest changes at the breaks

between scenes, and slightly less striking changes between the attacks.

Second, he has found the basic rhythm of the play, which is not something determined arbitrarily, but is inherent in the ebb and flow of the desires of the characters. The change of scene, with its sharp change of pace, energy, and quality is like the change from movement to movement of a symphony; the changes of attack are like the musical phrase, all part of one movement, but each distinct in itself.

Finally, he has acquired his most powerful tool for stimulating the actors' imaginations and emotions. By helping the actors to find the broad outlines of their characters' behavior, emotionally and physically, he can release them from strain and lead them to concentration and a sense of truth. He has begun the course advocated by Stanislavsky (*An Actor Prepares*, p. 265): "Put a role on the right road and it will move ahead. It will grow broader and deeper and will in the end lead to inspiration."

Assignments

Make detailed analyses of the following scenes:

1. *The Playboy,* Act I, Pegeen's row with the Widow.
2. *The Playboy,* Act II, Shawn's attempt to get Christy to leave.
3. *The Playboy,* Act III, Michael James's scene, from his entrance to the entrance of Old Mahon.
4. *The Glass Menagerie,* Scene 2, Amanda's scene with Laura over Laura's quitting school.
5. *The Glass Menagerie,* Scene 5, Amanda's scene with Tom, from Laura's exit to Tom's offstage "yes."
6. *The Importance of Being Earnest,* Act I, Algernon's spat with Jack over the "whole question of Cecily," involving the cigarette case, ending with "Here it is. Now produce your explanation, and pray make it improbable."

7. *The Importance of Being Earnest,* Act II, the last scene between Jack and Algy.
8. *The Importance of Being Earnest,* Act II, Miss Prism's courtship scene with Dr. Chasuble — to Jack's entrance.
9. *Romeo and Juliet,* Act I, Sc. 1, scene between the Montague parents and Benvolio, giving Benvolio's objective and attacks.
10. *Romeo and Juliet,* Act III, Sc. 5, second balcony scene to Lady Capulet's entrance.
11. *Romeo and Juliet,* Act V, Sc. 3, Romeo's farewell to Juliet, from, "How oft when men are at the point of death," to Romeo's death.

Reading List

Stanislavsky, Constantin. *An Actor Prepares.* New York: Theatre Arts, Inc., 1936, Chapters VII and XVI.

Cole, Toby and Helen Crich Chinoy. *Directing the Play.* Indianapolis. Bobbs-Merrill, 1953, pp. 291-295 on Bertolt Brecht and pp. 296-310 on Elia Kazan.

Chapter 8

Finding the Setting

After reading the play several times the director begins to think of characters moving in space. He realizes that there will clearly have to be the door, fireplace, sofa, or whatever functional elements of scenery the action calls for. He visualizes, perhaps, color and lights creating moods for certain scenes. Perhaps for some scenes he knows almost the whole business and properties and scenic elements. Before he can go much further in the study of the play, the space in which the actors move will have to be defined.

The setting described in the acting edition of a play is usually the setting of the original production simplified for "amateur" use. It is not always the best possible setting for the play; in fact, it is often a very bad adaptation. In any case, it was not designed for the conception of the play or for the particular stage that any specific director will use. It is always wise to ignore the ground plan offered in the acting edition, at least until one's understanding of the play and its requirements is fairly complete.

In the professional theatre, a highly skilled designer studies the play and presents sketches for the approval of producer, playwright, and director. In educational and community theatre, the director often has to design the scenery himself. In any case, he will have to help the designer, who may be able to create a handsome picture, but often does not know what will be useful and what obstructive to the actors. With pardonable concern for his own part of the theatre job, he is apt to forget Appia's brilliant advice that a stage setting should be "bare, empty, as if waiting" for the living presence of the actor.

Preliminary Study

Scenic design is one of the most exciting arts of the theatre, but, like everything complex, it is not learned overnight. To learn to design effectively, one should start by copious reading of general theatre history, then the books of great modern designers like Lee Simonson, Robert Edmond Jones, Donald Oenslager, and back through Appia and Craig to the history of specific periods. Since designs must be not only pleasing but also practicable — that is, able to stand up under use and to be shifted — one must also know a good deal about construction and rigging. Several texts on stagecraft and design are suggested in the reading list at the end of this chapter.

In hunting the setting for a specific play, one's imagination can be stimulated by travel books and books on interior decorating, with authentic pictures of the area or period of the play. A nineteenth-century Irish cottage does not look the same as a slum apartment in St. Louis. Floor plan, doors, windows, bannisters, ceiling, ground rows are different. In this research, unexpected details will turn up that not only give authenticity and flavor, but also help one to visualize the story in ways that are not trite.

Basic Requirements of Scenery

The director requires of scenery, first, of course, that it be appropriate to the play, architecturally credible, and satisfactory as design.

An appropriate design gives a good bit of information about the characters who use the space and about the mood of the play. *Romeo and Juliet* will need sunny Italian streets (if a representational production is planned), a moon-drenched balcony, a torchlit ballroom. *The Importance of Being Earnest* will need exquisite knickknacks in an overelegant drawing room. Crystal and gilt and gingerbread and pink light will be right for it, and Cecily will have a silly formal garden. *The Glass Menagerie* needs a few battered, time-eaten frivolities — a fringed lampshade, faded, pink-flowered cretonne — in Amanda's dim house. Even modern, "smart" comedies need arrangements of floor levels, furniture, details, and colors that reveal the nature of the people who live in the place. Stage design is never mere interior decoration. It is the shrewd creation of a space that reveals the characters and aids the telling of the story.

To be architecturally credible, the setting must create the illusion that it is made of the materials it purports to be made of, and that it could afford the uses to which it is put in the action of the play. If the production is to be realistic, doors and windows need thicknesses, and doors need weight. Openings must logically seem to lead where they are said to lead. Windows cannot be in the same wall as a door to an inner room without some kind of masking to indicate the logic of the arrangement. Staircases must not rise in directions where they would seem to lead past an open door or window. The same opening can hardly be used to lead to a kitchen and a bedroom, unless the opening is an alcove, with an exit on one side to the kitchen, on the other to the bedroom. Since openings always evoke curiosity, a set must not include doors that are not used. Top and sides of settings must be appropriately masked to prevent the audience from seeing backstage. In an interior, a ceiling piece and returns manage this easily, but in an exterior setting this problem is more difficult. One may use a barn to block in a field or yard, a porch or garden wall or summer house to block in a garden, with a tree or sky border overhead lighted properly. These points seem almost too elementary to mention, yet they are problems an unskilled director and designer may ignore, until they create havoc at dress rehearsals. They must be solved at once, along with the design of the setting, or, often, they cannot be solved at all.

Even if the production is to be realistic, one does not have to load the setting with gruesome wallpaper and pictures. The purpose of a stage setting is to create, not actuality, but an illusion of actuality, and one does this through a careful selection of highly characteristic details that will stir the imagination of the audience. Amanda's fringed portieres, the shape of the spindly whatnot that houses Laura's menagerie tell more about the Wingfields than a distracting litter of Victorian pictures and ornaments could do. What the designer can make the audience imagine is always more excellently real than anything carpentry and an eager property man can devise.

If the production is not to be realistic, the designer and the director must observe two or three cautions. It is wise to establish the unrealistic convention at the opening curtain, so that its shock value will be absorbed at once, and the audience can then concentrate on the content of the play. Also, it is essential to be consistent, using the convention in the setting, the properties, even in the acting, throughout the play, for inconsistencies re-shock and confuse the audience. It hardly needs to be said that any convention adopted by the director and the designer must be appropriate to the play, motivated throughout by the quality of the script itself, and subserving the playwright's intent of moving the audience in a certain way. It should never proceed from the mere whim of designer or director to be "different."

As a design, the setting requires unity, variety, balance, stability. If a large, heavy fireplace is on one side of the stage, some large unit — a bay window, double door, or large piece of furniture like a secretary — might be placed on the other side. The whole picture needs to be fastened to the curtain line by having some usable element of scenery or property at the downstage corners. The principle of stability is illustrated by two triangles. One seems entirely solid, with its base on the floor; the

Fig. 6

other, standing on its apex, seems about to keel over. Putting a chair or desk or some other useful bit of furniture at each downstage corner gives the design stability and has other advantages to be mentioned later.

It is easy to see why most textbooks on stage scenery contain only the most limited advice on stage design. Good design is not learned by rule of thumb, or by any common practice, but by long study of historical modes and of architectural and artistic ways and means. Yet the director must know something of stage design because the setting is the environment in which the actors must seem to live, and it can make the actor's job easier, or more difficult.

Scenery for Emphasis

Important as the appearance of the setting is to the play as a whole, there are other functions of scenery that can make or break the work of the actors.

The first consideration is that actors must move in the setting. There must be spaces suitable to accommodate the largest crowd scene and the most intimate scene the play contains.

The Irish cottage of *The Playboy* must contain the quiet little scene in which Pegeen Mike and Christy become acquainted, and the scene in which the crowd turns against Christy when Mahon beats him. It must contain spaces that will emphasize Christy's emotional change from the moment of the beating to the moment when he challenges, "I'm coming, but I'll stretch you first." When Christy is beaten to the floor, his nadir can be emphasized by getting some of the other characters high — on the bar, in the window seat, on chairs. His apogee can be emphasized by having him, perhaps, jump to the table, while the other characters take low positions. As the visual action on stage must reinforce the emotional relationships of the characters, the scenery must make these revelations of inner action possible.

The director is looking for ways to use his whole stage. The scenery can provide motivation for the actors to go into every area and can create playing areas. The unimaginative rectang-

Fig. 7

ular set, with furniture arranged left and right, gives at most four good playing areas. A setting that is broken by jogs, levels, alcoves, stair landings, and informally (but credibly) arranged furniture can create eight or nine good playing areas.

In dozens of ways, the scenery can create points of emphasis for the actor. Since an object near the eye seems larger and therefore commands more attention than one further away, all other things being equal, an actor in a downstage[1] area seems larger and is thus more emphatic than one upstage. The downstage actor is also in front of most of the furniture, and usually in a stronger light than he would be in upstage. Acoustically, too, he has an advantage. The downstage areas are therefore thought of as strong and are used for scenes of vital importance to the play — main crises, important exposition, strong complications, and characterization of main characters. Upstage, the actor is ten to fifteen feet away from the curtain line, and frequently behind furniture and in less strong light. This remoteness seems to make the upstage areas weak. They are used for transitions, for scenes between minor characters, scenes of secondary importance, lightly characterizing scenes, and simply for variety and contrast. In a stage setting, the furniture is usually arranged in such a way as to make it easy for the actors to use the downstage areas. To these generalities, there are many exceptions.

One of the first things a director learns about stage space is that, in many theatres, the upstage corners of a "box" set cannot be seen by all of the spectators. He learns to rake the corners in

[1] The terms "downstage" and "upstage" originated in the Renaissance, when the discovery of perspective was applied to stage scenery. Because they recognized that a flat surface, like a road, seems to rise as it recedes into the distance, the floor of the stage was raked upward toward the backdrop to make the setting look deeper than it actually was. Thus the actor actually did go up when he moved away from the audience, and down when he came toward the audience.

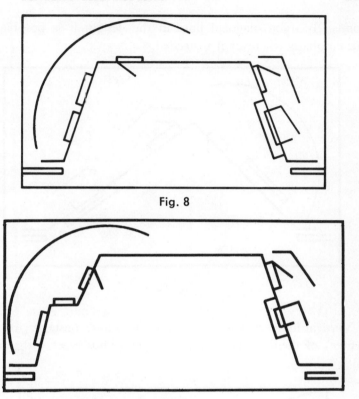

Fig. 8

Fig. 9

three or four feet, or to build angles in one or both corners that eliminate the useless space. If the sightlines are very bad, he designs a two-sided setting instead of a three-sided one.

The shape of the setting determines the main focus or actual "center" of emphasis. An asymmetrical setting puts the focus off center by making strong diagonal lines where walls join floor and ceiling. These diagonals create a new center. Other diagonals that create foci are staircases, drapes, pictures arranged diagonally, and furniture arranged in triangular space. The base of any staircase and the apex of any triangle are emphatic points. By using diagonal lines in the design, it is possible to put emphasis wherever it is needed.

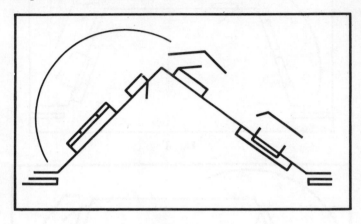

Fig. 10

Vertical lines emphasize an actor who stands onstage (toward center) of them, or downstage of them. Thus a set with many

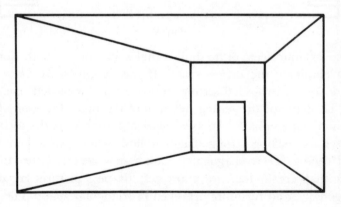

Fig. 11

jogs, or with columns, pilasters, trees, or any other vertical constructions, furnishes emphasis points off the actual center of the
stage.

Fig. 12

Even more forceful are framing units such as a large door or
window, a tall fireplace, or a huge piece of furniture like a

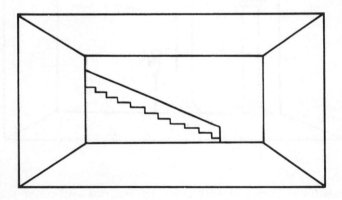

Fig. 13

secretary. The actor standing within the framing outline of such a unit is emphatic.

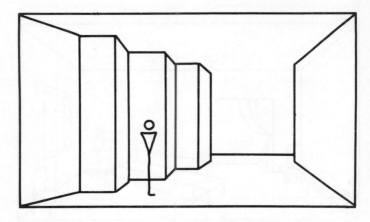

Fig. 14

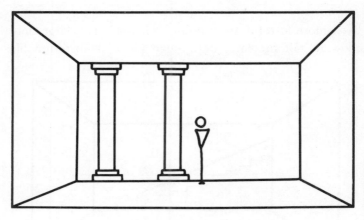

Fig. 15

Horizontal lines can emphasize by contrast. An actor standing against a low railing or at one end of a sofa seems tall.

Low ceiling beams can make an actor seem huge. But shoulder high horizontal lines cut the actor's head off.

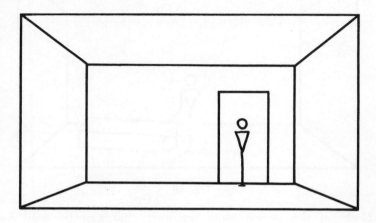

Fig. 16

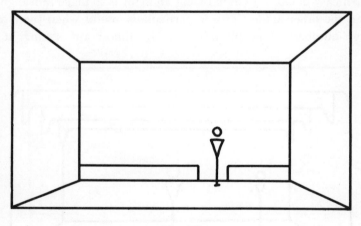

Fig. 17

The mass of large furniture, such as a table or a heavy chair, adds weight to the actor standing near it. It is thus useful to

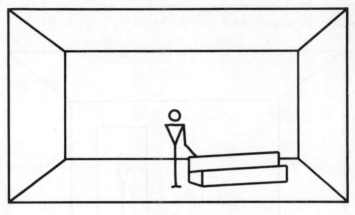

Fig. 18

include in the design some furniture that can be used for emphasis.

An easy device for emphasizing an actor is to place him higher than the other actors. This is particularly useful when there are large numbers of people on stage. In almost any setting, it is

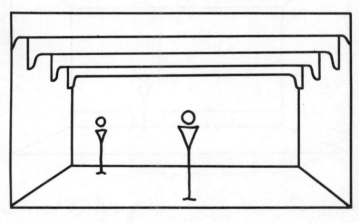

Fig. 19

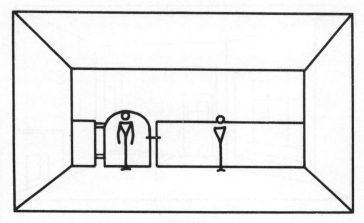

Fig. 20

possible to justify the inclusion of a platform, for houses are
not always built at one time, and ground is not necessarily level.
An oldish house might have an ell that would be up or down
a couple of steps — and it is generally helpful if the steps de-
scend toward center. A flat field might have a raised ditch-dyke

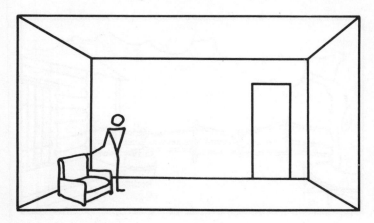

Fig. 21

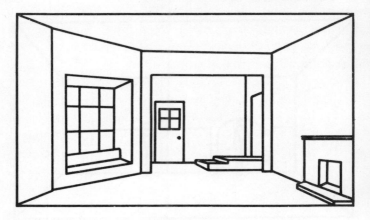

Fig. 22

across it, or a fence with a stile. A large window unit can be reached by one inconspicuous but infinitely helpful step up. A fireplace may have a raised hearth, useful for either standing or sitting on. Once the director has seen the tremendous advantage gained by even a little difference in level, he will utilize this device as often as he can justify it.

Fig. 23

Color is an important means of securing emphasis. If the setting is of a neutral color, the actor in a brighter or contrasting costume will be emphatic.

Finally, the focus of attention is always the point at which there is most light. In designing the action of a play, the director must keep in mind the capabilities of his control board. If he cannot light the downstage areas, if he cannot vary the intensity of light from moment to moment and from point to point on the stage to gain emphasis where he wants it, his problems of designing both scenery and movement will be redoubled.

One of the first problems in designing the setting is likely to be that two scenes of different quality have to be played in the same space. For example, a sofa facing a fireplace might be useful for a certain scene, but for another scene it would be better to have the sofa facing a window. In this case, the director must decide which of the two scenes is the more important, and set sofa, fireplace, and window for this scene, using whatever compensations he can for the other scene. The values of the play determine which scenes shall be given preference in designing the setting.

These values have to be considered in solving a major problem in *The Playboy*, the location of the outside door and window. Very important actions depend on the placing of these units:

1. Shawn crosses the door and the window, revealing his conflict as the play starts. If he cannot be seen, there are dead pauses while Pegeen writes, and Shawn's relation to her is not clear when he enters. Door and window need to be in the upstage wall for simple clarity.

2. Christy enters, "tired, dirty and frightened." This is a climactic entrance, with everyone on stage cowering from the dreadful sight they expect. The whole of Christy's *status quo*

is revealed in the lame entrance. The door needs to be upstage
for emphasis and in a weak area for comic effect.

3. Christy sees his father approaching, and Mahon enters,
a large and threatening figure. Christy hides behind the door.
Would it help if the audience sees him hiding? The door should
be in the upstage wall, for emphasis, clarity, and comic effect.

4. Shawn flees twice through the door, and Christy chases
his father through it. The door should be upstage and in a weak
area because the upstage and out cross is weak, especially if
Christy leaps from a high position on the table to a low position of beating his father just beyond the door.

5. Christy makes his last triumphant exit there. The door
should be upstage, because the last speech, delivered in the frame
of the door, with diagonal lines of actors turned to him would
be highly emphatic.

6. But the Widow and Mahon and the other men watch
the races through the window or door or both. This scene is
very difficult if the actors' backs must be toward the audience
and suggests putting as least the window in a side wall. But
Christy is sitting in the window for most of his long soliloquy
opening Act II and should be facing downstage.

The sum of the argument thus urges that door and window
be placed in the back wall, and the director is left to find means
of overcoming the problem of the races.

If both window and door are in the back wall, the four
actors watching the race will have their backs to the audience
through several supposedly exciting moments of the play. One
way of handling the problem would be to start the scene with
some of the actors on the window seat and some at the door
and to vary their positions as their excitement leads each to
communicate with the other group, moving from window to
door and vice versa. Another would be to have someone view
the races from outside the door and keep popping in to report
what he saw. Of course the widow would have to stay inside in

order to keep Mahon from getting too good a view, and thus recognizing Christy.

Since the action of the play varies from instant to instant, the setting is planned to give fullest value to the main actions of the play, and keen directing must compensate for deficiencies of scenery in the subordinate scenes.

Emotional Values through Scenery

The shape of the stage not only provides emphasis points, but also has much to do with the emotional effect of various scenes. In general, enclosed areas and broken spaces are less harsh than large empty spaces. A fireplace with furniture intimately grouped around it, an alcove attractively decorated in warm colors and invitingly furnished, a nook under a stairway, a cushioned window seat, or a warm drape can provide emotional background for tender scenes even in a fundamentally cold play. If large open space is essential, a design in curves is less harsh than a design in angles. Within a curve is a good place to play a warm scene, while an angular space may be more appropriate for sinister or harsh scenes. One point of caution should be observed in using curves on the stage: large curves are bland, soft, peaceful, romantic; but small curves, especially if numerous, are frivolous and comic. Their main use is, of course, in plays that are frivolous and comic.

The kind and arrangement of furniture has much to do with the emotional value of stage space. Furniture on stage has four main functions: to enable the actors to follow the playwright's stage directions, to create playing areas and emphasis points; to motivate movement; and to decorate appropriately. As in a room, intimacy is gained by grouping the furniture around points of interest — fireplace, coffee table, television set (if one is needed). A cold, formal effect often results from a symmetrical arrangement or from placing furniture parallel to the curtain

line. A bare, unsocial, institutional atmosphere is created by placing furniture against walls. This arrangement should be made
only in a very tiny set, for it denies one of the main functions of
furniture — breaking up space. Furniture placed stage center
usually divides a small stage into three downstage playing areas.
If placed right and left of center, it can make five areas.

It is practically a rule to place some furniture or unit of
scenery down right and down left. This is not only to give the
picture stability. Unless some reason is created for the actors
to use the outer corners of the set, two useful acting areas will
be lost, or the actor moving into these spaces will seem theatrical
with no reasonable motive to be there. A downstage fireplace, a
table or desk with properties that have to be used, a chair in
a corner that relates to chairs further onstage, or, out-of-doors,
a log, a well, a gate — any of these would help to weight the
picture and to motivate the actors into these spaces.

In arranging the furniture, if an entrance or exit is important,
it must not be blocked by placing large units of furniture across
it, for the actor is expressive only to the extent that he can be
seen. Instead of blocking the entrance, the furniture might be
arranged diagonally toward the important opening.

The amount of scenery and furniture usable on any stage
depends, of course, on the size of the stage. A comfortable
depth for a stage setting is twelve to fifteen feet, if many people
have to play in it. For a small cast, it is possible to use a ten-foot
depth. A proscenium opening of twenty-eight feet is not unusually small, though it is often too small for the stage plans
offered in the acting edition. On the other hand, an opening
of forty feet will demand more scenery and furniture than is
usually given in the plan the acting edition provides, or the stage
will look bare. If the opening is unusually large, it is often
possible to build a false proscenium, for by narrowing the opening, the play gains intimacy, and also a great deal of labor and
money are saved by reducing the number of flats that must be

built and painted. If the sides of the stage are blocked off by a false proscenium, however, it will also be wise to block off certain seats in the auditorium from which sightlines will be very bad.

Properties can also make a difference in the emotional values of a play. Cushions, flowers, draperies, objets d'art, all the paraphernalia of living, can warm up a cold area and add to the appearance of livableness of the setting, as well as reveal the kind of people living there.

A most important emotional aid is color. The audience responds to the "warm" and "cool" colors, perhaps unconsciously. Because their predilections are always conservative, dependent on the current styles, the director must be wary of his personal peculiarities of taste in color, lest they conflict too drastically with the common taste; for his objective in the theatre is not to startle but to control.

One elementary caution should be given here against oversharp contrasts of light and dark, especially of black and white, in the background. For example, in a setting of black drapes, an actor passing a white unit will leave the gaze of the audience on that unit instead of carrying attention with him. It is impossible for the actor to keep the attention of the audience if he must move across glaring light areas. If white and black are called for, it is customary to substitute a pastel shade, warm or cool as the mood indicates, for white, and a dark blue, green, brown, or purple for black. For the same reason it is unwise to decorate a setting above the heads of the actors. A high mural, unless very much spattered down, or a high rose window brighter than the area it surmounts, or a cyclorama too brilliantly lighted will call the eye of the audience up, away from the actor, instead of drawing it down to the stage.

The shape and color of light contribute powerfully to the emotional effect of the setting. A stage window, for example, is doubly joyous if a shaft of yellow sunlight comes through it.

A pool of light creates concentration and intimacy. Warm color, pink or straw, makes pleasant empathy. A cool light, blue, steel, lavender, gives a remote, harsh, lonely feeling.

All of these means of securing emotional values and emphasis in the setting are fundamental. They may not all be needed in every play, but they constitute the basic tools of the stage designer. If the director can learn how to use them, he will not only gain interest and variety in planning stage business, but he will also be able to reach into the subconscious responses of the audience, subtly evoking the empathies he wishes to create.

Practicability

Finally, in planning a play with more than one setting, shifting time is of paramount importance. The designer must learn to use unit settings, rolling units, and flown units before attempting a multiset play. Above all, he must learn to simplify without seeming to skimp. It is almost impossible to present a good multiset play until one's flights of imagination take practical shape *via* a good working knowledge of stagecraft and lighting.

Before finally determining on the setting, the director must know his own stage, in order to be sure that his idea will work, as well as to avoid insuperable problems for whoever is building the set.

Most useful to the director in planning his setting, stage pictures, and movements are two scale drawings of his theatre. The first is a ground plan that shows the exact size of the stage with all its openings and fixed furnishings — radiators, steps, scene dock, sink, anything that takes space — and also the first row of seats. This drawing enables one to fit his plan into the actual space it will have to occupy, to be sure that everybody can see all of the stage, and nobody can see anything backstage that is not a part of the setting.

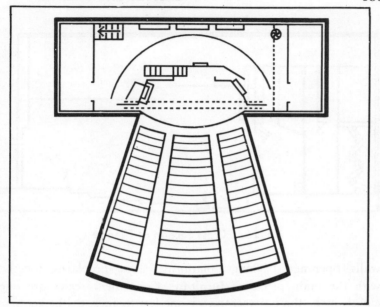

Fig. 24.   Ground Plan of Theatre·

The other is a cross section that shows the height of the grid and the arch, the rake of the auditorium floor, and the first and last seats in the house, including balcony seats if there is a balcony. This drawing is needed to trim the teaser and the borders (if needed) so that no one can see over the top of the scenery. It also enables one to determine the height needed for ground rows to mask the striplights that light the cyclorama.

If these drawings are not available, it is worth several afternoons' work for the director to make them, for only by knowing his theatre exactly can he be sure that his designs are wholly practicable.

The Elements of the Ground Plan

The ground plan, then, will be a scale drawing of the plan of the actual setting in the stage it will occupy. It will show all

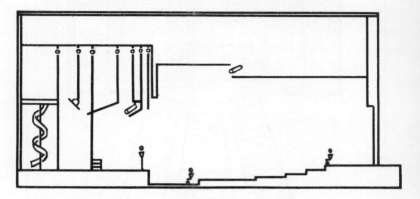

Fig. 25.   Cross Section of Theatre

walls, openings, backings, platforms, steps, fireplaces, together with the main pieces of furniture. Convenient scales are one-eighth inch, three-sixteenths, or one-fourth inch to the foot.

There are specific conventions for indicating the various elements of a setting. A solid line represents a wall, and there are conventional signs for constructions and openings.

Doors usually open down and offstage (hinges on the upstage side), except outside doors, which, as in a real house, open in. A door in the upstage wall usually has the hinges on the side away from center. A center door opens in whatever direction the action requires. One has to decide which way would be most helpful to the actors.

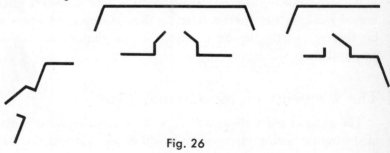

Fig. 26

Windows and outside doors usually have a cyclorama and a ground row to mask them. Inside doors must be masked to indicate the room to which they are supposed to lead. A fireplace must also have suitable backing. Any fireplace in which there

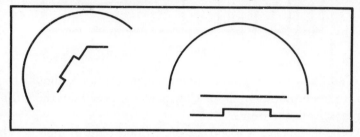

Fig. 27

must be firelight should be in the side wall, because it is extremely difficult to light it well in the upstage wall, and impossible to throw light from it on to the actors' faces.

Steps should be drawn to scale, indicating the exact number and size needed. Ten-inch treads and seven-inch risers are stand-

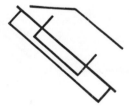

Fig. 28

ard, though stage steps are often broader and lower. The height of the platform is indicated by a circled dimension within the shape.

Large furniture is also drawn to scale on the ground plan. It may be somewhat shaped to distinguished it from a platform, or it may have an identifying label or a number which is explained in an accompanying key.

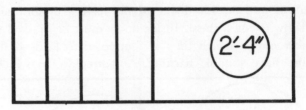

Fig. 29

In addition to the ground plan, the promptbook should contain a sketch, photograph, or elevations to show how the setting will look from the front.

As the technician works from the ground plan in building the setting, the director works from it in planning the visual images of the actors moving in space.

In plotting stage movements, the director often uses a shorthand derived from the ground plan. Rough drawings of the

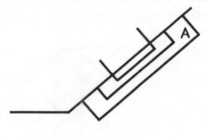

Fig. 30

locations of actors in relation to scenery and furniture are easier to read in rehearsal than paragraphs of writing. For example, by a sketch, the director can say that Actor A stands at the upstage corner of the fireplace, or that Actor B stands on the third step. He can show that Actor B stands at the up right end of the sofa and crosses down as Actor A enters the French doors. When many actors are involved, this kind of sketch can save a great deal of verbiage. A quick drawing shows Actor A

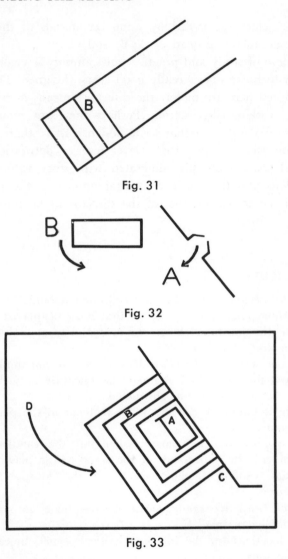

Fig. 31

Fig. 32

Fig. 33

sitting in a chair at the top of the steps, with Actor B at his right on the second step, Actor C below in the down left corner of the stage, and Actor D approaching from up center.

Of course, clarity is served by using the initials of the actors or of the characters instead of A, B, and C.

A lifetime of study and practice must amplify a vigorous imagination to make one a really good scene designer. The rudiments offered here are merely the director's means of making a practical, working stage setting. Perhaps these are enough suggestions to make it clear that scene design is more than a pretty or exciting picture, more than clever interior decoration. It is functional space, carefully integrated with story values, characterizations and the whole emotional impact of the play. As such, it is an important tool of the director as he pursues the playwright's intent.

Assignments

1. Try to decide where Laura's collection should be in *The Glass Menagerie*. List each scene that must be played near it, and tell why you have chosen the area and what limitations or problems your choice creates.
2. Find one scene in *The Glass Menagerie* that you think should be played upstage. Why? Arrange the furniture in such a way that this scene would not be obstructed.
3. Where is Laura's bedroom? What moment in the play determines your answer?
4. Where does the Gentleman Caller put the candlestick, in terms of (*a*) the importance of the scene to the play, (*b*) the emotional values of the scene, (*c*) the location of the menagerie?
5. In *The Glass Menagerie,* locate the telephone, record player, day bed. Give reasons.
6. Find locations for the following critical scenes, in each case giving reasons:
    (*a*) Tom's scene with Amanda at the end of Scene 6.
    (*b*) The dress-hemming scene, Scene 7.
    (*c*) The scene between Laura and the Gentleman Caller.

7. Find ways to create emphasis by using diagonal lines in a setting for *The Glass Menagerie;* for *The Importance of Being Earnest,* Act II.

8. Find vertical lines to emphasize Tybalt, while the Duke speaks in *Romeo and Juliet,* Act I, Sc. 1. How will the Duke be emphasized in this scene?

9. Use vertical and horizontal lines to emphasize Cecily in the scene in which Algernon proposes, Act II. What horizontal lines may be used for emphasis in Algernon's Georgian home in Act I, *The Importance of Being Earnest?*

10. Find a way to introduce levels into the setting of *The Glass Menagerie; The Playboy; The Importance of Being Earnest,* Act I; *Romeo and Juliet,* the street scene.

11. Design a setting that is logically correct, contains several means of emphasis, and offers useful acting areas for *The Importance of Being Earnest,* Act II. Select the colors you would use. Indicate the points you would emphasize by means of light. Revise these plans in the light of class discussion.

12. Use Kenneth Macgowan's *Continental Stagecraft,* Gorelik's *New Theatres for Old,* or any other books in the library and study one "style" and write a short paper outlining (*a*) the sociological sources, (*b*) the philosophy of the style, (*c*) its major characteristics, (*d*) acting techniques associated with it, and (*e*) chief proponents.

13. How did Shakespeare manage the quick changes of scene in *Romeo and Juliet?* How did the nineteenth-century melodrama manage to make quick shifts? In setting *Romeo and Juliet* on a modern stage, what shifting devices would you have?

14. Join the class in making a scale drawing of your theatre, taking all the measurements needed for sightlines and for producing a multiset play. Use a one-eighth inch scale, and have the two drawings duplicated for future use by the class.

15. Draw ground plans of each of the settings you designed in Exercise 11, adapting these to the dimensions of your own stage.

16. Use excerpts from your setting for *The Playboy* and show where all actors are when Mahon returns to beat Christy; where

Michael James, Pegeen, and Christy are just before the crowd enters; where the Widow and the three men begin to watch the races; where Mahon and the others are when he says, "It's Christy!" at the end of the race.

17. With excerpts from your setting for *The Importance of Being Earnest*, show where Lady Bracknell and Jack are in Act I, when she begins her interrogation; where everyone is during the lovers' quarrel in Act II, where Miss Prism courts Reverend Chasuble.

18. In *Romeo and Juliet,* what elements of scenery could help to reveal the intimacy and frustration of the lovers in the first balcony scene? What details of setting would help to create mood and clarify meaning in the second balcony scene?

Reading List

Appia, Adolphe. *Fifty-six Reproductions Reprinted by the Art Institute.* Zurich: Orell, Fuselli, 1929.

Appia, Adolphe. Memorial Volume, *Theatre Arts Magazine,* August, 1932.

Burris-Meyer, Harold and Edward C. Cole. *Scenery for the Theatre.* Boston: Little, Brown, 1938.

Craig, Gordon. *Scene.* London: Oxford University Press, 1923.

Freedley, George and John A. Reeves. *A History of the Theatre.* New York: Crown Publishers, 1941.

Fuerst, Walter René and Samuel Hume. *Twentieth Century Stage Decoration.* (2 Vols.) New York: Knopf, 1928.

Fulop-Miller, René and Joseph Gregor. *Das Russische Theater: sein Wesen und seine Geschichte.* (137 Plates) Zurich: Amalthea Verlag, 1928.

Gassner, John. *Producing the Play.* New York: Dryden Press, revised edition, 1953.

Gillette, Arnold. *Stage Scenery and Rigging.* New York: Harper and Bros., 1959.

Gorelik, Mordecai. *New Theatres for Old.* New York: Samuel French, 1941.

Jones, Robert Edmond. *The Dramatic Imagination.* New York: Duell, Sloan and Pearce, 1941.

Jones, Robert Edmond. *Drawings for the Theatre.* New York: Theatre Arts, Inc., 1925.

Macgowan, Kenneth. *Continental Stagecraft.* New York: Harcourt, Brace, 1922.

Macgowan, Kenneth and William Melnitz. *The Living Stage.* Englewood Cliffs, N. J.: Prentice-Hall, 1955.

Nelms, Henning. *A Primer of Stagecraft.* New York: Dramatists Play Service, 1941.

Oenslager, Donald. *Scenery Then and Now.* New York: W. W. Norton, 1936.

Simonson, Lee. *The Art of Scenic Design.* New York: Harper and Bros., 1950.

Simonson, Lee. *The Stage is Set.* New York: Harcourt, Brace, 1932.

Chapter 9

The Story in Space

The selection of the places the actors are to go and of the times at which they will move is called "blocking" or "staging."

In the Moscow Art Theatre under Stanislavsky, and in most European repertory theatres today, there is no great need to hasten the preparation of a play, because the company are attached by annual contract to the theatre in which they work. Time can be allowed for a great deal of experiment as maturation of the characters precedes the externalization of relationships by blocking. Indeed, a three-month period of rehearsal was not unusual for the Moscow Art Theatre, nor was it unusual for the dress rehearsal to be followed by a thorough reorganization of script, set, overall plan, and specific interpretations during another month's rehearsals.

The American theatre is always working against time. The professional company is on salary for a specified term and the theatre has been rented for a specific date. The players come from everywhere, with every sort of training. Most of the company have not previously worked either together or under the same director. They must become adjusted to each other's methods while rehearsing the play for which they are engaged. At the first rehearsal, they may read over the play around a table a couple of times, or they may read Act I and begin blocking it, or they may follow some other procedure. Usually the whole play has been blocked by the end of the first week in six or seven eight-hour rehearsals.

In the amateur theatre, too, the date of the opening has usually been announced in advance. On a certain evening a month or six weeks from the first rehearsal, the curtain will go up. The players are students or working people with limited time to rehearse. Often they are lacking in technique, unacquainted with the background of the play, and naïve as to the life situations in it. The director, particularly in the college theatre, is obligated to develop and train his actors; but he is also obligated to his audience, and must get these actors presentable in this particular play by the date announced. He must use time efficiently.

Considerable time can be saved if the director plans the blocking in some detail before going into rehearsal. Of course he must be able to explain to the actors the reasons for his directions in terms of motive, and he must always remain flexible enough to accede to the capabilities and limitations of his company, if change is advantageous or expedient. But for an inexperienced cast, progress is accelerated by well-planned blocking, which is usually an exciting revelation of meaning and relationship.

Many inexperienced directors ask, "How do you find things for the actors to do?" Others, when the script seems dull, get the actors to move about, to handle properties, light cigarettes, stand and sit down, with the sole intent of keeping the scene lively. The answer to both sorts of director is to find the life that is in the script and relate it to the life they can observe every day all about them. The director who can find no reasons for the actors to move must develop his powers of observation, for movement is life. The director who uses movement merely to command attention should realize that the attention of the audience must be rewarded by seeing what the movement accomplishes, to what end it is performed. Meaningless movement distracts and confuses. Rather than inject movement that means nothing, merely to keep the audience awake, it is better to study the "talky" scene from the point of view of the characters engaged in it, to find out who wants something in the scene and how he tries to achieve it. This process will suggest plenty of meaningful movements; in fact, there is always so much implicit movement in the interactions of characters toward a purpose that the main problem becomes: which of the possible moves will most accurately tell the story of these characters, and which moves should be suppressed as distracting. It is a problem of economy, not lack of resources.

There are four main sources of stage movement.

One finds reasons to move in the simple fact that the clearest evidence of life is movement. When an individual reacts fully to a stimulus, he moves in some way or other, however slightly.

One finds reasons to move in the story line of the play as a whole and of every scene of the play, for each scene is a minute pattern of the whole — someone is trying to affect the attitude or behavior of someone else. As these patterns emerge in the director's study of the play, they necessitate certain moves, if only for the sake of clarity, to keep the audience informed of what is happening.

One finds reasons to move in the nature of the characters in the scene, their desires, actions, reactions, inhibitions. The body of the character, his clothing, and his relation to his surroundings provide movement. Some of this movement is spontaneous with the actor and only needs to be channeled and controlled for clarity.

Finally, there are a few simple technical reasons for the actor to move in order to keep the audience seeing and hearing what is important for them to see and hear. These are as simple and clear cut and effective and unexciting as the tools on a carpenter's bench. One needs them for specific jobs.

If he knows what he is doing as a character, the actor will usually move more or less effectively; but not even in professional theatre does one often find actors with enough skill to block a difficult scene without the director's help. Therefore the director must learn as much as possible about movement as a basically human and also as a highly individual means of revealing life.

The Kinaesthetic Nature of Meaning

The actor who merely speaks words is not very interesting. He is more so when he understands the words. The really exciting actor is alive to his toes with meaning.

Meaning is, of course, not merely the dictionary substitute of other words for the word in question. Look up the word "ant," for example: "any of certain social hymenopterous insects constituting a family (Formicidae); an emmet, pismire." The dictionary may include a picture, which helps, because it at least evokes an image of the creature *one has bent above, watching.* The completion of the meaning may be the memory of a burning ankle, a trip to the shed for ant poison (blue), a feeling of triumph in the destruction of the hive. Thus, meaning includes, besides a concept, a kinaesthetic element. Even a biologist may complete the meaning of "ant" by a mental turning of files to catalogue the insect. In other words, meaning involves some kind of personal, muscular response. Full meaning is *something that happens within oneself.* Thus, "love" may mean cuddling an infant, a passionate embrace, delight in a beautiful object, satisfaction in a profession, or something else, depending on the experiences (that is, kinaesthetic memories) that produced the feeling a particular individual calls love. "Plate" to the Renaissance soldier meant something to wear into battle; to a woman of 1850 a silver utensil to polish; to the photographer it means a film for taking pictures; to the gourmet something to eat from; to the waiter something to carry. Always, when an actor has a strong awareness of meaning, he recognizes some muscular involvement.

As scientific evidence of Langfeld's theory of empathy, a most fascinating discovery was made by Edmund Jacobson in using relaxation as a therapy for speech disorders. A patient trained to relax completely lay on the couch in the laboratory. In his right biceps muscle and at the bend of the right elbow, very fine string galvanometers were inserted. The patient was instructed that at a certain signal he was to imagine he was slowly lifting a three-pound weight with his right arm. Dr. Jacobson then retired to watch the patient behind a one-way glass. As was anticipated, at the signal the patient made no perceptible move. But the electrodes, attached at the other end to a graph, recorded tremors of the right biceps. Other experiments of this kind were done on this patient and many others. Of all the patients tested, 50 percent revealed tremors of the muscles involved in the imaginary acts, though not in other muscles. In other words, this was not mere general tension, but a specific response of exactly the muscles needed if the imaginary act had been really performed. It proved that for this 50 percent of the patients imagination is clearly kinæsthetic. To complete the story, the other 50 percent were given further tests that showed that about half of these subjects had tremors of the eye muscles and the other half had tremors of the vocal bands during the imaginary acts, indicating that they had either a visual image of someone performing the act or an auditory image of the words describing it. In every case, some muscle was involved.

It is the first 50 percent that concerns us primarily, however, for it is by recognizing these tendencies to move that we are able to understand some very deeply hidden wants and feelings in our civilized and inhibited fellow creatures; and it is by utilizing them that we are able to reveal the inner life of the characters in a play. It is this recognition of the hidden that we call insight.

Movement as a Response to a Stimulus

In a play, as in life, one never "just moves." One moves because something stimulates him to do so — the telephone, a responsibility, a desire, a thought, a pain, a memory, the sight of a friend or an enemy, a beautiful or an ugly object. The stimulus, whatever it may be, sets up a need, which in turn causes action to satisfy the need. This view, elaborately set forth by Hegel in his *Philosophy of Fine Art,* has been more recently stated by H. A. Murray:

> A need is a construct (a convenient fiction or hypothetical concept) which stands for a force . . . in the brain region, a force which organizes perception, apperception, intellection, conation and action in such a way as to transform in a certain direction an existing, unsatisfying situation. A need is sometimes provoked directly by internal processes of a certain kind . . . but more frequently (when in a state of readiness) by the occurrence of one of a few commonly effective press (environmental forces) . . . Thus it manifests itself by leading the organism to search for or to avoid encountering or, when encountered, to attend and respond to certain kinds of press. Each need is characteristically accompanied by a particular feeling or emotion and tends to use certain modes . . . to further its trend. It may be weak or intense, momentary or enduring. But usually it persists and gives rise to a certain course of overt behavior (or fantasy) which . . . changes the initiating circumstances in such a way as to bring about an end situation which stills (appeases or satisfies) the organism.[1]

[1] H. A. Murray *et al., Explorations in Personality* (New York: Oxford Press, 1938), pp. 123-124.

In life and in plays, the number and kinds of stimuli are endless, each moment containing new ones or re-emphasizing old. At the perception of the stimulus, the response is whatever the particular stimulus moves the individual to do in the particular time and place. A hornet in a classroom, for example, makes certain people cringe and cry out; others follow the insect with their eyes; others smile with a kind of pride while seeming to concentrate on the lecture. In another place, these individuals might behave quite differently. They might flee, strike out, or even try to capture the hornet, depending on what the meaning of "hornet" was to each of them.

Modern psychology finds three types of reactions to stimuli: (a) toward, (b) against, (c) away from.[2] These basic types of action, carried to extremes, are the acts of taking into oneself (as in eating, grasping, embracing), snuggling (being taken into), killing, and fleeing in panic.

A savage coming on food or a small bright object reacts like a child, by cramming it into his mouth. He seizes the woman he likes. Any desirable object causes him to move immediately toward it to take it into himself. Of course, civilized adults inhibit this primitive impulse. The modern young man entering a dining room salivates discreetly. He does not kidnap his dinner partner and drag her to his cave, but he reaches for her with his eyes and respectfully asks her for a date. Predatoriness, the impulse to grab, to gather in to oneself, is behind John Worthing's cool, "I don't propose to discuss modern culture . . . I simply want my cigarette case back." Unless Romeo is a singularly bloodless lover, the impulse to gather in is also behind such an exquisite speech as:

> If I profane with my unworthiest hand
> This holy shrine, the gentle fine is this:
> My lips, two blushing pilgrims, ready stand
> To smooth that rough touch with a tender kiss.

[2]Karen Horney, M.D., *Neurosis and Human Growth* (New York: W. W. Norton, 1950), p. 190.

The impulse toward has another aspect, the move *to be en-folded*. This is the nuzzling of the savage into his bed of reeds or fur, or of the cub against his mother. It is the homing impulse, the wish to belong. Romeo dramatizes his dejection over Rosaline in order to get Benvolio's sympathy. Laura and Amanda show opposite responses to the same desire: Amanda frankly grabs for the Gentleman Caller; Laura flees him because she wishes to be enfolded. Pegeen Mike tries to make Shawn come and get her with, "You're making mighty certain, Shaneen, that I'll wed you now." In Reverend Chasuble's, "But is not a man equally attractive when married?" he succumbs to a suppressed wish to be captured by Miss Prism. The wish to be enfolded is the basis of all coquetry, all plays for sympathy, and of the death wish. The impulse to nuzzle into security and warmth is the feminine or childlike counterpart of the basic human impulse toward.

The second basic movement, according to Dr. Horney, is against the stimulus, to destroy or obliterate it. The savage, in his quest for food or love, slays his rival. The infant hurls to destruction the objectionable toy. Pegeen slashes at Christy with words. Capulet flattens his young cousin Tybalt with "Goodman boy." Gwendolyn and Cecily duel with poisoned feathers:

GWENDOLYN
Are there many interesting walks in the vicinity, Miss Cardew?
CECILY
Oh yes, a great many. From the top of one of the hills quite close one can see five counties.
GWENDOLYN
Five counties! I don't think I should like that. I hate crowds.
CECILY (Sweetly)
I suppose that is why you live in town.

Thus, although civilized man is prohibited by law from

slaying his fellow man, he inflicts injury in many ways, both legal and socially acceptable.

The third kind of impulse recognized by Dr. Horney is the impulse away from a stimulus. The savage flees screaming from a great beast he cannot fight. John Worthing, as the epitome of civilized man, cannot flee after rousing Lady Bracknell with, "I don't actually know who I am by birth. I was — well, I was found." Yet he recognizes in her not entirely metaphorical snorts the impulse of a jungle tiger to slay in defense of her caste, and Jack's one step backward is symbolic of full screaming flight.

In the complexity of modern life, the completion of these basic actions is rare. Manners, mores, hygiene, questions of security of different kinds, religion, laws, whatnot, operate to inhibit us from grasping immediately every object that seems desirable; we do not slay every evil person or break every ugly object we see; sometimes we avert our eyes or move away to avoid our own half-recognized impulses to destroy. We rarely flee screaming, but everyone has felt the muscular "set" of flight in guilt or failure or embarrassment. We stiffen our backs for the purely verbal blows. Even the impulses that keep us alive are hedged about with inhibiting stimuli. We laugh when we jump out of the way of approaching traffic; we plunge into danger in subways and airplanes and across busy streets; our love-making is hedged about by legal, social, and hygienic considerations; and a whole code of mores and aesthetics surrounds our digestive practices. Civilized man is usually responding to many stimuli at once. For us, meaning is almost always a primary muscular set that means, "I must," plus a secondary set that means, "You had better do something else."

In summary, if an individual really recognizes a stimulus, even if his nature or the circumstances inhibit him, his body responds in some way. There is at least incipient movement toward, against, or away from, whenever one experiences full meaning. Thus, whether there is much or little movement, it is vital for the director to distinguish the stimuli inherent in the speech or the scene, for it is by making use of the basic impulses corresponding to these that he is able to visualize the play in space for the audience.

If the three basic movements, toward, against, and away from, seem to limit the possibilities of picturizing a scene, it must be pointed out that each move can vary in several ways. First, moves can vary in direction. For example, one can go toward by spiraling in from the perimeter of a circle, or even by taking a step away in order to get a good spring forward. Moves can also vary in extent, from a mere turn of the eyes to a cross the full diagonal of the stage. They can vary in rate, in tension, and in number. All of these variables actually indicate differences in the meaning of the stimulus to the reacting character, and a sensitive actor may use them spontaneously.

Movement to Tell the Story

The nineteenth-century melodrama and the early motion picture thrived on the story-telling value of practically wordless pantomime. The audience of today still depends for understanding on what it sees more than on what it hears. One believes what the characters say because the body of the actor reinforces the speech. Romeo is a cold lover if he does not lean toward Juliet as he says, "If I profane with my unworthiest hand this holy shrine . . . ." Shawn, the poltroon, takes a step backward as he says, "Will I strike him with my hand?" and one knows that he does not intend to strike at all. In each case, the audience understands what the character means not by what he says, but by what he does.

There are almost infinite ways of saying nearly any words. "Good morning" might mean "Get out of here!" or "I hope you like me," or "How wonderful to see you again," or "I guess you feel pretty lousy after your binge last night," depending on who says it to whom and under what circumstances. If one tries to say "Good morning" to convey each of these meanings, one becomes aware that he does it by the way he looks, by his facial expression, above all by the set of his body in some variant of the basic patterns toward, against, and away from.

Fig. 34

In trying to convey a play to the audience, one of the most simple and powerful tools of the director is the mere line of the actors' bodies. In relation to the basic patterns of bodily action, one could actually invent a bit of dialogue for the three pairs of lines above. By adding a head, arms, and the other leg, the dialogue comes more easily.

Fig. 35

The human figure is highly subtle in its revelation of meaning. It can move away while reaching toward. The foot can belie the head. A hand or the angle of the head can express, while the rest of the body remains rigid.

Stick figures are useful in preparing the promptbook because they furnish the director with a convenient system of annotating his interpretation of characters in their relationships. The figure consists of a round head, a triangular torso (wide at the *top* to denote shoulders), two arms with elbow and wrist joints, and

Fig. 36.   Stick Figures — Various Poses

two legs with knee and ankle joints. The overall figure is about eight heads high. By adding a nose, one can tell which way the figure is looking, which is often important. By adding a skirt, the gender can be changed. By shifting the angle of the figure in relation to the floor and bending the joints as human joints bend (not backwards, like the joints of dogs and horses), the figures can be made to express all of the gross actions and some rather subtle actions of human beings.

A few symbols for properties and scenery are also useful: a bench, chair, sofa, three-legged stool, desk, fireplace, door, window, tree, column. With these symbols it is easy to invent others as necessary.

Stick figures should not, of course, be thought of as pictures; they are merely directors' notes, helpful as one tries to visualize changes of relationship that are hard to define verbally, or when

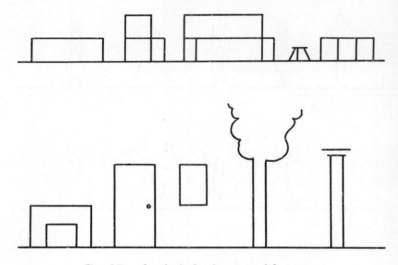

Fig. 37.   Symbols for Props and Scenery

most of the actors' moves are shifts of weight and the angle
of the body. At a long scene at a table or in restricted space
such as a jury box or the fire escape in *The Glass Menagerie*,
every move must be meaningful, and variety is extremely hard
to achieve. The figures provide a convenient shorthand that
can be read rapidly when one is working with the actors.

Of course these figures are never to be shown to the actor
as a picture of how he should look. To dictate the angle of the
head or arm or body would achieve exactly the wooden result
that a third-rate photographer gets when he poses his subjects
too carefully. The director uses the figures merely as notes to
help his own thinking and to help him motivate the actors,
who, if they *are* well motivated, will probably behave somewhat
like the pictures — or may do something much more true and
subtle.

A second potent tool of the director in revealing changing
motives and relationships is the distance between the characters.
The figures below represent six-foot men on a thirty-foot stage.

Far apart, they do not seem to have any relationship at all; members of the audience sitting in the first few rows would have to turn their heads to get the whole picture in two separ-

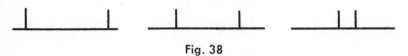

Fig. 38

ate images. The nearer the characters stand, the more definite they seem to be related. In the last figure, the relationship is close enough that they can be called a pair.

Even if motivational direction is indicated, distance makes a great difference in the apparent urgency of the relationship of the two characters. In the first pair of figures, there is a mild

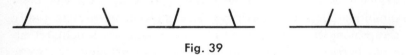

Fig. 39

feeling that the two characters must get together. This feeling is more urgent when they are closer. In the last figure, they are so close that a fight or an embrace seems imminent, for if the figures do not get together they will fall on their faces.

There can be no rule about how far apart actors should stand, for each scene creates its own necessities, and within the scene there are many changes of urgency. It is good to remember, though, that distance is related to urgency. If the actors are very far apart, their relationship generally does not seem very critical. When they come into close proximity however, it appears that the scene has reached a crisis and must soon come to an end, unless a reason can be found to wrench them apart. Generally, in a critical scene, the actors need to be at least some of the time within reach of each other, so that one step forward by either of them would enable him to seize or kill. The possibility of taking this one step keeps the objective in the mind of the

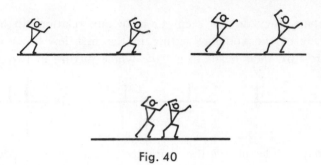

Fig. 40

audience and doubles the crisis-tension in both actors and audience.

A shrewd director will prevent this close proximity until the scene has progressed to the point of crisis. He will find ways of drawing the actors out of close range, using not only emotional inhibitions, but also providing some physical barriers to justify the prolongation of a scene. The playwright has usually set up some barriers, psychological, at least, to concluding the scene before he is ready to conclude it. The director takes advantage of the setting and properties to reinforce these intrinsic barriers.

Fig. 41.   Some Visual Barriers

A lover finds his objective more difficult to accomplish if the quarry is seated. A vase or a lamp in the girl's hands fends off the moment of the embrace. A table between two combatants prevents their coming to blows. Even though these are only momentary barriers which could be quickly overcome, they

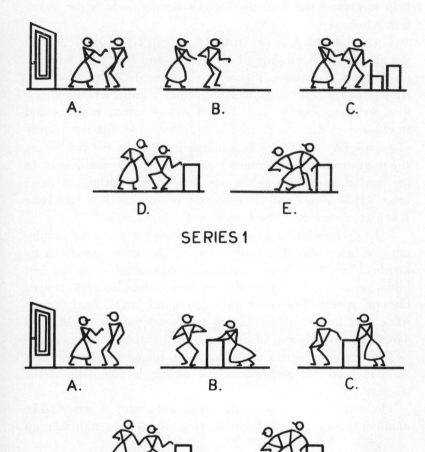

SERIES 1

SERIES 2

Fig. 42.   Blocking for Crisis Tension

help to express the dramatic struggle through which the objective is achieved.

The use of barriers can make very important differences in the apparent relationships of characters, and hence in the overall progress of a scene. Figure 42 on page 179 represents two ways of blocking the same scene, in which a girl is trying to get a man to make love to her. The man has serious scruples and rejects her in the first picture of each series. In the last picture of each series, she forces herself into his lap. In the first series, the man makes the first move from position A to position B. In the second series, the girl moves first. Which series has more crises? How soon is it clear what the outcome will be? How much resistance does the man reveal in each series?

Relationships continuously change during a play, the dominant role being played sometimes by one character, sometimes by another. In Christy's love scene with Pegeen, he takes the first initiative, but, after Pegeen's acceptance of him and his "mitred bishops" speech, Pegeen's motive dominates. In Michael James's scene that follows, dominance is taken successively by Michael James, Pegeen, Shawn, Christy, and finally Michael James again.

The relative positions of the actors on stage can help in many ways to show the audience whose motive is dominant at the moment.

The larger an object is, the more important it seems. The dominant character can be made larger by having him take up

Fig. 43

more actual space. That is why the full front or full back position is emphatic. He can seem larger, because he is downstage
and nearer the audience than his partner. The stage area he oc-

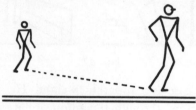

Fig. 44

cupies can give him dominance. He can assume a higher level

Fig. 45

than his partner. He can utilize reinforcement of the scenery
and furniture, such as vertical lines repeating him, framing, the

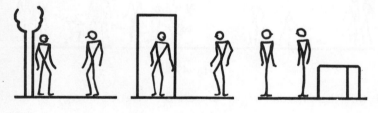

Fig. 46

contrast of horizontal lines. He can utilize the diagonal lines of
drapes, stairs, the angle of furniture. He can use the mass of

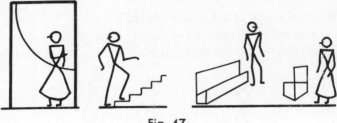

Fig. 47

furniture to increase his apparent weight. He can be emphasized by other actors, through repetition, isolation, and contrast.

Fig. 48

According to Alexander Dean, an actor moving with the eye
of the audience from left to right (of the audience) seems to
encounter no resistance, and therefore seems less strong than
a character moving against the eye, from right to left. As a test

Fig. 49

of this theory, one might discuss the relative energy revealed
by the two figures below. Which seems to have the more pressing objective?

In the next set of figures, one of the standing figures may
seem more powerful, and one of the kneeling figures may seem
to offer more resistance than the others. By reversing the right-

Fig. 50

left relationship of the figures, it may be possible to detect changes in the emotional relationships of the characters.

Fig. 51

The matter of right-left dominance is debated; some directors do not feel that it has any validity. Yet, in the design of a scene, a change in relationship, whether for better or for worse, can actually be indicated by the mere shifting of an actor from one side of his partner to the other. In a fight, which must be blocked very carefully, if it is to look real without causing injury to the actors, the theory of right-left dominance is useful. If the challenger stands right center and the baited character is left center until his tensions catapult him into the fight, the move right seems overwhelmingly powerful. Several changes of right-left relationship during a fight also keep it exciting. A fighter driven up right or down right by his opponent seems to be in grave danger, and a knockout blow suddenly delivered from up left of the opponent is shocking and seems fatal. Perhaps the real reason that these moves seem exciting is that the right-handed fighter moving from stage left to stage right faces downstage in a stronger body position than his opponent. In

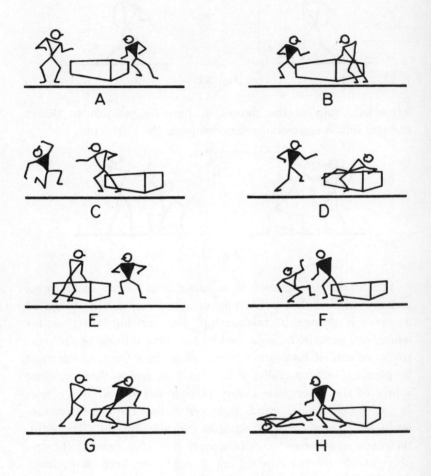

Fig. 52.   Dominance in a Fight

any case, if the theory seems valuable in a fight scene, it may prove equally so in a scene of less violence, for every scene is an attack on an objective.

An animal moves toward its objective directly and completely. A person, however strong his motive, moves only as far as his inhibitions permit. Often he is reacting to two stimuli (motive and inhibition) in such precarious balance that he cannot move at all; and he conceals his conflict so well that he seems quite calm, when he is actually in emotional turmoil. By translating the paralyzing effect of equally strong motives and inhibitions into alternating positive tendencies toward the objective and negative tendencies away from the objective, the director can relax and free the actor, while giving the audience a clear picture of the emotional state of the character.

The patterns toward and against are usually thought of as "strong," and the move away "weak." A strong move is toward the objective, toward a strong stage area, higher level, or better body position. A strong move usually initiates attacks or occurs in moments of determination or success. A weak move is away from the objective, toward a weaker area, lower level, or less emphatic body position. Weak moves reveal insecurity, hesitancy, failure. Both weak and strong moves are good, if they express what the play means. If an actor says, "I'm sorry," with his head high, he is not apologizing, but defying. If he says it and then sits with his head in his hands, he means that he is defeated. The proper move is weak or strong, whichever reinforces the meaning of the speech.

When a sequence of stage moves contains both weak and strong elements, the total effect is strong if the last move in the series is strong. For example, an exit through an up center door is weak. But if the character pauses full front, framed in the door, to deliver his last speech or for a farewell gesture, the exit is very strong, especially if the other actors roughly form a diagonal line toward him, or if most of them are looking at him. An up right door seems to engulf Shawn as he flees without looking back in Act I of *The Playboy*. The same door gives

Christy a very strong final exit, as he turns, framed, his verticality duplicated by Mahon, who is behind him, and the whole crowd of villagers in the room ranged in roughly diagonal lines to listen to him.

When a character sits (weak) and then straightens his back and raises his head, the move is strong. When a character rises (strong) and turns upstage or away from center, especially if his shoulders sag, the move is weak. A weak move, if motivated, is often valuable for contrast, because a character coming out of a weak position into a very strong position has double emphasis.

From this discussion it must be clear that an understanding of the weak-strong principle serves both the actor's need for expressive movement and the director's need for clarity and emphasis.

When a weak or strong move is needed to clarify, one may select from the whole range of the compass plus up and down in order to avoid monotony. It is not necessary to keep the characters moving into and out of center. Variety comes from a wise selection of weak moves; for the strong move can come from any weak position, and the direction can easily be controlled, once the actor is motivated to move at all. He can turn upstage instead of right or left, or he can move behind furniture or into profile, or he may sit down or lie down if any of these are appropriate. Or, if the speaker has any effect on his partner, the partner can move to reveal the effect, and thus secure an entirely new pattern of movement. Nothing is more helpful to the director than a clear understanding of the values of weak and strong movement.

This understanding is particularly important in a pacing scene (when a character moves over the same path several times while talking or listening). The purpose of such a pattern is to reveal emotional tension, without distracting the audience with wondering where the actor will go next. The important parts of the speech must be said during a strong cross, while the weak cross can be used for transitions, repetitions, or to allow the audience to digest the joke after a laugh line. The most emphatic points in a pace pattern are just after the turn into the strong cross and just before the turn into the weak cross. When the pacing is done by the listener rather than by the speaker, each turn is a response to something that has been said and is evidence of the effect of the speaker on the pacer. The weak move must occur when the listener has been scored upon, the strong one when he feels resistance; and time must be allowed for the move which punctuates the speech.

As an example, here is a triangular pattern developed for Capulet's tirade against Juliet in *Romeo and Juliet* Act III, Sc. 5. Juliet, down left center, furnishes one apex for his triangular path; Lady Capulet and the Nurse, falling back to down right, provide the second point; and the third point is a point to which Capulet flees, up right center, to prevent himself from

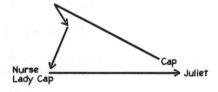

Fig. 53

harming Juliet. He overshoots this apex as he vents his anger but rebounds to it with a slight threat to Juliet before taking the downstage cross. The use of a pattern is justified by the fact that Capulet is in the tradition of the Pantalone of *commedia dell'arte*, a generally comic character, and the pattern, being somewhat rigid, is comic. It is not crassly comic, however, for it has enough variety to prevent it from becoming too obvious and from seeming contrived. It is based on three motives: the down left cross on his wish to force Juliet to do what he wants; the up right center cross on his flight from his own violence; and the down right cross on his need for the support of his wife in his convictions. It keeps all of the characters on the stage involved in the scene and is thus not merely mechanical, but fully dynamic. It should be needless to say that this is not presented as the only way of staging the scene but merely as a workable way, in illustration of a method of finding stage business. The pattern is used as follows:

CAPULET

Standing DLC near Juliet.

God's bread, it makes me mad!

EXPLOSION

X-ing rapidly URC as Nurse and Lady C fall back to DR.

Day, night, late, early,
At home, abroad, alone, in
company,
Waking or sleeping,

Slight threat toward Juliet, bringing him to begin the pattern.
XDR to Lady C.

still my care hath been
to have her matched.
And having now provided
A gentleman of princely parentage,
Of fair demesnes, youthful and nobly
trained,
Stuffed, as they say, with honorable
parts,

Slow threatening X to Juliet.

Proportioned as one's thought would
wish a man,

EXPLOSION

Rapid XUR.
Threat toward, returning to
pattern.

And then to have a wretched puling
fool,
A whining mammet in her fortunes
tender,

X to Lady C.

To answer, "I'll not wed, I cannot
love,
I am too young, I pray you pardon
me."

Slow threatening X to Juliet.

But an you will not wed, I'll pardon
you.
Graze where you will, you shall not
house with me.

EXPLOSION

Rapid XUR, threat toward, return-
ing to pattern.
X to Lady C.
Facing Juliet.

Slow threatening X to Juliet.

Look to't, think on't. I do not use
                              to jest.
Thursday is near.
        Lay hand on heart, advise.
An you be mine, I'll give you to my
                              friend.
An you be not, hang, beg, starve,
                die in the streets,
For by my soul I'll ne'er acknowl-
        edge thee.
                    EXPLOSION

The pattern is broken — He turns
downstage so that neither Lady C
nor Juliet can see how moved he is

To Lady C, X-ing to door.
Turn, at door, to Juliet.

Nor what is mine shall ever do thee
                              good.
Look to't.
Bethink you. I'll not be forsworn.
                         EXIT

A crowd scene presents special problems of dominance, for each character who speaks must secure immediate attention. By keeping all of the means of emphasis at his fingertips, the director can manage to place the actors in strategic positions, so that by a step or a gesture each can draw attention at the proper time.

In Romeo and Juliet, Act I, Sc. 5, Capulet's ball, there are seven major changes of emphasis before Romeo and Juliet meet. (1) The entrance of Capulet is no problem, for he talks as he enters (probably wearing a strikingly rich robe) and moves through center to the brief scene with old Capulet. This scene must leave the old men seated in a prominent area, for later it contains the conflict with Tybalt which motivates the fatal duel. Old Capulet's white hair also calls attention to this scene. (2) The dancers take over the stage for a brief while. (3) Romeo and his friends enter. By being out of the pattern of the dance they gain some attention. However, to insure emphasis for this important moment, it may be useful to put the entrance on a definitely higher level, and in the emphatic UC area. (4) Romeo must be prominent in his short scene with the servant. If Mercutio and Benvolio have left the stairs and joined the dance, and Romeo is still on the platform, and if the dancers move briefly out of center as the servant crosses, Romeo has attention as he points out (5) Juliet dancing with Paris. A

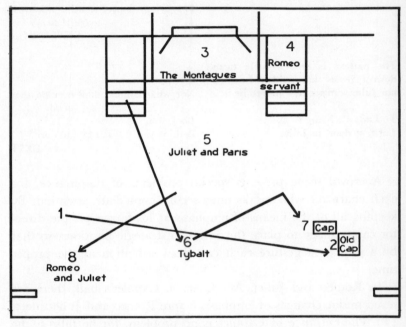

Fig. 54

figure in the dance that would permit Juliet and Paris to move from a relatively weak position into center would solve this problem. (6) Tybalt may have been ranging without a partner during the dance. As he says, "This, by his voice, should be a Montague," he must move to focus, well downstage. (7) The scene with Capulet is no problem, if Capulet is in an emphatic area and Tybalt moves into it. (8) Finally, Romeo draws Juliet out of the crowd and into an emphatic isolated area. The lights can help a great deal throughout this scene, but especially here, by subtly dimming on the dancers and coming up a few points on the lovers.

The diagram shows possible solutions to these problems of emphasis.

The characters who do not speak in a crowd scene must look alive and seem part of the situation, yet they must not distract. Of course the director begins by characterizing every member of the scene, helping each one with relationships that motivate him to think of individual business. On the other hand, the crowd has specific functions, which can be served only by giving each member exact cues and exact business to perform on these cues. It is often wise to invent their *ad libs* for them; otherwise, they either may not speak at all, or they may tend to use anachronisms. The aural pattern of a crowd must be rehearsed like choral reading until it is accurate.

The basic functions of a crowd are:

1. To create excitement. In the opening scene of *Romeo and Juliet,* the stage rapidly fills with dueling, brawling groups, to get the audience alert for the quiet expository scene which follows. In the fight scene between Mahon and Christy in *The Playboy,* the excitement of the main crisis of the play is redoubled by the pushing, jeering, cringing, and rush of the mob.

2. To make transitions. In the party scene of *Romeo and Juliet,* the forceful cross of the servant through center to Romeo leads attention from Capulet to Romeo. A set of dancers clearing center gives focus to Paris and Juliet, who move into center as Romeo points them out.

3. To emphasize a situation. The crowd who watch Christy being beaten spread out over the room. As he flees from Mahon, they scatter out of the way, and their fear of him emphasizes the notion that Christy may win this fight. When

Christy chases his father from the house, the crowd, repeating the pattern of his cross, emphasizes the sweeping defeat of Old Mahon.

In rehearsal a great deal of detail will come to mind that does not occur to the director during the planning stage. But the major blocking of a crowd scene must be planned before rehearsal, in order to avoid a bedlam of actors offering suggestions while the director is trying to make decisions.

In arena staging, obviously some of these methods of securing emphasis are useless. For example, in full arena, there is no setting to provide emphasis points, though the furniture helps, through its mass, contrasting line, and arrangement. In arena, as on the proscenium stage, isolation and reinforcement from other actors can also be used.

Unless the auditorium is well raked, one must seek motives to keep the actors on their feet more in arena than on the conventional stage, and most important or critical scenes must be played standing. The actors can sit on the arms of chairs or lean on tables. If they must sit at certain points, the chairs must have high seats and low backs. The patterns of movement must be planned to avoid favoring one part of the audience while neglecting another. A triangular pattern is often helpful, the actors crossing at the main breaks in the scene as in the proscenium pattern. In order to reveal to the audience (all around) what happens to all of the characters, Capulet's triangular pattern, illustrated above, would have to be broken by, perhaps, moving Juliet at the attack breaks, so that the audience could see her reactions.

For example, Juliet might cross away on "proportioned as one's thoughts would wish a man," and Capulet might cross in the opposite direction, changing his physical pattern, but not the basic emotional pattern of the scene. Lady Capulet could still provide the focus of his need for support.

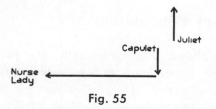

Fig. 55

On "You shall not house with me," Juliet might again cross away to a bench and sink down, and Capulet would then deliver the rest of his threat from behind her, facing in a new direction for the benefit of the audience on another side.

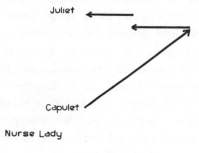

Fig. 56

Thus two moves of Juliet, fleeing from her father's rage, would block the scene for arena.

Probably the reason that not much is written on acting and directing for the arena is that the basic techniques do not differ very much. The actor is concerned with an honest interpretation of his role, and the director is, as always, concerned that the audience see and hear and respond in the desired way. In arena, the fact that the audience are all around instead of on one side makes a few techniques more useful than others; but they are not basically different techniques, and anyone who can direct a proscenium play honestly and skillfully can also direct for arena.

Movement as Punctuation

It has been shown that, structurally, the play moves in a
series of related scenes, each of which is in turn a series of
attacks on an objective. These divisions are not unlike the
chapter, section, and paragraph divisions of a book. Since the
audience do not have the printed page to help them, another
sort of symbol is needed to indicate the break at the end of
a chapter or paragraph. On stage, we use a punctuation of
time and space, more various and subtle than the printer's
spaces, but quite as essential for clarity. This punctuation is
not a bag of director's tricks if it is based on a thorough
understanding of and respect for the human values inherent
in the play. By keeping the audience aware of the progress of
the story, it helps to build the tension-release rhythms that
create crisis and climax; and, as it becomes more and more
highly individualized during rehearsals. it reveals the personalities of the characters who move. The concept of movement as
punctuation is as intensely related to the bases of characterization as to the action of the play.

Perhaps the first directions that are written into the promptbook are those that mark the beginnings of new scenes, large
shifts of area designed especially for clarity. These transitional
movements that lead from one scene to the next are often provided by the playwright, in the entrance or exit of a character
or in some transitional dialogue or stage business that allows
the audience time to digest a scene and anticipate the next
one. In general, it is a good idea to indicate the start of a
new scene by moving the actors to a new place.

Such a moment occurs after Shawn's first exit in *The Playboy*. As he is to return immediately in the same mood, one of
terror, Pegeen merely snatches his coat, reprimands Michael
James, and restates her objective as she flounces up behind
the counter. Interest centers for a moment on the table where

the men return to pick up their drinks. But Shawn's return heralds the first entrance of Christy, perhaps the most important moment of Act I. A great deal of movement accompanies and follows the three short speeches of this transition. Shawn opens the door, sticks his head in — and there is surely some responsive movement of the people inside, which the playwright does not give. Shawn looks back over his shoulder, runs into the room. The people inside, since they are cowards, probably move to a safe distance. Christy coughs outside. There is another tiny scramble of movement, and then they are dead still, every eye upon the door for a perceptible moment — a moment which the audience shares. Christy enters, "tired and frightened and dirty."

Another moment calling for a rather long transitional break is the one in which Pegeen has raucously got rid of Shawn in Act I. As she bolts the door and takes off her apron, the audience has time to think, "That's the end of Shawn for tonight." Then she hangs her apron across the window for a blind, opens a chest, takes out a blanket, and brings it to Christy at the fireplace, while he and the audience wait for the scene ahead.

Moments like these effect a definite renewal of audience interest. Listening, one can hear them stir, and see heads and shoulders rise as a new scene starts. In confirmation of this point, a valuable description of audience behavior was made by Murray Stahl.[3] After a long training period in which he developed a shorthand to describe behavior, he took a position from which, unseen, he could watch the behavior of the occupant of a certain seat in the auditorium from a distance of about eight feet. In four nights of viewing the member of the audience who sat there, he found a clear pattern of settling

[3]Murray W. Stahl, "An Evaluation of Observation as a Method of Reporting Audience Behavior," Master's thesis (University of Alabama, 1951).

down as a scene progressed and sitting up again as a new scene started, while the fixation of the eyes indicated that there was no lapse of attention. The audience evidently needs time for the unconscious relaxation of muscles between scenes.

The time required and the amount of business needed to mark the end of a scene and the beginning of the next probably depend on the amount of emotional change from scene to scene and on the extent to which muscular strain must be maintained in the audience in the process of suspense. If a quiet scene is to follow a scene of great tension, then a good bit of transitional movement may be desirable in order to be sure that the audience is relaxed and ready for the quiet scene. But if suspense is to be increased, the scene must move ahead with energy and with little opportunity for the audience to relax. The movement that sets the scenes apart is not just any move; it derives from what has happened, the characters involved, and the requirements of the scene ahead.

The punctuation of the attacks may be less in space and duration than that between scenes, but there will be at least a definite loss of tension in the actor as he fails to accomplish his objective through one attack, and a definite change in the line of his body as he starts a new attack — at least a tendency to move toward, against or away from. The audience shares the actor's changes of tension.

As a matter of fact, it is extremely helpful to think of all business as punctuation, no more artificial than the printed punctuation which clarifies the meaning of the following sentence:

> I'm so glad you're home, Mary.
> I'm so glad you're home — Mary!

Mary could be anyone to shake hands with in the first sentence; in the second, she is someone to go toward and enfold.

On the stage, the dash is indicated by a pause long enough to take a breath. The action of going toward and enfolding replaces the exclamation point. The whole business is motivated and the meaning is clear.

An amateur actor is often shocked to realize that every move is significant, but the professional is so alert to the meanings he conveys that he studies deeply such questions as, "When do I set down my gloves?" "At which word should I rise?" — or sit, or turn away. Challenged by, "I'm so glad you're home — Mary!", his full plan might be: "I'm saying hello to the children. I pick up the littlest one on the word 'home.' He is high above my head when I see Mary. I slowly set him down as I look at her. We love each other so much. I say 'Mary' very quietly. Then I walk over to her and sweep her into my arms." This really makes the most of a dash and an exclamation point.

Shakespeare rarely gives us these directions. On the Elizabethan stage a Shakespearean scene begins when a character enters and ends when all characters leave the stage — a definite, though monotonous punctuation. However, in a long Shakespearean scene there are, of course, changes of objective — in other words, more than one scene in our sense. These need to be punctuated by movement.

As an example of how precise business enhances the meaning of a speech, while inadequate and ill-timed business obscures it, part of Juliet's potion scene may be studied. The only direction given by Shakespeare in the first twenty lines is ("Lays down a dagger"). Obviously, however, Juliet moves a great deal in the beginning of this speech. If two students will perform the experiment of memorizing it, the first using the lettered directions given in the right-hand margin, the second using the numbered directions at the left, several points will become clear.

1. She stands middle of room looking after mother and Nurse who have just left

2. X slowly toward bed, stop, take deep breath

3. Run to door while saying next line

4. Stop, relax
5. Turn toward bed

6. X to bed, get vial from under pillow on "Come, vial."
7. Sit on bed, open vial

8. Close vial, cross on "No, no," to prie-dieu, get dagger from bible
9. X to bed on speech
10. Lay dagger on night table
11. Open vial, sitting, smell bitter opiate

12. Start to set vial down
13. Bring it back to lap

---

(1) Farewell! (A) God knows when we shall meet again. (2)

I have a faint cold fear thrills through my veins that almost freezes up the heat of life. (3) I'll call them back again (B) to comfort me.

Nurse! (4) (C) What should she do here? (5) My dismal scene I needs must act alone. (6) Come, vial. (7) (D)

What if this mixture do not work at all? Shall I be married then tomorrow morning? (8)

No! No! (E) This (9) shall forbid it. (10) Lie thou there. (11) What if it be a poison (F) which the friar Subtilly hath ministered to have me dead, Lest in this marriage he should be dishonored Because he married me before to Romeo. (12) I fear it is. (13) (G) And yet methinks it

---

A. X slowly toward bed while speaking

B. Turn toward door

C. X to bed and sit while speaking

D. Take vial from under pillow

E. Take dagger from under pillow, set it on night table

F. Look at vial

G. Open vial

should not
For he hath still been
tried a holy man.
I will not entertain so
14. Raise vial to   bad a thought. (14)
mouth

First, it will be seen that the actress using the numbered directions throws the more light on Juliet's feelings, because these directions are the more sensitive of the two sets.

1. Juliet's dread seems much less if she moves before rather than after "God Knows when we shall meet again."

2. Running to the door while she speaks (suiting the action to the word) reveals her panic more clearly than if she merely turns, later, as in the lettered series.

3. The direction, "Stop, relax," marks the end of the attack more clearly than the cross in the other series.

4. If she has to get up for the dagger, the rush of panic seems much greater than if she merely turns and picks it up, and great determination is expressed in her slow and wordless cross as she carries it to her bed. Moreover, it is illogical for her to have the dagger under her pillow. The lettered directions miss these points completely.

5. Directions 12 and 13 reveal her mounting panic and stringent effort at control, a conflict to which she alternately yields and gives fight throughout the scene, if the ultimate drinking of the potion is to be convincing and moving.

The more elaborate plan also gives the actress time to build some of Juliet's feeling. Taking time to think a speech fully and to relax when possible is the indispensable step toward a sense of truth for the actor. Even an actor who seems a little insensitive will give a presentable performance if the director can get him to study in this way, completing one step, with clear visible and aural punctuation, before going on to the next.

Also, this process builds crisis-tension in the audience. Each time Juliet raises the vial, the audience expects her to take the potion; when a new fear delays her, the audience must wait.

It is this process of anticipating and being made to wait that creates suspense, in the same way in which one excites a child by making him guess in which hand the lollipop is.

In actually working with the actress playing Juliet, one would hardly direct her this minutely, for she herself might do something out of her feelings and her sense of truth that would be more expressive. The point of the illustration is that emotionally correct movement, precisely executed, enhances a speech for the audience and for the actor, whereas emotional values and meaning are obscured by vague and ill-timed movement, in much the same way that punctuation can make a printed page easier or more difficult to read. It also shows that a better performance can be given by even a poor actor, if the director can help him to do logical things accurately.

A Scene in the Promptbook

As a final illustration of the director's visual means of clarifying the action of the play and keeping the words always dynamic, a full promptbook is presented of Mercutio's Queen Mab speech (*Romeo and Juliet*, Act I, Sc. 4). This speech is one that regularly challenges and terrifies the actor who must play it. It is fifty lines of fantasy, the hardest kind of imagery to make interesting in our literal-minded times. It has been played with brilliant voice work and nimble swirling of cape in a hundred different ways since Thomas Pope first brawled through it in 1591.

The speech must not be thought of as a soliloquy. It is a part of the attempt of Mercutio and Benvolio to get Romeo to cheer up and join them in crashing the Capulet party, a typical collegians' prank unto our own day. This motive dominates the scene in the behavior of Romeo and Benvolio as well as of Mercutio. The single speech each of Romeo and Benvolio might indicate that they are bored, but their responses to the

Queen Mab speech must not lead the audience to think it is boring. Both Benvolio and Romeo are devoted to Mercutio (one of the reasons that his death is so keenly touching), and they delight in his humor, as their other scenes together indicate. Benvolio shares Mercutio's motive here and will cooperate rather than throw cold water on Mercutio's exuberance. Since Romeo does change his mind at the end of the scene, one must conclude that the Queen Mab speech had some effect on him, penetrating his real and deep premonition of death. This scene is thus more than a display of histrionic pyrotechnics on the part of the actor who plays Mercutio; it is also more than a delightful bit of Shakespearean fantasy; it is a struggle between Mercutio (aided by Benvolio) on the one hand and a gripping devil of fear on the other hand for the possession of Romeo's mind.

With no speeches, Romeo and Benvolio must make clear their positions in the struggle, through visible behavior which furnishes Mercutio cues for his attacks and indicates his progress. This kind of approach to the scene makes it unnecessary to seek very far for stage movement, for it is inherent in the relationships of the three characters. In rehearsal it should also go a long way toward removing the actor's fear of the "long speech" by turning his attention from his own delivery to his effect on the other characters. It will also help him to memorize the speech, since the behavior of the others gives him cues as clear as words, and he can thus learn the fifty lines in what Stanislavsky called "small bites." The director may well take the point of view that there are no "long speeches."

Before presenting the scene, it should be made clear again that the purpose of the example is not to show pontifically how the scene must be interpreted, but to illustrate a method of study that will make a "speech" into a dramatic, suspenseful struggle.

Music Continues

1.

2. arm around Romeo

3. Run fingers over Romeo's nose, X-ing to Ben.
   Romeo sit, steps R L

4. Attack 2

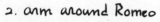

5. Romeo turns. Mercutio rises, enlisting Ben's
   help

5a Sit on wall, driving chariot

6.

Fig. 57A

Mercutio's objective: to get Romeo to crash the Capulet party. Benvolio supports him. Romeo hangs on to his dream of Rosaline and the disturbing dream he has had of death.

Mercutio begins by playing the "medico", "The Doctor" of commedia and of other plays of Shakespeare, a pedant, loaded with irrelevant, meaningless circumstantial details.

Attack 1: Diagnose the case
1. Romeo is surprised at this game, turns. Mercutio warns him of the seriousness of his disease.
2. Romeo feigns alarm at This. Benvolio begins to Think Romeo is now with them.
3. Deceived by his own cleverness, Mercutio thinks he has won easily
4. He and Benvolio laugh and turn to Romeo to find he has lapsed into the doldrums.

MERCUTIO
Oh, then I see Queen Mab (1) hath been
with thee.

She is the fairies' midwife (2) and she
comes
In shape no bigger than an agate stone
On the forefinger of an alderman,
Drawn with a team of little atomies (3)

Athwart men's noses as they lie asleep. (4)

Failure

But the attack seemed to be working and may again. Mercutio pursues it.

Attack 2: Treat the ailment by thaumaturgy
5. Romeo listens to "moonshine" and "film", Mercutio is encouraged to let his imagination go. He seeks concurrence from Benvolio, using less romantic, more masculine images. Benvolio loves nothing more than Mercutio's fooling.
6. But when they look at Romeo again, he has stopt listening.

Her wagon spokes made of long spinners' legs,
The cover of the wings of grasshoppers,
Her traces of the smallest spiders' web,
Her collar of the moonshine's watery beams,
Her whip of crickets' bone, the lash of
film, (5)

Her waggoner a small gray coated gnat
Not half so big as a round little worm
Pricked from the lazy finger of a maid.
Her chariot is an empty hazel nut
Made by the joiner squirrel or old grub,
Time out of mind the fairies' coachmaker. (6)

Failure

Mercutio must hastily remind him they are discussing his illness.

Fig. 57B

6a Attack 3

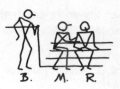

B.   M.   R.

7. Call on Benvolio

8. Ben bows, very fancy

9. Seducing in Romeo's ear

End Music

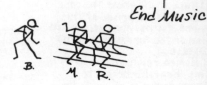

B.   M.   R.

11. Mercutio and Benvolio pantomime, playing
    for Romeo's attention.

12.

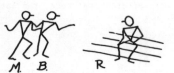

M.   B.   R

Romeo turns away

Attack 5

13. Seduce

Fig. 58A

Attack 3. Wrestle with The disease.

And in this state she gallops night by night
Through lovers' brains and then they dream of love.

(This is sure medicine) Romeo responds, and Mercutio tries a new attack

Attack 4. Minimize the illness, which is epidemic but not fatal
7. He grabs help from Benvolio.

(7) O'er courtiers' knees that dream on curtsies straight. (8)

8. Benvolio might pantomime. Mercutio thanks him with a laugh,
9. and gets to work on Romeo again,
10. casting a mischievous aspersion on Rosaline

O'er lawyers' fingers who straight dream on fees, (9)
O'er ladies' lips who straight on kisses dream, (10)
Which oft the angry Mab with blisters plagues

11. Romeo laughs, a bit embarrassed, and Mercutio again thinks he has won. His exuberance leads him to clown with Benvolio. Both are working hard to get Romeo to laugh with them.

Because their breaths with sweetmeats tainted are. (11)

Sometimes she gallops o'er a courtier's nose,
And then dreams he of smelling out a suit.
And sometimes comes she with a tithe-pig's tail
Tickling a parson's nose as 'a lies asleep,
Then dreams he of another benefice.
Sometimes she driveth o'er a soldier's neck
And then dreams he of cutting foreign throats,
Of breaches, ambuscadoes, Spanish blades,
Of healths five fathom deep; and then anon
Drums in his ears; at which he starts and wakes,

12. Benvolio and Mercutio laugh heartily exhilarated by their clowning. But Romeo is gone again. (The audience laughs)

And being thus frighted, swears a prayer or two
And sleeps again. (12)

Failure

Attack 5. Make Romeo see the ridiculousness of his attitude by being deeply mock serious.

This is that very Mab
That plats the manes of horses in the night
And bakes the elflocks in foul sluttish hairs,
Which once entangled much misfortune bodes (13)

13. Romeo is caught by "misfortune", and gives full attention.

Fig. 58B

Attack 6

14. Romeo turns away

15. Relax, not pushing any more

Attack 7.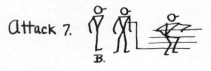

16. Ben x to steps

                                                Slowly fade in
                                                    Dance Music

17. Hand on Mercutio's arm, but alone

18. Turn to Mercutio. M. slaps him on shoulder

19. Slap Mercutio on shoulder
20. Start into house, flanked by Ben and Mercutio

                                               Music up as lights
                                                  fade

Fig. 59A

Attack 6.
Mercutio presses his
advantage by culling his
next example from the
basic interest of the male
in women.

This then is that hag, when maids lie on
their backs,
That presses them and learns them first
to bear,
Making them women of good carriage.
This is she -- (14)

14. Romeo is caught em-
barrassed. In courtly
love, one does not admit
carnal desire.

ROMEO
Peace, peace, Mercutio, peace.
Thou talkst of nothing.

Failure

---

15. Mercutio gives up,
making very gentle fun of
Romeo's romancery. He
loves Romeo, and this is
The most intimate moment
of the scene. Mercutio
did not realize that this
is the very method that
would work. He takes
heart, and

(15) True, I talk of dreams,
Which are the children of an idle brain
Begot of nothing but vain fantasy
And more inconstant than the wind,

Attack 7. Urges Romeo to
try more satisfying fare.

who woos
Even now the frozen bosom of the north,
And being angered puffs away from thence,
Turning his face to the dew-dropping
south. (16)

16. As Romeo rises, turning
to Mercutio with friendly
gratitude, Benvolio gets
impatient.

BENVOLIO
This wind you talk of blows us from our-
selves.
Supper is done and we shall come too late.

17. Romeo is quietly ser-
ious as he forces Mer-
cutio to understand the
depth of his premonition.

ROMEO
I fear too early. (17) For my mind misgives
Some consequence yet hanging in the stars
Shall bitterly begin his fearful date
With this night's revels, and expire the
term
Of a despised life closed in my breast
By some vile forfeit of untimely death.
(18)

18. Mercutio does under-
stand, perhaps claps him
on the shoulder. Romeo con-
fides his fears to God.

19. Claps Mercutio in
manly thanks and (20)
starts into the house.

But he that hath the steerage of my course
Direct my sail. (19)
On, lusty gentlemen. (20)

Success-Climax

Mercutio's success is climactic, but his affection for his friend prevents him from an expression of triumph. Benvolio, as less involved,
would be the one to express their pleasure at getting what they wanted.

Fig. 59B

Assignments

1. Think of the meaning of the following words: wind, breeze, zephyr, tornado. What does each make you want to do?
2. State the tendency to move (there is no actual move) of the characters in the following speeches:
    JULIET (*Romeo and Juliet* Act III Sc. 5)
    Well, thou hast comforted me marvelous much.
    AMANDA (*The Glass Menagerie,* end of Scene 7)
    Yes, I know — the tyranny of women. Goodbye, Mr. O'Connor. I wish you luck — and happiness — and success! All three of them, and so does Laura! — Don't you, Laura?
    CECILY (*Earnest,* Act II)
    It would distress me more than I can tell you, dear Gwendolyn, if it caused you any mental or physical anguish, but I feel bound to point out that since Earnest proposed to you he has clearly changed his mind.
3. Copy the figures on page 175 until they are easy to draw. Then picturize: man taking thorn from foot, man who has just over-heard his best friend betray him, man presenting woman with gift, mother welcoming son from college, father saying goodbye to son who is going to prison, two children reading before open fire.
4. Picturize the moment after Jim has kissed Laura when he calls himself "stumble-john."
5. Picturize the quarrel between Capulet and Tybalt in Act I, Sc. 5:
    TYBALT
    It fits, when such a villain is the guest. I'll not endure him.
    CAPULET
    He shall be endured. What, goodman boy? I say he shall.
6. Picturize a scene in which a man and woman are at lunch in a restaurant: (1) They are casually acquainted. In the course of the meal they find out that (2) they differ radically on some matters but (3) fundamentally like each other. (4) The man realizes he is falling in love. (5) The girl is engaged to someone else. Draw stick figures to show all these relation-

ships. The setting is a restaurant booth. The woman is at the man's right.

7.   Use any logical elements of scenery you can think of and find as many pictures as you can for two people on the fire escape of *The Glass Menagerie,* an area six feet by eight feet.

8.   Find barriers for Scene 3 of *The Glass Menagerie* when Tom invents a secret life in order to terrify Amanda. Picturize the following moments in this scene:

What do you think I'm at?

Every time you come in yelling that Goddam "Rise and shine."

I'm going to the movies (second time he says it).

On those occasions they call me El Diablo.

9.   In the scene between Jack and Algernon about the cigarette case, find all changes of dominance and picturize each of these changes, using as many of the means of emphasis as you logically can.

10.   Block Christy's soliloquy opening Act II of *The Playboy.*

11.   Find a pace pattern (include furniture) for Algernon as he explains Bunbury to Jack in Act I and show how he would use the pattern.

12.   Study the short scene in which Tom and Jim O'Connor first come into the house in *The Glass Menagerie.* There is a stage direction for Tom that is incomplete, — "Lights cigarette and crosses back to fire escape door." See if you can tell when and why he thinks of lighting the cigarette, break the scene into its beats, and show each part of the process of lighting the cigarette and crossing to the door.

Reading List

Baldwin, Thomas W. *The Organization and Personnel of the Shakespearean Company.* Princeton: Princeton University Press, 1927.

Bergson, Henri. *Laughter.* New York: Macmillan, 1913.

Cole, Toby and Helen Crich Chinoy. *Directing the Play.* Indianapolis: Bobbs-Merrill, 1953.

Duchartre, Pierre Louis. *The Italian Comedy.* New York: John Day, 1929.

Dean, Alexander. *Fundamentals of Play Directing.* New York: Farrar and Rinehart, 1941.

Gorchakov, Nikolai. *Stanislavsky Directs.* New York: Funk and Wagnalls, 1954.

Hall, Calvin S. and Gardner Lindzey. *Theories of Personality.* New York: John Wiley, 1952.

Horney, Karen. *Neurosis and Human Growth.* New York: W. W. Norton, 1950.

Jacobson, Edmund. *Progressive Relaxation.* Chicago: University of Chicago Press, 1929.

Houghton, Norris. *Moscow Rehearsals.* New York: Harcourt, Brace, 1936.

Murray, H. A. *et. al. Explorations in Personality.* New York: Oxford University Press, 1938.

Nicoll, Allardyce. *Masks, Mimes and Miracles.* New York: Harcourt, Brace, 1931.

Stahl, Murray W. "An Evaluation of Observation as a Method of Reporting Audience Behavior." Master's Thesis (University of Alabama, 1951).

Chapter 10

The Characters in Space

The two variables of movement that have been discussed —
direction and distance —tell the story as it might be acted
by any human beings. Four other variables modify the movement to make it that of specific characters. These variables
are extent, rate, tension and number. They reveal the character, because they show *how* he moves.

The Bases of Characterization

A character, on the stage as in life, is highly complex. It
is impossible to discuss how movement reveals character
without first summarizing the sources of characterization. One
must know why the individual moves before being able to say
how he moves.

To describe a character in terms of adjectives, as some actors
try to do, is to fragment him. It does not help the actor to be
told that Shawn Keogh is shy, for Christy is shy, too, at times.
Both of them are also aggressive at times; yet they are quite
different characters. The adjectives do not describe enough of
their behavior to enable the actors to play these roles.

Nor is it enough to invent a few mannerisms as the sole means of presenting the character. It is significant that of his entire book, *Building a Character,* Stanislavsky devotes only six pages to the external means of characterization. Most of the rest of the book is devoted to the training of the actor's voice and body, in order to make him flexible and responsive *to the promptings of his spirit.* With a trained and flexible voice and body, a good actor will begin his characterization not with fragmentizing adjectives or superficial mannerisms, but with a systematic exploration of the dynamic sources of his character's behavior. He will first seek the basic human needs that impel him to act, then the individual goals, the experiences that created them, the specific actions he takes to satisfy them, and the conflicting desires that inhibit his action.

Our hope of understanding our fellow creatures lies in the fact that we are biologically, psychologically, and socially much alike. Everyone wants something — physical comfort, emotional security, growth, approval. But our specific goals and our specific ways of achieving them are apparently quite different. For example, everyone needs the approbation of some fellow being; one seeks it by becoming a football hero or a movie star, one by writing a poem, another through a profession of service, another by surrounding himself with possessions or a family, another by conformity, another by crime or suicide. To understand the specific goals, one must understand the causes of differences between human beings.

Even minor biological deviations affect the needs of an individual and his means of satisfying them. A young person with elastic muscles and active glands will move differently and toward different objectives than a person whose muscles and glands tend toward atrophy because of age. The motives and behavior of a beautiful young woman will be colored by her beauty as much as a blind person's by his defect. Tallness, shortness, crooked or beautiful teeth, flat feet, all leave their mark on the possessor's way of facing life, his goals, and his method of operation. An individual thinks and acts in a particular way because of his biological individuality.

Differences of family background, of course, create differences of need and of action to satisfy need. Wealth, poverty, literacy or the lack of it, the closeness or looseness of family ties, fear, jealousies, security, pride, embarrassment experienced in childhood color the adult's outlook and behavior even if he has moved into quite different circumstances. The great mushrooming of psychiatry is ample evidence of this fact.

The place where one grew up has had an effect on his goals and behavior. Although cinema and television have tended to eradicate many surface differences of people in the United States, a person who has lived all his life with the quiet goals of a country town, the life circumscribed by neighbors who knew his family and forbears, is a different individual from someone who spent his childhood amid the frantic pursuits of a large city, where no one ever heard of him or his ancestors. A person whose childhood was passed near the ocean or in the mountains is different from someone who grew up on inland plains. One's standards of excellence and opportunities to develop are also conditioned by the people he has known and by the institutions provided by his community for the well-being of its citizens.

Even the time at which an individual grew up makes a difference. A sixteen-year-old girl in 1900 behaved quite differently, and thought differently, from a girl of the same age today. A man of 1560 might dream of flying to the stars, but he had to make a profession of something else. Today, he can spend his life training to this end.

One's occupation and particularly his hobbies not only reveal but also help to form as well as to satisfy his needs, and strongly modify his behavior.

An individual is also partly a product of his experiences of success and failure. If he has received few rebuffs, perhaps he can name his goals and set about working toward them with confidence, whatever they may be. On the other hand, someone who has seldom enjoyed the successful pursuit of a goal may have no confidence in his power to achieve, and sometimes, as a result, his power to desire atrophies, as Pavlov discovered in the second part of his classic experiment with the dog.

Even certain chance experiences modify objectives and behavior — a hurricane, a personality, a trip, a book, an idea in a newspaper. Shakespeare's career in the theatre may have been sparked by the annual fair that came to Stratford. Appia revolutionized stage design when he saw the wing and groove setting and the fat singers of Wagnerian opera.

Part of the understanding of an individual must be an understanding of his inhibitions. Inhibitions are almost always of social origin, from the need to live with one's fellow man. Some inhibitions stem from clear prohibitions of the law with their threat of punishment, or from those of the church with its threat of immediate as well as eternal disapproval. Some exist because of the need for approval of specific individuals, — parent, friend, lover, business superior. Some inhibitions seem to be related to self-approval, especially those that contain ethical or aesthetic elements. Some, of course, are the result of a need to protect the body, or from the body's recognized incompetences. The causes of inhibition are not always apparent, for inhibitions are initiated from infancy or from any other period in life, in highly complex ways. In the study of a character, one needs to know his inhibitions and their sources, for they are the negative expressions of motives; the penalty for breaking them is the failure to achieve some goal, whether it is overt or not.

An individual is thus a system of biology modified by experience, with certain drives and certain inhibitions based on these, and certain behavioral patterns deriving from them. He

moves in his specific way because of what he is. His movements
differ from those of all other people because he actually is
different.

Individual Differences in Moving

One individual's moving differs from another's in terms of
the extent of the moves he makes, the rate and tension of the
moves, and the number of moves made.

A move may be a mere turn of the eyes, a very slight hand
gesture, a step or two, or a full move into an entirely different
space. In general, the extent of the move depends on the
strength of the motive (toward, against, or away from), modified by the inhibiting factors of the character in his environment. Michael James and Pegeen move more fully than the
other characters in the first act of *The Playboy*, because they
live in the shebeen and have unlimited rights and duties there.
Shawn makes small movements because he is afraid of his
own feelings toward Pegeen, and Christy because much punishment has taught him to be as inconspicuous as possible.
Jimmy and Philly move in restricted space as a matter of good
manners, Mahon because he wants to be elsewhere in his search
for Christy. The rate, tension, and the number of moves of
these characters would vary, but each has a reason to make
moves of limited extent. All of these characters are also capable
of large moves when the inhibiting circumstances are removed
or when the situation becomes critical. Christy, once he has
had the experience of being admired, can move in quite a large
area, counting glasses at the opening of Act II, perhaps pantomiming his story to the girls, and using the longest diagonal
of the stage when he drives his father out.

In a modern American play, few characters move broadly,
for most Americans fear attracting attention. People who use
large gestures seem flamboyant or ill-bred or over-excited. We

cultivate a blasé manner, sangfroid. Mercutio, the uninhibited Elizabethan, moves freely as his great sense of fun drives him. Thus the extent of the move indicates something about the relative vigor of motive and inhibition.

Incidentally, textbooks caution us against the use of a long cross, as it is likely to create a dead pause. It is often wise, in fact, to break a long cross by finding earlier motives to make part of the cross. Probably this is because the average actor does not move well enough or has not enough emotional energy to keep control of the audience for the time that it takes to walk fifteen or twenty feet— the length of an average-sized room.

One use of a long cross is to indicate great release of emotional energy in success or failure. The long cross thus sometimes proves useful to mark the end of a scene or a major change of attack within the scene. If the long cross is emotionally right, the motivated actor can be taught to hold it.

Very small moves also require some caution, for they tend to pass unnoticed. If the move is significant, even though small, time must be allowed and attention thrown toward it, for no move is of the least value to the audience if it is imperceptible.

A person moves as rapidly as he must under the stress of an impulse and as rapidly as he may in terms of his age, health, and other inhibitory stimuli. Thus, rate and tension must be considered together, for speed indicates the force of the motive, while tension reveals the power of the inhibiting factors.

In general, a young person moves more rapidly than an old person, a happy person than a sad one, a healthy person than one who is ill. But whatever the physical condition of the individual, under certain kinds of emotional stress, movement tends to be rapid; for example, in strong anticipation of a pleasant experience, or in the sudden perception of danger, or in an overwhelming impulse to complete any of the basic emotional patterns toward, against, or away from. Observation of life only will tell how much tension and how great speed are appropriate in a given situation. As a general principle, one may say that difficulty increases tension. If the motive and the inhibiting factor are both strong, there will be strong tensions. But one thing is certain: the amount of tension on stage will be felt in the audience and can be used toward the effect the playwright wanted, whether this be crisis, as in conventional drama, or the other kinds of empathy desired by some less conventional playwrights.

The number of moves a character makes, large or small, tense or relaxed, also reveals something about him. The strongest object one can think of, a rock, does not move at all. Thus poise, which we associate with strength in a social situation, is characterized by freedom from random, purposeless movements. A poised person sits or stands well-balanced, with relaxed neck and quiet hands, and moves with efficiency.

On the other hand, motionlessness is also characteristic of the dead. Old age, illness, hopelessness, and a generally phlegmatic nature prompt relatively few movements, and a thoroughly scared person is sometimes paralyzed. The number of moves must be planned in connection with all the other variables in order to interpret and portray character. A few heavy, slow, awkward moves may indicate a stupid person; the same number of slow moves made dexterously may indicate great power.

The number of moves seems related to the energy level and control of the individual. In Christy's scene with Pegeen in Act 1, he moves very little, fearfully trying to seem what she would have him be. In Act II, with the girls, he moves a great deal more. He is freer, more sure of himself, and the experience exhilarates him and gives him more energy. He has also had a good night's sleep to replenish him.

A sample analysis of the characters of Christy and Shawn may help to show how one arrives at characterizing behavior. The text of *The Playboy* makes it clear that both Shawn and Christy are afraid. Their inhibitions are about as strong as their positive impulses. Yet the flight of Shawn as he leaves his coat in Michael James's hands in Act I is quite different from Christy's flight at the first approach of Old Mahon in Act II. Shawn is fighting his devil of temptation in the person of Michael James. Christy has no way of fighting his father face to face.

Both young men are healthy and strong — Shawn from taking care of himself, Christy from hard work out-of-doors. Christy is small, lean, dirty; Shawn is probably somewhat better looking, plumper, soft, and well-dressed for courting in his second-best coat.

Shawn was probably the only child in a family of comfortable means for that area. His father probably died while Shawn was in school ("Your father that you're used to"). His mother was probably intelligent enough to hang on to their property. She may have pampered Shawn, for his petulance indicates that he is accustomed to getting his own way; but his timidity with Pegeen suggests that his mother may also have dealt him a quick backhander upon occasion. It is clear that he has always been able to buy what he wanted — decent clothes, good farm stock and equipment, and now, Pegeen Mike. He is his own master, a solid farmer with perhaps more adipose tissue than muscle, who never uses his hands to fight or make love, and ducks a fight with Christy. At Father Reilly's parochial school he has learned the three R's without acquiring an appetite for more knowledge. His imagination has been inflamed to terror by Father Reilly's eloquence on the subject of hell-fire and he is therefore fanatically rigid in his practice of the negative virtues.

Christy comes from a "stony divil's patch of a field" which he and his father worked themselves. Christy's mother must have died in his infancy, for he seems not to have any memory of snuggling into security. Surely his father drove him out to work as a little boy, scolding and cuffing and becoming even more irritated at the boy's submission. Christy is used to hardship just short of starvation. He has nothing to call his own except his "old dog and cats," and, until he reaches Michael James's shebeen, his only dream is to be quiet and safe, to be let alone. His education is limited to the Sunday lesson of the priest, who gave him a simple notion of the difference between right and wrong. Hell-fire is not so real to Christy as the hell his father keeps him in.

Since Shawn has never occupied himself with very difficult goals, he has always been successful enough to think well of himself. He has experienced ridicule, but only from people toward whom he felt superior because he was a little richer and much holier than they. He therefore has a sense of personal dignity which he strives to maintain. Christy has been too beaten to formulate any satisfactions other than an occasional night of fishing or poaching, free of his father's taunts. He has watched other men enjoying their freedom and ease, without much notion of gaining this happy state for himself. His experience of strangers has been mainly as the object of their ridicule. He has no personal dignity.

Shawn, if only because of his wealth ("my drift of heifers and my blue bull from Sneam"), must have been eyed by the mothers of local girls, who may have thought of him as a "catch." Christy was known to the village girls as "the looney of Mahon's." Both Shawn and Christy are therefore rather lonely, Shawn because he is a little too rich, Christy because he is too poor both in purse and in spirit.

Shawn's physical actions must reflect his three motives: his male desire for Pegeen, his terror of hell-fire, and his frantic determination to maintain his personal dignity. His biology is pulling in one direction, his imagination in two others. In dealing with business matters in the village he moves with ease, perhaps rather amply, but, because of Father Reilly, his spurts of movement toward Pegeen are likely to be rather rapid, short, tense, with elbows rigidly at his sides, knees together, forbidding the embrace he desires. His impulses to flee are also likely to be quick and tense, because he also wants to stand on his dignity. To select this kind of tight movement for Shawn merely as a mannerism might tend to make him seem effeminate. Actually, it is caused by the paralyzing effect of three powerful drives.

Christy also, in Act I, makes hesitant short moves, but fewer than Shawn, and without much tension. His motive is deeply biological — rest, food, security. His body is bone-tired, and his full acquaintance with blows and ridicule has made him both agile at ducking and impervious to pain. He huddles into himself with the quiet of a dumb animal.

Frustrated, Shawn grabs, slaps, and pinches like an angry child. He absolutely cannot fight. Since he is as adult at the beginning of the play as he is likely to become, his behavior in new situations can only regress. Christy matures during the play, and hence learns new behavior. His dumb quiet slides from him as he gains the respect of people, and his gestures become larger and freer. He spreads out and reaches up, even to pitying the Lord God. His childish terror and clinging to the Widow in Act II end in a man's curse, and, when he has to fight, he slugs with positive deadly intent.

Another useful comparison might be drawn between Mercutio and Algernon Moncrief, for both of these young men are, to use adjectives, rich, wellborn, and willful, seeking their own whims regardless of the other people involved; but the social conditions under which each was reared make a difference in their behavior.

The Elizabethan young nobleman left the care of his female relatives at puberty and entered the service of an experienced knight who brought the boy up in a man's world. The concept of "honor" was instilled into him by example and by practice. He learned to be edgy toward anything that might impugn his courage and sought opportunities to prove his mettle in swordplay. The practice of the arts of love, courtly and otherwise, was part of his adolescent training, and he was frankly proud of his achievements in both kinds. He could dance and turn a sonnet as neatly as he could fence, but Mercutio was more gifted at wenching than at wooing, to judge by his various advices to Romeo and his bawdy scene with the Nurse.

His clothing, too, would affect the way he moved. The ruff that kept his chin high, the rich fabric of his doublet, the decorated hose that revealed his well-shaped thigh and aristocratic ankle, the cape that swung in velvet folds behind, and particularly the sword, on whose hilt his hand habitually rested, would have made him walk and sit and stand quite differently from a modern young man. He would have been sent to France or Italy to complete his education, but Mercutio rejected the foreign education that he ridiculed in Tybalt. In his own estimation, he was a plain Englishman. In the scene with Benvolio in which he ridicules Tybalt, he might affect a rather rough stance, copied in boyhood from some soldier relative he admired; he might sit carelessly. His hands, ringed by a pleated linen ruff, would be strong and male, but he would ride in gloves. One might expect him to carry himself well and to move with well-simulated nonchalance, for he was always proving that nothing could touch him. Under stress, he would move nimbly, with no tensions except those that would accomplish his purposes — the quick embrace, the pinking of his foe. Shakespeare gave a clue in the name, Mercutio. He would do unexpected things — madcap, impulsive things. There would be vast differences of behavior from moment to moment, depending on whether his jealous defense of his honor or his zest for life was dominant. But he would always move with the control and agility of a skilled swordsman.

Mercutio does not seem to have any inhibitions, from society, scruples, biology. He can move freely toward whatever whim pops into his head. Algernon is so loaded with social inhibitions that he has adopted them as positive motives. He wishes to reveal himself as the epitome of what is correct.

Algernon was reared in a matriarchal society (Gwendolyn says in Act II: "The home seems to me to be the proper place for a man."), with a backlog of possessions and advantages and the conviction of his right to these, even though the time had long passed when the family could afford them (Lady Bracknell says of land: "It gives one position and prevents one from keeping it up."). His values are feminine, selfish, irresponsible, and charming. He likes to possess exquisite objects and fine clothes (Jack refers to him as "being always overdressed," and Meriweather reports that his luggage consists of "Three portmanteaus, a dressing case, two hatboxes and a large luncheon basket."). But he does not seem to enjoy these things with his eyes and hands; only his high head and his full chest would reflect his pleasure in fine things. Exquisite surroundings are merely an extension of himself; they are his setting, they exist to enhance him. He himself is the work of art.

In the fashion of his time, he would wear tight trousers gallused high, and narrow shoes, so that he sits and walks rather stiff-legged; one might think of a pompous crane. He has little tendency to move, for he is basically a stand-patter, the last word in conservatism. To Jack, he is dead weight. Whatever he thinks of to do is for his own comfort. In his intense appreciation of himself as a work of art, one might expect him to drape himself effectively over a becoming chair, with delicate posing and some demonstrative hand gestures. If his knees are rather stiff, his wrists are relaxed and graceful.

When his appetites are aroused, he has no scruples (though his appetites are limited to those mentionable in mixed company); his way of moving is to dip and seize, again like the image of the crane. His instant decision to investigate "little Cecily" is quite of the same character as his confiscation of Aunt Augusta's cucumber sandwiches, as his resentment of Jack's eating the muffins, and as his appropriation of the name "Earnest," even though Jack had used it for years. He can be nimble enough in taking possession.

His behavior to his aunt is entirely ritualistic, for he is quite aware that she has no money to will him. He condescends to Jack, even when demanding an invitation to dinner. His behavior to Cecily is also ritualistic, somewhat impeded, no doubt, by the fact that he is unaccustomed to moving across grass and under trees. He would almost surely be awkward at times in the country, but he would regard this as the fault of the country rather than of his own inflexibility, and he would forgive it.

Since Algernon is very close to caricature, it might help the audience if he would take an instant to get attention before moves like sitting or rising or showing the cigarette case; a moment that would say, "See, I shall now move with astounding grace." This is not quite the same as mere superficial exaggeration; it derives from the fact that to himself, Algernon is the center. His actions are supremely important, and all peripheral things flow after him.

Thus motive, environment, and experience determine the kinds of movement Algernon and Mercutio would use, as definitely as they do for Shawn and Christy.

From these examples, it must be clear that stage movement can never be described solely in terms of external behavior. A mannerism is the result of a complex of causes. The adoption of a mannerism by an actor without considering its causes can, at best, chance to affect his inner characterization; at worst it reduces him to an automaton. But when the whole character, past and present, with all its dynamic causes and manifestations, is known, any mannerism that develops is the reflection of a live individual. And any adjectives used to describe moments of his behavior are bound together by a dynamic unifying concept of the character as a whole.

Additional Sources of Characterizing Movement

Characterizing movement may also be derived from the immediate environment of the actor. Properties provide an endless source of business. Pegeen can find any amount of characterizing activity in wiping glasses and straightening the shop. The neighbor girls handle their own properties and pry into Pegeen's cupboards as they make tea. Their handling of Pegeen's cups would be furtive, for they are interlopers. Cecily waters flowers and plays with her books and her diary. Algernon always has food to munch and to toy with. The Reverend Chasuble has his prayerbook and his eyeglasses — handling, cleaning, and putting them in the case. A very little reasoning about what is appropriate in a given case will provide properties to motivate stage business. The sooner the actor begins to think where he is, the sooner this business will come to light.

Costumes create stage business. Mercutio uses his cape, Tybalt his sword, in ways that reveal their natures and also punctuate their speeches. Amanda removes and hangs up her old coat in a way that tells us she must be careful of the little that is left of her better days. Tom thrusts his hands deep into the pockets of his Mackinaw, huddling away from his home environment. Gwendolyn's large hat, furs, purse, gloves, lorgnette, used with great deftness, reveal her extreme social skill and help to make her "points."

Among the most easily available sources of stage business are moves related to the character's own body. Pains and defects, of course, affect movement. Frequent references to hair, nails, makeup, clothing; scratching, rubbing, tapping, flexing, stretching all reveal something about the character's relation to himself — his degree of satisfaction with himself, and whether he is dominated by the physical, emotional, or intellectual side of his nature. His way of sitting, leaning, or sprawling on furniture also reveals his psychological personality.

All of these ways of finding stage business suggest themselves whenever one thinks of a character as a whole living individual, instead of as someone who says certain lines.

Economy in the Use of Business

Many amateur actors are lost in admiration at the ingenuity of a director who loads a play with endless properties and business. Actually, the trick is to know so much that one can find a few of the most telling bits of characterizing business, and then to use these for all they are worth, not only to characterize, but also to tell the story and to punctuate. A plethora of details leaves the audience as confused as a plethora of details in a book. Accuracy and economy are virtues infinitely more to be desired. And it is interesting that when the actor is packed with meaning — the invisible tendencies to movement — this tension is communicated to the audience with a minimum of means.

An example of the economical use of stage business occurs in the opening scene of *The Playboy*. Pegeen is signing her letter as Shawn enters. She has still to address and stamp the letter and seal it into the envelope. She does all of this to put a wall of glass between herself and Shawn, behind which she is unapproachably desirable. At the end of the little scene, her cross to the bar raises the wall, inviting Shawn.

1. Invite him in
2. Directing the envelope — the wall rises

3. Lick stamp
4. Put stamp on letter, thump stamp

5. She rereads letter — she glistens behind the wall

6. Put letter into envelope

7. Lick envelope

8. Press envelope, rise, X, and put letter on corner of counter, turn to Shawn — The wall is down

SHAWN: Where's himself?
PEGEEN: (1) He's coming. (2) To Mr. Sheamus Mulroy, Wine and Spirit Dealer, Castlebar.
SHAWN: I didn't see him on the road.
PEGEEN: How would you see him (3) and it dark night this half hour gone by? (4)
SHAWN: I stood a while outside wondering would I have a right to pass on or to walk in and see you, Pegeen, (5) and I could hear the cows breathing and sighing in the stillness of the air, and not a step moving any place from this gate to the bridge.
PEGEEN: (6) It's above at the crossroads he is, meeting Philly Cullen and a couple more are going along with him to Kate Cassidy's wake. (7)
SHAWN: And he's going that length in the dark night?
PEGEEN: He is, surely, (8) and leaving me lonesome on the scruff of the hill.

CRISIS

As with everything else in directing, much study and thought go into plotting the movements of the actors in a play. First one seeks to discover when a move is necessary in telling the story or in punctuating for clarity; then when it is needed to reveal the motives of the characters; and then one studies what sort of move is both true and effective for the characterization. But eventually the promptbook is in order and the director is ready to answer the first questions the actors will ask.

It seems appropriate to repeat one warning: actors are human, alive, sensitive. They often find out much more about the play as they rehearse the scenes together than the director can, sitting alone in his study. However rich his acquaintance with life, however imaginative and sincere he may be, he could be wrong. He may find that the actors do better things than he has indicated in his promptbook; or he may need a new plan to fit a specific actor. The promptbook is not graven in stone; it can be changed if it must be. The plan is good if the basic patterns feel good to the actors and they begin to invent, within the pattern, moves of their own that indicate the character is coming to life.

Assignments

1. Study the scenes in which Jimmy and Philly are on stage in *The Playboy* and find all evidence which characterizes each. Invent an appropriate background, motives, and relationships that reveal the differences between them. How would these affect the behavior of each?
2. Invent at least five characters who might appear in the crowd scenes of *The Playboy*. Characterize each in terms of his age, sex, occupation, his part in the races, his relation to Christy and to Pegeen, his relation to at least one other character in the crowd.
3. Find characterizing behavior for Amanda in the scene with Tom in which she plans the entertainment of the Gentleman Caller. Block the scene.
4. Find characterizing behavior for Lady Capulet in her first scene with Juliet; for the Nurse in Act II, Sc. 5; for Friar Lawrence in the tomb scene. Justify these actions.
5. Find characterizing business for each character on stage while Jack searches for his handbag in the last act of *The Importance of Being Earnest*.
6. Find a dynamic objective for Friar Lawrence's first speech (Act II, Sc. 3), analyze the speech, and picturize each beat, seeking vitality and variety in the moves he makes. What characterizing behavior makes him different from Friar John?

7. Make a full promptbook of *Romeo and Juliet,* Act II, Sc. 5.
8. Make a full promptbook of Jack's proposal to Gwendolyn in the first act of *The Importance of Being Earnest.* Remember that Algy is helping Lady Bracknell select music in the next room.

Reading List

Armitage, Merle. *Martha Graham.* Los Angeles: Linton R. Kistler, 1937.

Crain, Harold C. "Characterization in the Plays of Modern Dramatists, Techniques and Practices." Ph.D. Thesis (State University of Iowa, 1947).

H'Doubler, Margaret. *Dance: A Creative Art Experience.* New York: F. S. Crofts, 1940.

Kris, Ernst. *Psychoanalytic Explorations in Art.* New York: International Universities Press, 1952.

Kluckhohn, Clyde and Henry A. Murray. *Personality in Nature, Society and Culture.* New York: Alfred A. Knopf, 1948.

Stanislavsky, Constantin. *Building a Character.* New York: Theatre Arts, Inc., 1949.

PART THREE

Working
with the Actor

Chapter 11

Casting

The director's first contact with the company occurs during casting. This is a crucial time not only for the play at hand, but also for the theatre as an organization because it is at these announced auditions that new people come into the theatre, unless casting is confined by custom or expedient to the students registered in a department or to members of a community theatre.

Methods of Casting

In the commercial theatre the audience are so accustomed to being baited with "stars" that very few producers will risk a play without one. In the non-commercial theatre, generally the audience come to see the play. Even in community theatre, "box-office" casting is frowned upon unless the popular public figure is also a reasonably good actor. The audience for the non-commercial theatre also seem to tire of seeing the same actors frequently; they like change. Thus, even a very valuable actor must be used judiciously in a variety of parts, and not frequently presented in the same kind of role.

Although, of course, before selecting a play the director must be fairly sure he can cast the most difficult parts, precasting in the non-commercial theatre is usually not a wise procedure. A reputation in the director for precasting any parts at all tends to deter many people from entering tryouts, and thus the acting potential dwindles from play to play. The amateur actor usually does not have either the confidence or the determination to get a part if he thinks it already "belongs" to someone else.

Auditions are a healthy means of finding new actors for the theatre and the best actors for the roles to be cast. Auditions also bring into the theatre people who have no interest in acting but would like to belong to the theatre group, offering talents that range from scene design and carpentry to giving good parties that help the morale of the group. They volunteer at audition time because it is the one announced time when someone is sure to be in the theatre who could take their names and give them assignments. Auditions should therefore be planned to absorb new people of all kinds. Crew heads should be on hand and taking notes as carefully as the director.

Many plans have been tried for auditions. Some directors like prepared auditions to which candidates bring something they have memorized and probably played elsewhere, to give an idea of their finished work. This is often a waste of time, for, while a few amateurs have had excellent previous training, most of them have not, and along with their virtues, they also betray their glaring faults as they present "finished" readings.

Some directors make copies of the script available so that the candidates can get an idea in advance what the play is about. This helps some actors; others get a mistaken conception of the play, or become "sold" on certain parts for themselves to the exclusion of roles for which they might be better suited. Also, scripts disappear under this system. But when an actor independently secures a copy of the script and familiarizes himself with the play, it is an indication of his genuine eagerness, independence, and intelligence. It is a good sign. If some of the other candidates feel that he has taken unfair advantage of them, it might be remarked that they had the same privilege; the play is in print.

Other directors like a "cold" (unprepared) reading. They argue that an untrained actor lacks not only skill to study the play, but also understanding of his own range. They feel that they can tell more about the actor from a simple sight reading than from a possibly wrong interpretation after a quick reading of the play.

Private readings are not very helpful except in special cases, and should never be granted merely as a favor. A poor sight-reader or an extremely shy candidate may lose some of his fears in a more intimate situation; but the actor who cannot manage to get to announced auditions, especially if there are two or three of them, is likely to be unable to attend rehearsals faithfully.

An interview with each new actor is often helpful in revealing hidden emotional springs, the little hopes, conceits, fears, that must be taken into account in working with the actor. It is often possible to abolish tensions and establish rapport more quickly in an interview than in the rehearsal group. It enables one to check up on grades, in a school situation, and on the amount of distracting social responsibilities the actor will be subjected to; and to indoctrinate the newcomer in a friendly way into the rehearsal requirements and theatre discipline and customs.

Planning the Tryouts

Whatever plan is chosen, announcements must be made early enough, and there must be enough tryouts for people with prev-

ious commitments to arrange to read. The publicity should include the name of the play, the time and place of readings,
what (if anything) is to be prepared, and where the script is
available (if it is). Posters help to advertise tryouts. A good
news story or two makes for prestige and good public relations.
The greatest help is to have some of the active workers pro-
mote tryout attendance by speaking at meetings of other local
or campus groups.

Meanwhile, to help in remembering the new people and to
acquire a file of those who want to work, a questionnaire may
be prepared on a five by seven card, to be filled out by the
candidates upon their arrival and handed to the director when
they read.

APPLICATION FOR MEMBERSHIP

Name   Telephone
_____

Street Address
_____

Sex   Height   Weight   Age
_____

Occupation
_____

Interests: (Check as many as you would like to do)
    Building_____, Painting_____, Lighting_____,
    Sound_____, Props_____, Costumes_____,
    Publicity_____, Acting_____

Skills: Can play piano_____, violin_____, guitar_____,
    Other musical instrument (Please name)_____
    Can sing_____, dance_____, paint_____
    Other skills (Please name)_____

(on reverse side)

Please list previous theatre experience:
    Place   Play   Role

A questionnaire for a student organization should include the hometown of the student and the name of his hometown newspaper, for the benefit of the college press bureau. Instead of occupation, it should include college status — to what class he belongs — and his major subject.

With the questionnaire, the candidate might be given a copy of the tentative rehearsal schedule, so that he can see approximately what will be expected of him if he is cast and will not try out if he cannot meet the schedule. It may be a good idea to hear him read anyway, in order to get a notion of his qualities, even though he will not be considered seriously for this play.

It is important to make people feel at home and hopeful when they come into the theatre for the first time. Nothing can freeze a potential talent more quickly than for a newcomer to find himself alone and inconsequential while the "old members" congregate happily and confidently together. The active group can organize themselves to put the new people at ease, helping them with the questionnaire, introducing them to others, and above all, taking an interest in what the new people have been doing. The mute evidence of well-displayed playbills and photographs is a better introduction to the standards of the theatre than the reminiscences of the actors.

Although the director in any theatre must make the final decisions about casting, the admission of a new member to an established group is always somewhat critical. Therefore an advisory committee of a few sincere and tactful members of the organization has one value: to indicate the response of the working members toward the new person as a teammate. Good morale is one of the first essentials of rehearsals, and one must recognize and deal with bad attitudes promptly and as skillfully as possible, in both new and old members. No matter how charitable everybody may try to be, a person with markedly odd social attitudes is a risk to the play and to the organization. A conscientious, intelligent advisory committee can help to prevent or to correct disrupting influences.

Conducting the Readings

At the beginning of the readings it is a good policy to remind everyone that casting must serve the best interests of the play. The director may sketch the plot very briefly, describe the characters, and tell what effect the play is likely to have on the audience. Since nearly everybody at tryouts wants "the lead," it is a good idea to describe the challenges offered by the shorter (and often more difficult) roles in order to engage interest in these. The introductory remarks should be as brief as possible, for the candidates came to try out, not to listen to a lecture.

The newcomers may be asked to read "cold" at first, not necessarily for particular parts, but just to give the director a notion of their voices and general characteristics. Later they will be asked to read for special parts. They should be encouraged to say what they want to read, so that they realize that everybody has equal rights and equal chances to show what he can do. They should be forewarned that when the director has learned enough about them he will stop them, to give others a chance to read. They should be urged to pay attention to others' readings so that they will learn about the play from listening and thereby give a second reading better than their first; and they should especially be exhorted not to imitate what they hear, but to think about it and give their own interpretation. It may help to remind them that this is not the only play of the year, and that if they are not cast in this play they may have some particular gift for another one; that a good way to learn is by watching others work, and that the prompter has a particularly good opportunity to do this; that their services are in demand for all sorts of tasks around the theatre, and that the person who is around is the one who is remembered.

It would be delightful if tryouts were always attended by vital and well-trained actors. This is not the case in most non-commercial theatres. For each vital and well-trained actor there are many who are definitely not well trained and who even seem to lack most of the qualities that make an actor. Since many of these candidates may develop into highly valuable members of the company and since it is the specific function of the director to find them and to give them training, all must be seen, heard, and evaluated. In the non-commercial theatre, except in a few long-established and highly professional community theatres and in colleges where training of professional calibre is offered, the company which is finally assembled from the candidates at tryouts is mainly distinguishable by its sincere desire for training. There are almost always a few members of the company who are only "the best we could find." It is the director's task at tryouts to find the best, the actors most likely to develop well enough to move the audience as the playwright hoped it would be moved.

In casting, one looks for an actor who might be able to imagine the role. This is sometimes partly based on one's earlier experience with the actor, but usually it is based on hunches — insight, the knack of surmising the hidden. One has an image, not too rigidly defined, of the physical requirements of the parts, mainly the shapes and relative sizes of the characters. One has a notion, not too rigid, of the voices needed. Beyond this, one seeks more subtle qualities. If it is necessary to adjust one's initial images to the actors who can play the roles, one must do so. The director must find a company in whose power to develop he can believe.

Two considerations seem to be paramount: real ability in the actors who must carry the heaviest burdens, and balance in the company as a whole.

In what does this "ability" consist? First, in intelligence, energy, and a "dramatic" quality.

A stupid person, slow at comprehending the values of the script, insensitive to relationships, unable to focus his imagination, unwilling to use his mind, does not make a good actor even in a bit part, however amiable he may be and however hard the director tries to help him. He wastes rehearsal time that might be more profitably spent on other actors. The play could progress more rapidly if the slow learner were not in the company. An actor simply must be intelligent.

In the promising actor, there is a vitality that seems to stem from physical strength (of one kind or another), plus an unusually keen interest in things and people. The vitality of an actor is perhaps different from that of an athlete — the whole problem of the quality and amount of the actor's energy challenges investigation — but this vitality is evident in the actor's eyes. He is alert and attentive. He has a control over his own mental workings and a kind of moral force that engages his partner while they read. In a series of uninteresting candidates, the director is suddenly called to attention; and the other candidates also notice a person with the kind of vitality that indicates a promising actor.

Sometimes one is deceived by a strong voice and excellent speech. These are essential attributes, of course, but they can be acquired. The energy that is specific to actors is the result of a *capacity to react strongly* to all kinds of stimuli *and to enjoy these strong reactions.* If this can be acquired, it will be through some event more tremendous than one can count on providing in a month of rehearsals. An example is Garrick's acting partner, the great tragic actress, Elizabeth Barry, who was almost ludicrously incompetent as an actress until after her love affair with the Earl of Rochester, one of the most shocking rakes of history.

Laziness is concomitant with feeble will power. Since the crux of acting is the ability to channel his will into the desires of the characters, the lazy person as an actor is dead weight.

"Dramatic quality" is hard to define. It certainly is not flamboyance; it is not a delight in showing off or a need for shallow admiration. Perhaps most concretely it is a capacity to put oneself in another's shoes, to imagine another's situation, to find oneself strongly stirred *in the way in which someone else might be stirred*. Sometimes, it is true, his quick, sharp response makes a young actor seem over-colorful in a group of emotionally shallow, unimaginative contemporaries, but the "dramatic quality" often exists in a quiet and retiring young person. In casting, the director must be alert for the quality, for it is very valuable.

Given intelligence, the actor can probably understand the role; given the "dramatic quality," he may be able to play it; given energy, he can convey it to the audience, all other factors properly contributing.

Several other characteristics are of at least secondary importance in the selection of a cast.

An actor should be a good teammate. At casting, the actor is likely to present his most ingratiating side. He may display a modesty which the company may never see again. Often one can judge the social or sociable qualities of a candidate by noting how the rest of the candidates react to him. If they seem to like him, he will probably "fit in." But sometimes the actor is shy, or overconfident, or simply unacquainted with the mores of the theatre. One has to estimate to what extent his withdrawal characteristics or his tendency to create hostilities will persist and affect the play. An example of the ill effect of a poor teammate occurred in a college freshman company of *Green Grow the Lilacs*. The lad cast as Curly had talent and good looks, plus a high degree of group feeling. He had probably never been really disliked in his life. But the girl who played Laurie, cast because of her happy vitality, disliked him, and he sensed her feeling. His vitality ebbed, and within two weeks he was having nervous indigestion from trying to cope with his first rejection. After talking the situation through with the director, the girl made an effort during rehearsals to conceal her dislike with sociable behavior, but neither the actors nor the director felt that any truth ever developed between these two characters whose relationship is the core of the play. The company must become a family as soon as possible, in order to get all work done with a minimum of friction.

If, aside from congeniality, a candidate seems to have desirable characteristics, one might cast him and make plans to get him group-conscious at a very early date by working both with him and the group toward this end. But this kind of casting is always risky.

Another advantageous trait in an actor is a combination of independence and flexibility. The actor who listens during tryouts and duplicates what he sees or hears another candidate do, adding nothing, is a weak prospect. More promising is an actor with a positive personal interpretation, even if, lacking acquaintance with the play, he is wrong. If a suggestion from the director can put him on the right track, or even if it merely puzzles the actor and makes him think, he is not inflexible and may be trainable.

In the non-commercial theatre the actors with the best voices are likely to be cast in the longest roles, and every actor must be able to make himself heard and understood at the back of the auditorium. But a shy, inexperienced actor may not be able to reveal his vocal potentialities on a first or second reading. If he seems to have imagination and some of the specific qualities needed for a part, one can test his potential ability by listening to him in offstage situations. If he has an expressive voice in conversation, free of breathiness, stridency, and other signs of tension, and if he has reasonably interesting pitch range, his power to project may be further tested by conversing with him across the auditorium. Usually an actor without serious vocal defects can reply easily when he is relaxed and not thinking about his voice. A really weak voice is hard to cure in a month.

On the other hand, poor diction may be treated with some hope of improvement if the candidate has a good ear and is willing to try. If, by listening, he can tell the difference between the way he makes certain sounds and the way a better speaker makes them and can duplicate the correctly made sounds, he is trainable, provided he has the will to try. To test this, one might begin by asking him to master one fault by the next tryout. Intervocalic "t" is a good sound to start with, as nearly all careless speakers say "ciddy" and "liddle" instead of "city" and "little," regardless of regional influences. If he makes progress, he need not be regarded as untrainable. If no progress is made, he obviously lacks the will to try; he is a weak prospect.

Needless to say, each actor must be tested in the whole gamut of the role for which he is a candidate. If the role has comic elements, he must be able to sense the comic as well as the more serious passages. If he has to sing, dance, or play a musical instrument, he must have had some previous training, no matter how solemnly he assures the director that he will learn.

A director inevitably operates on hunches. A hunch is something one "knows" without being able to say how he knows it. In casting, it is a more or less vague impression that some quality of an actor is related to a quality of the character for which he is cast. One thinks, for example, of Benvolio as a collegian, amiable, ready for fun, and, particularly, capable of binding himself in warm friendship. In Shawn, one might look for a degree of self-satisfaction and a kind of rigidity of spirit. Not knowing the actors intimately, the director studies them as they read and casts by means of very minute and partial signs. Since the reasons for hunches are not easy to name, the hunch is often wrong.

Good hunches come from thousands of subconsciously stored experiences such as everyone garners from his earliest moments

of contact with the outside world — some psychologists say
even from prenatal life. The power to use these memories seems
to be related to Freud's superego[1] or Sullivan's self-system[2],
the censor that withholds from consciousness what seems harm-
ful to one's deepest personal objectives. The extent to which
an individual can reach these memories seems to depend at least
partly on a frank i.e., ("uncensored") acceptance of his own
motives and fears. In his creative work with actors, beginning
with casting, a keen director seems to have a certain control
over his controls, which enables the hidden memories to float
into or near consciousness so that he can use them.

It may be possible to improve the ratio of right to wrong
hunches by developing a habit of conscious observation at all
times. Many an artist can recall periods in which he deliberately looked about him and tried to remember his impressions, as "The Creature" did in Boleslavsky's fifth lesson.[3]
Hours on street corners, in railway stations, at parades, in
church can be rich in evidence of human hungers, delights,
failures, strivings. Carried into every moment of one's life, the
habit of keenly noting people's behavior makes one adept at
adding a tiny detail like, for example, tension of the muscles
around the eyes to other minute signs in diagnosing the springs
of a person's behavior. In using hunches, one must remember
that any knowledge derived in this way must be used always
as an artist seeking to understand the complexity of a personality, not as the critic or moralist weighing the character of the
individual.

When one has applied what one knows of the play and of
people in casting and has strong hunches about who could play
each part, it is extremely important, further, to see that the

[1]Sigmund Freud, *A General Introduction to Psychoanalysis* (Garden
City, N.Y.: Garden City Publishing Co., 1943).
[2]Henry Stack Sullivan, *The Interpersonal Theory of Psychiatry* (New
York: W. W. Norton, 1953).
[3]Richard Boleslavsky. *Acting: The First Six Lessons* (New York: Theatre Arts, Inc., 1933).

company is well balanced. The actors must be credible together; they must reinforce each other to create the necessary
unity of impression. Size takes attention. A very large actor,
tall or stout, is hard to cast except in character roles. A big
voice also commands attention and must be used where it will
be helpful, not distracting. Michael James and Old Mahon are
both drunks, but each commands his own empathies. It is
almost essential that Old Mahon be larger and louder than
Michael James, or, indeed, than anyone in the play, though
Jimmy and Philly need not be smaller. Also, Mahon is crude
and dirty and spiritually callous. Michael James is soft and
(for his milieu) proper and cleanly. It is also essential to
balance Jimmy and Philly among the elderly drunks of this
play. They are positive men, and the actors need skill and
imagination to play them. But Michael James is the pivot in
their first scene, and Mahon and the Widow are the pivot in
their scene in Act II.

As a matter of balance, it is sometimes a good idea to put
the greatest skill in the most difficult parts, not necessarily
the "leads," but the parts most difficult to characterize. The
actor playing the "lead" generally feels great responsibility and
works hard to acquire his role. An unskilled bitplayer is often
a trial in rehearsal because his sense of responsibility is often
in direct proportion to the number of lines he has to say. He
has to be taught that in playing a scene one acts, even when
not speaking. To cast power in the bit parts is not always
successful, however. In a college production, one very talented
young actor cast in a one-line bit as a secretary, commanded
too much attention in rehearsal simply by his intelligent concentration on the secretary's objective of taking accurate notes.
Directed into negative positions in the group and into weak
body positions, he saw the point. By the next rehearsal he had
created for his character a new objective: to apologize for his
incompetence. He thus became such a very negative secretary

that by his very weakness he took more attention than the role justified.

Voices are tremendously important in balancing a company, for voices create powerful impressions of characters. A slight breathiness may be valuable in a repressed or nervous character, nasality in an acrimonious one, and full resonance in one who has physical strength or moral virtue in a high degree. Since it is very difficult to change the quality of a voice in the brief period of rehearsals, one must be extremely cautious in casting voices.

Appearance matters very little, except that the company must be convincing together. Any physical abnormality which cannot be concealed is, of course, out of the question except in a role that calls for that kind of deviation. One must also be alert to minor defects which may not show up at tryouts but which affect the general health, fatigability, and mental outlook of the actor, such as a slight curvature of the spine, flat feet, or sinus trouble. A stutterer, on the other hand, need not be eliminated, for he never stutters memorized material if he is sufficiently rested.

Final Readings

The number and length of the readings depends, of course, on how many parts must be cast and how many people come to tryouts. A play with a large cast may take a week of daily tryouts. A few characters can usually be cast in two three-hour readings. Final tryouts may be by invitation. If so, this should be mentioned in all announcements.

As the candidates read the second or third time, it is wise to give a little direction to two kinds of readers — those who are impossible but believe they can play the role and those who look like good prospects. In the first case, the actor may improve surprisingly (and a strong wish to play is a great asset) but generally he is unable to make the suggested changes and begins to realize he will need more than inspiration to play the whole part. As the prospect either responds or does not respond to direction, one can tell how much of a liability he will be as a member of the company. In this preliminary direction, one must be careful not to rob the candidate of confidence in himself. He must feel sure that he is rejected on artistic grounds, not personal grounds. Friendly laughter is a good way to relieve his tension at his failure.

In studying the best prospects together to be sure of getting the best possible combination, one may do a good bit of directing, seeking the actors who respond most successfully. The end sought is a balanced company, whose vocal, visible, and emotional characteristics will work together to create the unified impression required by the playwright.

Before announcing the cast, it is wise to mention again the responsibility of all to the play and the audience, in the hope that those who are cast will feel their obligations and those who are not cast may experience a certain relief. The script may then be given to the actors who are cast, while the others may be reminded that there are many jobs open to them on various crews if they really love the theatre and that they may be cast in another play.

The actors who are cast should be urged to keep good health habits and regular study habits, for a worried, exhausted, ill actor lets the company down at rehearsals and ruins the performance. Sometimes it is a good idea to remind the company that they hurt the theatre if their public behavior is offensive to others.

The schedule should be thoroughly discussed, so that, if really essential, the rehearsal dates can be changed to accommodate any very important engagements. It must be made clear that actors who want to maintain standards will be willing to sacrifice a good bit for the play. Rehearsals, however, can be scheduled around labs and ROTC nights, and, for the sake of good feeling, even a really major social event might justify changing a rehearsal date. Of course in planning any theatre schedule, the company must be allowed to attend major cultural events, particularly in communities where these are infrequent. But before the company leave the last tryout meeting, the schedule must be in its final form, and no actor can be cast who does not firmly agree to it.

Some directors manage to double cast or to use understudies. Double casting involves either double rehearsal time for the director, or for an able assistant who can spend enough time with the first company to learn motivations and business as well as the necessary time with the second company. Understudies in professional theatre attend all rehearsals, memorize lines and business, and usually rehearse for the first time during the out-of-town tryout, with the stage manager as director. Learning by watching is actually a great help, but for the young actor it must be amplified by doing. In the amateur theatre a faithful understudy is so rare that he should be cherished, for he has a great love for the theatre, and possibly some gift.

Casting is possibly the most critical task of the director. In non-commercial theatre it is almost inevitable that the company will contain all degrees of aptitude and past training. When he has done the best he could, the director utters his confidence that they are all able to master their roles. He then goes home and studies how to use all he has learned about each actor in order to help him bring the script alive on the stage.

Assignments

1. Plan an interview with a new actor. What would you try to find out about him? What questions would you ask him? What would you tell him?
2. Make a detailed plan for helping new candidates feel at home in your theatre group.

Chapter 12

First Rehearsals

When the director walks into the first rehearsal he is armed with relatively full — not complete — knowledge of the play. Certain objectives have been laid down for each rehearsal, and, in general, these objectives must be achieved in approximately the order and time named. However, in rehearsal the director is no longer dealing with stick figures as he did in his study; he is faced with real differences among sensitive individuals. Exactly what will happen in each rehearsal can be only approximately guessed. His first task is to become acquainted with the company.

Actors are people, with all the inspiration, limitation, pride and nervousness of people. They come to the theatre for all sorts of reasons and with all sorts of qualifications. In the non-commercial theatre, acting is generally one of many diversions of the participants. In addition to his responsibilities at rehearsals, an amateur actor has a job or schoolwork as the main objective of his life. He also has social and family responsibilities that he is either sacrificing or handling under extra strain for the sake of this activity. He is paid for his services in the theatre only in terms of some kind of inner satisfaction.

3. List all scenes needed at tryouts to reveal the gamut of Friar Lawrence's character. What scenes would you have to hear candidates for Christy read? For Lady Bracknell? For Amanda?
4. List the characteristics you would hope to find in an actress playing Lady Capulet, in the order of their importance.
5. Plan the speech you would use in introducing *Romeo and Juliet* to the actors at tryouts.
6. Improve your ability to make sound casting decisions by listing the evidence for your impressions of people after observing them for one hour in (*a*) a public place, (*b*) a party, (*c*) in the library, (*d*) at the scene of a fire or accident.
7. Recall an incident when you saw someone under acute emotional stress and list in detail how you knew how he felt; how others around him behaved. If you find yourself moved again as you recall, can you tell how you reawakened this emotion in yourself?
8. Name some characteristics of people that would make you hesitate to cast them in a play. Can you think of any compensating characteristics that would make you willing to cast them even with their faults and problems?
9. After watching a whole rehearsal, describe the overt signs that reveal that a certain actor is a good teammate.
10. Point out evidences of unbalance in the company of the last play you saw.

Reading List

Boleslavsky, Richard. *Acting: The First Six Lessons.* New York: Theatre Arts, Inc., 1933.

Freud, Sigmund. *A General Introduction to Psychoanalysis.* Garden City, N. Y.: Garden City Publishing Co., 1943.

Gibson, William. *The See-Saw Log.* New York: Alfred A. Knopf, 1959.

Sullivan, Henry Stack. *The Interpersonal Theory of Psychiatry.* New York: W. W. Norton, 1953.

Young, John Wray. *The Community Theatre and How It Works.* New York: Harper and Bros., 1958.

Zimmerman, Joe. "An Experimental Study of the Psychological Characteristics of a Group of Superior College Actors." Ph.D. dissertation (Northwestern University, 1948).

Sometimes an actor is motivated to enter the theatre by a need for approval. The illusory glamor of the theatre, the applause, telegrams, compliments serve as support to his ego. *To be* an actor is his desire. The director must subtly change him so that he wants *to become a good actor.*

Sometimes it is the *camaraderie* of the theatre that draws the actor; he wants to belong to something. This need ranges in intensity and kind from that of the seriously maladjusted, unsocial person to that of the social climber. The actor with this objective must discover, through rehearsals, that belonging means contributing. To this kind of actor must come the joy of making the play with others, appreciating their work as much as he wants them to appreciate his.

Sometimes the actor seeks a creative outlet for ill-defined emotional urges, and once in a while this is a real need to reach into the nature of other human beings. This is the stuff of which actors are made. One of the problems in working with actors who have this motivation is that they sometimes reject technique as false merely because it is technique. They have to be patiently shown that technique is like a language which helps them to share the truths they have discovered and that failure to use an honest and applicable technique of communication results in something that *seems* confused and false.

There are even actors in the non-commercial theatre from sixteen to sixty who wish to become professional actors. Some of these are merely wishful thinkers. Some have realized too late what they might have been. A tiny few have the combination of talent, industry, and nerve to head into the commercial maelstrom; they are dedicated. The director may tend to think of these young actors as his most serious responsibility; but in his enthusiasm he must keep a level head, encouraging once in a while, but never urging anyone to enter the precarious profession of acting. Perhaps one should demand a little more of these people than of the others, both for the sake of their development and to test whether they can stand the limitless demand for perfection that the theatre makes. Certainly one should seek every means to make their paths easier if they are determined to attempt a theatre career.

The previous training of the actors in the non-commercial theatre is varied. They come from high schools, from college, from the community. They have had all amounts and kinds of acting experience, starting with none at all. They report that they have not acted since high school, that they have attended drama school, that they have been apprentices in summer stock or performed in summer outdoor theatres. Once in a while a non-commercial theatre is enriched or embarrassed by an ex-professional actor who gave up the career for some reason.

The easiest company to work with is one in which many of the members have worked together with the director before. But many in a large cast and someone in every cast may be totally lacking in stage experience; and in college theatre some are likely to be too young for their roles. The great divergence of motive and experience makes problems for the director because he must weld the individuals into a company, breaking down old, comfortable habits in some cases, in order to make the play an integrated whole; and he must do this without detriment to the actor's confidence, but rather by showing him the pleasure of conscious growth. For the director's task is to present, in the three to five weeks' rehearsal period, a play in which all the actors look and sound as if they were equally talented and well trained, so that the audience can concentrate on the play without being distracted by the actors.

Such as they are, the company await the moment when they will be on stage. The ground plan of the set has been taped on the floor. The director now shows the actors a colored sketch of the finished setting and walks them over the stage, taking them through all "doors" and describing what is to be imagined outside of each window. He points out where the steps and platforms and fireplace are indicated, and what each piece of rehearsal furniture means, and blocking begins.

Objectives

The first series of rehearsals has three clear objectives:

The actors must master the play intellectually. The main motivations and the basic pattern of movement must be got out of the promptbook and into the understanding and behavior of the actors. By the first run-through they should know at least what their objectives are in each scene, including, of course, their relations to their playing partners; and they should know what areas, in general, they are to occupy. Usually an adult company can go a long way in early rehearsals toward mastering the major beats of many of the scenes, with their concomitant visual changes. They know where the main crises are, even though they are not yet able to make them. They recognize the difficult scenes and understand most of the jokes. Since every direction is presented with its motive, whatever the actor learns in the first week of rehearsal adds to his understanding of his character.

The actors must begin to acquire dependable new habits of mind and body. They must learn to concentrate on *why* they move at each repetition of the pattern, so that thought, feeling, and action become firmly associated. Three important effects of the association are quickly apparent:

First, through the discharge of energy in the mere use of the large muscles in moving about the stage, the actor is physically relaxed. Since a logical physical pattern is easier to learn than lines, the actor quickly develops a feeling of competence and confidence. Moreover, in associating the motive with the move, he loses *self-* consciousness and gains concentration — his first step toward creativity.

Second, as more and more of the actor's mind and body become involved in the repetition of the scene, a well-known psychological principle (*Gestalt*) operates to make memorization of the lines easier.

Finally, many inexperienced actors are embarrassed when they must pause to think what comes next. A small lapse of memory shatters their concentration. The discovery of the beats in the scene and the movement associated with the change of beat gives them moments when they not only may, but must stop and think. Therefore, instead of feeling rushed and tense, they learn to use these moments to relax and gather their energies for the next beat. This conservation of energy is essential later, when they are trying to sustain and build the whole play emotionally.

These three results, the loss of physical tension and growth of power to concentrate, easier memorization of lines through the establishment of a more and more complete *Gestalt,* and the conservation of energy through the basic rhythm of the play, are brought about by means of carefully building habits in rehearsals.

Problems with Actors

Because actors are individuals, not automata, the progress of rehearsal in the first week is often thorny. While the actors are learning what the director already knows, he is trying to learn how to deal effectively with each one of them and hoping that as they gain independence they will add to his knowledge of the play.

If the company is inexperienced, it will save time to show them in advance how to write directions into their scripts and to give them a bit of stage shorthand — L, R, and C for left, right, and center, U and D for upstage and downstage, X for cross, etc. The actors must be urged to take time to get all of their business into their books clearly and accurately. Unless the director insists on this, the unskilled actor will not do it; and at next rehearsal, his forgetting what he was told to do will so confuse the other actors that sometimes the blocking has to be done all over again.

A little time is also well spent in helping the inexperienced actor to read without keeping his nose in the script while his partner speaks. As in life, he should hear, rather than see, what is said to him. The old-fashioned use of "sides" had one advantage: the actor was forced to listen because the "side" contained only his own speeches and his cues. Unless he heard what his partner said, his own lines did not mean very much. The actor also finds it helpful to look at his partner during his own speeches. A good technique to acquire is quickly to read a sentence and then say it to his partner. In this way, the actor begins memorizing without being aware of it. He is forced to be alert because he is performing more than one process: he is reading, listening, responding, memorizing, thinking, and speaking. A further advantage of reading in this way is that the actor does not develop a habit of dependence on the book, but throws it away of his own free will when he is mentally ready.

Another habit to guard against with the nervous actor in his first reheasals is turning to the director for approval. He must learn to keep his objectives within the stage, and that he is never right when his objective is the director's approval.

An important step toward relieving the actor's sense of insecurity is to see that good relations exist between the members of the company and between the company and the director. This has been started, of course, through fairness at tryouts and through the give and take of modifying the rehearsal schedule together. The first direct move for rapport is in making it clear that director and actors have the same objective: to make a fine play for the delight of the audience. They must understand that every actor's best work depends on and contributes to the best work of all the others. As a company, the actors must realize that the time spent on every actor is for the good of all; that no one, not even a highly talented actor, can make the play single-handedly, but that any single member of the company can ruin it. A good time to point this out is the first time that the flow of a scene is broken by one actor's inattention, or the first time an entrance is missed in the run-through of a scene, whether it be a main actor or a bit player whose negligence is responsible for the break in continuity. After the moment of reprimand, which the actors generally recognize is deserved, the company seems to draw together in a new understanding of their individual responsibilities. The "lead" recognizes his dependence on the rest of the company, and the bit player gains a sense of his own value.

Occasionally directors declare that they do not use a prompter. The reason they give is that actors tend to rely on him instead of learning their lines. The prompter, however, is generally conceded to have many values. In the first place, the prompter in the non-commercial theatre performs approximately the functions of the assistant stage manager in the commercial theatre. He keeps the book up to date, recording cuts and alterations in the script and noting all stage directions. Because he has a record of decisions that were made or changed in rehearsals, he enables the company to avoid pointless arguments. In the line-learning stage of rehearsals, he keeps the rehearsal moving, so that the actors do not bog down in lines but keep progressing from thought to thought of the play and get a feeling of continuity at run-throughs. The director, likewise, at run-throughs, can see what scenes build and where emotional continuity is lacking, if he has a capable prompter to keep the actors moving ahead. Even in performance, the prompter is not superfluous if he gives the actors a feeling of security. For even in professional performances, even after a play has been running several weeks, a tiny thing may happen and the star "blanks out." There is no sense in letting actors "get themselves out of it" with awkward floundering, if a single word from the prompter can bring them instantly back to the text in emergency. It should not happen; it generally does not happen; but it does happen occasionally, even on the professional stage.

If a prompter is appointed, it is wise to make him feel a part of the company at once by explaining to the company the value of his help. If the company know and like the prompter as a person, later on they will accept his help gratefully instead of resenting it. A really good prompter is rare in non-commercial theatre, for often the job is done by someone who has no understanding of the needs of actors. The prompter will be more efficient and will also feel more like part of the company, if the director coaches him when he needs it. He should be instructed in advance how to correct and amplify the prompt-book during rehearsals, and he should be shown how to help each individual actor as need arises. Above all he should be praised, just as the actors are praised, when he does a sensitive and efficient job.

One of the worst problems that may arise in the first rehearsals is that some member of the company has had no experience of precise direction. This individual may feel that he is under fire and may be completely unable to concentrate. Once in a while someone becomes resentful or hopeless and stops trying to do anything more than say the lines and move where he is told to go. The confusion of actors like this may be mitigated by letting them know in advance that all rehearsals are frequently interrupted, not because the actor is hopeless but because the director believes the actor can do better than he himself realizes. His injured feelings may be assuaged if he knows that the director, too, finds first rehearsals slow and painful, but that careful motivation and precise building of good habits prevent him from having opening night "jitters." Sometimes an actor becomes reconciled to his first experiences of minute direction when he is told that professional rehearsals are conducted in exactly this painstaking manner. The most effective help for the actor who is confused by and hostile to precise direction is to go over each attack and then each scene as a whole until he realizes that he is behaving logically and has actually memorized the scene. He then becomes comfortable and can take further direction.

It is inevitable that the actor's most personal concept of self is threatened in the first rehearsals. He finds that he does not move well, speak well, even breathe well. He does not understand the script or the character. He does not know how to concentrate on the character's objectives. He has lost the forest in the leaves. Thus, while teaching the script, stage technique, and bodily behavior and speech, the director must help the actor to enjoy his growing pains.

To some of the actors, the director becomes an emotional prop, someone to whom they can tell personal problems. This function is subtly flattering, but it should be avoided as far as possible. With firm habits of observing people, one comes to know a good bit about actors during rehearsals, but never enough to take over the functions of a psychiatrist. Advice, moreover, is often sought without being heeded and often given with ill effect. Of course, if the actor's emotional problem or his personal behavior impede the progress of the play or harm the relation of the organization to the community, there is some reason for the director to try to help the individual toward a solution. Most directors have a friendly personal concern for each member of a company. But the collective problems of producing a play are enough of an emotional load without accepting personal problems unrelated to the theatre.

One other ugly situation occasionally arises. The selection of a cast is something like marriage; one cannot possibly know the actors without having lived with them a while, and once they have been cast it is hard to get rid of them. The professional contract usually contains a clause permitting the actor to be dropped from the company at the end of five days, if he does not develop as expected. But in considering the dismissal of an actor in the non-commercial theatre, one is concerned with the effect on the actor's morale if he feels that he has failed. Yet, if one is sure that he has done all in his power to help the actor and still does not get results, a simple arithmetical calculation will nerve the director to inflict the pain, as gently as possible. Is the work of a whole company to be vitiated by the incompetence of one individual? Is an audience, perhaps several hundred people, to be deprived of an excellent entertainment because the director made one mistake in casting? Is the actor to be allowed to fail publicly, whose inadequacy at this stage is known only to the company and (invariably) to him? The non-commercial theatre may have incidental therapeutic effects, but its function is to delight the audience as well as to train the company, and the training function is not served if the audience is not served.

The actor can understand that the director is concerned about him, that the company like him, that he may be needed in another play or another capacity. He can be shown that the mistake in the first place was the director's. He can be let out gently, but he must be let out while there is still time to repair the director's error.

Some Principles and Techniques in Training the Actor

The major concern of rehearsal is to translate the meanings and motives of the play into kinaesthetic terms for the actors. From the beginning it is right to insist that every actor mean what he says as far as his understanding goes at the moment. Although in the first rehearsals meanings may be somewhat general and shallow for some actors, good initial blocking usually clarifies meaning and paves the way for their full kinaesthetic experience later on.

In naming the objectives and attacks for the actor, it is always helpful to keep as near as possible to basic patterns of bodily action and to phrase the directions in the most vivid terms, in order to stimulate the actor's feelings. For example, a direction, "Tell him to go away," does not elicit the vital reading that might result from "Kick him out," "Freeze him out," or "Wipe him from the face of the earth." Especially where the content of a scene seems to be intellectual, the actor is helped by directions related to the basic bodily patterns. Instead of "Persuade," for example, one might direct the actor, "Take possession of his mind," or "Climb into his mind," or "Hold him and pour this into his mind," depending on the situation and the characters involved. Shawn does each of these things in the scene in which he tries to "persuade" Christy to leave.

Dynamic directions have many advantages, not the least of which is to involve the listener as well as the speaker. In following directions of this sort, the speaker attempts to get a response from his partner, and finds that the response, verbal or kinaesthetic, stimulates him as a cue. Moreover, if the actor understands a group of speeches as a vital attack on an objective, he is likely to make spontaneous weak or strong moves toward, against, or away from his partner, and it is easy, if necessary, to modify these moves or to change their direction for purposes of emphasis and variety.

If the directions are dynamic and the actor still does not move spontaneously, he may be helped by being made aware of the tension-release pattern of the scene with, "That attack failed; you have to stop and think what to do next." He gains assurance when he realizes that the character must relax and think at the exact spots where the actor's memory blocks because there is a change of thought and feeling. When the next thought comes, as a new attack, he is sometimes able to move spontaneously because inhibitions and fears have been removed.

It is here, in the earliest stages of rehearsals, that the basic rhythms of the play are built in. Of course the actors are not aware of anything so sophisticated as "rhythm," and certainly they do not yet feel very strongly the alternation of motive-tension and response-rest. But the foundation for the full experience is being laid from the start, by allowing the actor time to formulate his purposes and his means and to study his partner's responses as the cues for his next attacks. It is this kind of deliberate, motivated thinking that prevents actors from "going blank."

The precise timing of an action is extremely important, both in reinforcing the motive and in gaining the audience's attention. Two old saws are generally applicable. One is the oversimple rule, "Thought precedes action precedes speech." Psychologists express much the same thing when they distinguish between three phases of response to a stimulus: sensory awareness, recognition, response. This, too, is an oversimple statement, for it does not take into account varying degrees of alertness in the responding individuals, or varying degrees of urgency in the situation. However, it has general value and the one specific value of allowing the actor time to think and the audience time to attend to what the actor is doing.

The other old saw says, "Move on your own speech." This is also generally true — unless the actor is being spoken to or about, in which case he may have to move either as a response to the speaking character, or simply as a means of keeping the audience aware of him as the topic of conversation. If what is said is very important, the speaker must, of course, wait until the move is completed before continuing to speak.

These two "rules" are useful because the eye of the audience is more alert than the ear. If there is anything to watch, the audience will watch rather than listen. A skilled actor becomes habituated to making his motive coincide with the moment when it is theatrically effective to move. By keeping words and movement subtly but cleanly separated, he keeps the audience's attention always where it should be.

In these early rehearsals, two psychological principles are depended on to a high degree in working with the actors. The first is the James-Lange theory,[1] which, though somewhat discredited by psychologists, seems to work in general for actors. The theory is that conscious emotional states *follow* emotional behavior. On perceiving a threatening stimulus, one runs automatically and then feels afraid, or one strikes out at a stimulus and then feels anger. It follows that if the actors have acquired the mere physical behavior related to a given stimulus, a conscious emotion is likely to be experienced.

A few classroom-tested exercises generally bear out this theory, though not for everyone who tries them.

> Put one foot back, both knees bent, weight on the back foot but balanced so that you could move easily in either direction. Raise the arms tensely as if protecting your head. Increase the general tension. At a signal, run as rapidly as possible in the direction of the back foot to the opposite end of the room.

The result of this steady increase of tension and sudden explosion of muscular activity is, of course, a change in the rate of breathing and heartbeat, with trembling, perspiration, and probably an increased secretion of adrenin, the biological symptoms of emotion. The consciousness of "fear" may also be present.

[1] John Dolman who was probably the first to describe The James-Lange Theory for the theatre, did not document his material. Konrad Lange was the author of *Das Wesen der Kunst* and William James (brother of Henry) of *Principles of Psychology*. Most accessible work on the theory is W. B. Cannon's article, "The James-Lange Theory," in *American Journal of Psychology*, XXXIX (1927).

For people who do not respond with a feeling of panic to the mere physical pattern, the exercise may be repeated, adding a fear-stimulus, the image of a baseball or airplane propeller coming at their heads or a homicidal maniac or stampeding elephant, or any image of their own that induces fear. The combination of the image and the appropriate bodily pattern usually secures the desired results in the actor's consciousness.

To complete the illustration, exercises are given to evoke emotions appropriate to bodily patterns toward and against.

> With both hands forward, palms facing each other, arms relaxed, take two quick steps forward, close the fists and rapidly bring them in to the chest.

The actor should feel a sense of happiness or triumph. If he does not, let him imagine that he is grabbing something he likes to eat, or picking up a puppy or a child, or catching a piece of china about to fall, or saving his purse from falling into the river.

> Stand with feet apart, knees bent, hands clasped at the right side (unless you are left-handed). Tense the arms and clench the fists. Slowly and with great tension, raise the clenched fists together above the head. Then suddenly and very rapidly and tensely bring the clenched fists down in front of the body to waist level and quickly relax.

If this does not leave the actor feeling angry, add an image of killing a snake, breaking a hideous vase, throwing an insulting letter into the fire.

These exercises do not work for some people, but they work generally, enough to justify early blocking as a valid means of stimulating the actors' emotions. Thus, even if the actor's imagery is unclear, the mere process of walking through the stage business with appropriate energy and speed is sometimes enough to evoke the feelings the actor is supposed to have. This does not, of course, mean that one should ever be satisfied with the blind following of directions, but it justifies using stage business to illuminate a scene and gives the actor, if not full emotional response, at least the confidence that he is doing something right; and it helps the other actors by maintaining continuity and giving them something that they can believe in, at least superficially, in the early stages.

A corollary to this principle is useful. Since the physiological symptoms of emotion are much alike whether the feeling be fear, anger, or delight, by merely changing the actor's tension level and breathing rate one can sometimes affect the actor's feelings. For example, Shawn's second entrance can be made convincing, and perhaps even sincere, if he is directed to run at top speed from the farthest corner of the stage house, dodging the inevitable backstage hazards — masking, braces, ground rows, prop table — and if he is given the arbitrary, but not illogical, direction to gulp air at the two points marked by dashes in the speech,

The queer — dying fellow's beyond looking over the — ditch.

With these directions, however phlegmatic the actor may be, he is likely to feel some excitement comparable to fear; in any case, he gives a good illusion of being terrified.

The other psychological principle that begins to operate in these first rehearsals is Pavlov's principle of the conditioned reflex. The dog which was given a bell-sound along with his steak learned to salivate at the sound of the bell without the steak. At first the principle may operate on purely physical and intellectual levels; certain word groups become associated with certain actions. But as soon as the physical habit is established, some actors also include specific thoughts as the beginning of a subtext, and, by the operation of strong imagery and the James-Lange theory, their emotions become habitually involved.

The object of the rehearsals is to involve the whole physical and psychological being of the actor in a set of complex and dependable habits from the beginning to the end of the role.

As the converse of the Pavlov theory, even though first rehearsals are inevitably slow, it is vitally necessary to take time to root out any wrong connections before they become habits. The interpretation at the end of the blocking rehearsal may be incomplete and shallow, but it must be logical and consistent if the next weeks of rehearsal are to bring enrichment instead of frustration.

Scenes That Need Specific Handling

Certain kinds of scenes need special handling — love scenes, fights, crowd scenes, for example.

Some directors block love scenes at private rehearsals to save the young actors embarrassment, for naturally they will concentrate more easily on their characters' objectives if they are not distracted by wondering what their confrères think of them as people and as actors. On the other hand, it sometimes makes for rapport to handle the wolf calls of the watching company by indignantly insisting that they show respect for their fellow actors and try to learn from what they see, so that *they* will not be awkward if they are ever lucky enough to get a romantic role. This is one instance where asperity on the part of the director is effective. By showing the two people engaged in the scene that he understands their feeling in the difficult job of playing a love scene, the director can often gain a highly professional attitude from them. In any case, it is a mistake to postpone blocking the scene, on the principle that the longer one hangs over the springboard the harder it is to dive.

The visual pattern of a particular love scene must be derived from the nature of the scene and the characters in it. It may be anything from the light, formal kiss that Algernon might give Cecily in *The Importance of Being Earnest* to the deep, clinging embrace of Romeo and Juliet. The director will have visualized it very carefully before asking the actors to rehearse it.

Whatever the plan, it must generally be learned first as pure pattern. One begins by seeing that the couple are firmly balanced, so that no unplanned move will destroy the mood of the scene; they learn first the best position for their feet. Then they learn how to stand with their hips together, so that the wish to touch will be clear. They are shown exactly what to do with their hands. The book is cast aside and they practice moving into the embrace and executing it without words until they are reasonably skillful. Then they are given the book again and shown at what points in the dialogue each move is applicable, and they are walked through the scene. Generally the actors lose self-consciousness in the simple technical mastery of the job, for the more interesting and original the pattern and the more difficult the execution, the more accurately they must cooperate with each other at each step. Indeed, the actors often need both strength and agility to make a love scene look spontaneous to the audience. As the actors master the basic pattern, they realize that they must learn the lines of this scene early so that they can begin to motivate and to add details.

Since there is an endless variety of possible patterns, it seems pointless to describe a few different kinds of embrace. One special caution about the use of hands, however, seems worthwhile. Hands tell a great deal about the quality of love expressed in the embrace. They should hold the partner in the way that that particular lover would hold his partner. In a prolonged embrace, the tendency of the young actor is to move his hands a good bit. Unless the embrace is supposed to be fiercely passionate, he should be made to keep his hands still.

With very young actors, it may help to conceal their awkwardness behind furniture and well upstage. In many comedies, the love scene between young people is written to be amusing, and the director will deliberately plan awkward business, including loss of balance and neat recovery. Of course even the awkwardness is skillfully executed by virtue of long and exact rehearsal.

Fight scenes may be blocked at private rehearsals, largely because they take a good bit of time and it seems pointless to make the company wait.

A good stage fight must be carefully planned, both to excite the audience and to avoid injury to the actors or the scenery and properties. The actual moves to be used must depend on the characters fighting and on the space which they must occupy. The relative importance of the fight to the play as a whole determines how long the fight is to be and how many moves are needed. If the fight must last as much as thirty seconds, suspense is increased by changing dominance several times, so that the final blow, through being anticipated and withheld, comes as a climax.

Whatever pattern is planned, it should be drilled simply as a pattern until the actors connect when they are supposed to connect and stagger to exactly the spot where they should stop. When they know the pattern, they learn the word cues, if any, for shifts of dominance. By keeping the emphasis on accuracy of execution, one avoids the wild feelings that cause excessive energy and accidents. It is essential that the whole fight become habitually accurate before the actors may be permitted to let their emotions become involved at all. When complete accuracy of movement has been established, the extra energy they gain by admitting their feelings completes the illusion of the fight.

Unskilled actors are likely to ridicule the notion of telling them how to fight. But if the director has planned the fight well and can describe it well, and especially if there is something showy or difficult, like falling over a table or down a stair, they can be intrigued into learning it. The first time someone is bruised or furniture is knocked over in an unrehearsed pattern, the actors recognize the value of planning the fight.

If the fight is rehearsed privately, a test of whether it is good or not is the response of the company when they see it for the first time. If they gasp in spots, or if at the end there is a burst of released breath and of talking or laughing, the fight promises to be good.

Crowd scenes need special rehearsal. Since some of the extras involved in the scene are not needed at other times, it is wise to concentrate these rehearsals as much as possible in the interest of saving everybody's time. From the point of view of rapport, it is also valuable to get the principals rather good in their parts before bringing in the crowd, so that the extras are not ignored for long periods while the director works on the "leads."

The first problem in a crowd scene is to give each extra a sense of his personal importance to the play by grouping the extras into social or family groups and making up or helping them to make up enough of a story to put them into relationship with each other and with the main characters. It helps to find a piece of business in which the main characters may relate to the extras. For example, in the crowd scene that brings Christy home victorious from the races, there might be a hero-worshipping boy who carries Christy's prizes for him; and one who is jealous and perhaps throws Christy a towel and walks away rather pointedly. Each of these fellows might have his own coterie so that they could instigate mass moves. The coteries might also be differentiated, in terms of the actors cast in the scene. There might be the little brother or sister of the leader, his pal, a girl who likes or dislikes him. Relationships must be broadly established at first rehearsals and in more and more credible and interesting detail at each successive rehearsal.

The first moves they learn are likely to be group moves — small groups that make up the whole and yet differ from each other. Then, within each group there may be individual actions that punctuate specific moments. All of this has to be carefully tied in with speeches and with their own ad libs — which, by performance time are written into the script, for they are not ad libs any longer.

All of this is drilled and refined and redrilled and further refined until it comes alive and each actor at each instant feels his part as a character and makes his modest but very definite contribution to the whole. However well the director has planned the scene, he has to make some adjustments in terms of the people he has cast; and others because, each time they play the scene, he finds new ways to create variety and add energy.

Since members of the "mob scene" are usually the least experienced actors, in the non-commercial theatre, the director is wise to use, if he can, some seasoned actors as nuclei of the various groups. The seasoned actor will provide the less experienced ones with an example of concentration, furnish them with a source of energy, and show them how to pick up cues promptly.

A very important part of rehearsing a mob scene is to do it in good spirit so that the actors enjoy it. They must be glad to realize that more is expected of them than mere bulk. It is good if they leave with the feeling that their scene will be one of the best in the play.

In summary, the qualities needed to direct a crowd scene well are: a clear and detailed plan that becomes richer as the actors work on it, perfect discipline combined with good nature and a sense of fun, patience and determination in dealing with the actors. It has been said that the ability to direct a crowd scene well is a test of a director. It is certainly a test of his emotional stability.

The question is often asked, "Should the director ever show the actors what to do?" Some directors think nothing could be more shockingly bad.

The simple fact is that one has to show sometimes. An actor who knows nothing of stage technique must be shown the weakness of crossing behind furniture and other actors, getting himself into weak positions to talk to actors upstage of him, making feeble entrances or exits. Even a fairly skilled actor may need to be shown how to execute a difficult piece of business, especially one that contains complex problems of taking and releasing attention or problems of balance and physical skill.

The director who has to show the actor how to express emotions must confess that he has failed to stimulate the actor to suitable spontaneous behavior. Yet sometimes he actually does fail to get the actor to act. In giving him something to imitate, the director takes a last chance that the James-Lange theory will operate. This kind of showing, however, is to be used only when all other means have failed with a stolidly unresponsive actor.

If precedent is needed for showing, Gorchakov in *Stanislavsky Directs* reports an occasion when Stanislavsky, in introducing to the Moscow Art Theatre Company a French farce quite uncongenial to their method, read and acted out each part to help the actors understand the nature of the play.

Run-through

Accuracy, even in the broadest movements and timing of the play, involves a great deal of repetition. One repeats over and over, each attack, the whole scene, the whole act, and finally one repeats the whole play with no interruptions from the director. The first big run-through comes at the end of the series of blocking rehearsals, with books still in the actors' hands and the director banished to the auditorium. This rehearsal is a welcome one to the actors and reveals that progress has been made in several important respects.

First, the play now makes sense to the actors. They can see what they are working toward. They like what they have learned and have a feeling of competence. In this state they are relaxed and ready for more learning.

Next, they find that they have remembered much more than they anticipated. This is partly the result of breaking each scene into related bits, like Stanislavsky's[2] turkey, each bit being easy to learn because it is small, but partly because the thread of relationship to the whole ties it into the actors' memories.

Finally, some of the actors find that their feelings have become involved in some parts of the play, through the operation of the James-Lange theory and the complex conditioned reflexes they have acquired.

Assignments

Since these assignments are based on attending rehearsals, the best plan for doing them well would be to get connected with a play in progress as bookholder or assistant director. If this is impossible and you must merely visit rehearsals, some cautions may be needed. (1) Always ask permission, explaining why you want to attend. Some directors do not like visitors at rehearsals. (2) Sit close enough to the stage to be sure you see and hear what is happening. (3) Attend enough rehearsals to understand the effects of the director's techniques. Even the actors do not know after only one rehearsal. (4) Never tell the director how to solve a problem. (5) No matter how strong your convictions, never try to help an actor; you will only confuse him.

1. Study the actors in rehearsal, and see if you can list the main motive of each for participating in the play.

2. Try to determine each actor's difficulties in relation to the director. How could the director improve his relationships with the actors? (Do not discuss this with the actors; it is an exercise in using your judgment.)

[2] *An Actor Prepares*, p. 105 f.

3. Find actors in the company who do not seem to have good relationships with the rest of the company. What could the director do to improve the situation?

4. Does the company contain an actor who is hostile to precise direction? Follow him through several rehearsals, until he accepts direction willingly. What caused his change of attitude?

5. Note examples of directions that were effective during blocking rehearsals. What was the evidence of their effectiveness?

6. Note instances when "dynamic direction" did not work. Can you tell why?

7. Note the spots at which certain actors memorized unconsciously during blocking. Can you explain how this happened?

8. What instances of random movement did you note at a specific rehearsal? What did the director do about it? Why?

9. Can you recount an instance in which the director attempted to use the James-Lange theory in getting an actor to feel his part? What effect did it have on the actor?

10. State all the difficulties encountered in blocking a love scene. Describe the actors' attitude toward the scene before and after blocking.

11. Describe in detail the director's methods of blocking a crowd scene. A fight scene.

12. Cite occasions on which the director showed an actor what to do. Justify the showing.

13. At the first run-through take notes of points at which the rehearsal objectives are incomplete.

14. Describe in as much detail as possible the differences between the methods advocated in this text and those used by the director you have been watching. State the positive values of the method you have been watching — what does it teach you?

Reading List

Cannon, Walter B. *Bodily Changes in Pain, Hunger, Fear and Rage.* New York: D. Appleton, 1929.

Cannon, Walter B. "The James-Lange Theory," *American Journal of Psychology,* xxxix (1927).

Dietrich, John. *Play Direction.* Englewood Cliffs, N. J.: Prentice-Hall, 1953, Chapter 20.

Gorchakov, Nicolai M. *Stanislavsky Directs.* New York: Funk and Wagnalls, 1954.

Pavlov, I. P. *Conditioned Reflexes.* London: Oxford University Press, 1927.

Pavlov, I. P. *Experimental Psychology and Other Essays.* New York: Philosophical Library, 1957.

Stanislavsky, Constantin. *An Actor Prepares.* New York: Theatre Arts, Inc., 1936, Chapter 7.

Watson, John Broadus. *Behaviorism.* New York: Henry Holt, 1914.

Chapter 13

Training the Actor's Body and Voice

In casting "the best available" talent, the director has rejected the least promising candidates. The people who are cast in plays are normally competent people. Because they have an unusually high degree of energy, they generally look and sound a little stronger than average.

Yet in practically every play, some work has to be done to counteract the inhibiting effect of ordinary social living on the bodies and voices of the actors. A child under six almost always moves well and speaks in a clear voice that projects without effort, until he begins to live in the competitive world of his peers. Fashion, the fear of seeming "different," the mass of pressures and unfulfilled desires create tensions, and, in compensation, an affectation of slovenliness in speech and stance that often becomes ingrained. The behavior that has evolved under social strains has generally served fairly well for ordinary social purposes, so that the actor thinks of his everyday behavior as "natural" behavior. On the stage, however, it not only looks and sounds bad, but often seriously impedes an actor's work. For example, an actor may know he is supposed to feel sad enough to throw himself on the ground, but when he does anything that reveals his sadness, he feels silly. He may know that he is supposed to be glad another character is entering, but when he tries to make a quick cross toward the arriving character, he feels awkward and frustrated instead of glad. Lively and powerful emotions simply do not come into a lazy and awkward or hypertense body. A voice that fails to respond to the actor's feelings tends to interrupt his feelings.

The actor who moves or speaks inadequately usually does not have any very serious problems in correcting his behavior, *if he wants to improve.* But such as they are, the problems must be dealt with early, so that good habits can solidly replace the old bad ones before the feelings begin to flow, making it impossible to interrupt the actor to correct these minor details. Acting is something like playing the piano; one must learn to play the instrument before he can play the music.

Motivation

Speech and posture are so tied up with a person's image of himself that he feels false and affected when he attempts to change. This feeling is aggravated by the tendency of his non-theatre friends to tease, or even, to a degree, to reject him as he tries to acquire behavior different from theirs. One of the surest ways to motivate improvement is to reveal to the actor that his everyday behavior actually does not convey to his friends what he thinks it conveys, that the slovenly voice and carriage which he permits people to see and hear represent his most commonplace self, something a good bit inferior to what he knows himself to be. Thus he sees that it is his habitual behavior that is false, not the good behavior. This idea usually shocks people; they really do not want to deceive anybody; they are willing to seem what they believe themselves to be. Students, in particular, accept this idea readily. They realize how very much they change in their college years and are willing to change the outer man as a symbol of the inner change.

A motivation that works with some college adolescents is to remind them that, while they know themselves to be the same Jim or Mary who was "a kid" in high school last year, here no one knows anything of their life as children; people think of them as young adults with a great deal of poise and dignity. This may be the first time they have ever faced and accepted the fact of their growing up; their behavior almost automatically becomes more adult.

If an actor fancies he is going to make a career in the theatre, or even if he plans to do a good bit of work with the local group, the teasing of his friends of the moment will not be as important as the satisfaction of knowing he has improved. To the college student, sometimes one has to point this out with appropriate examples of the evanescence of college ties.

Each actor will respond to different motivation. Sometimes the evidence of greater efficiency of good habits is plain to him. He can see its effects in his better-trained fellow actors. Some improve by watching the faults of others, some by ridicule, some by the prestige that good speech and carriage give in social and business life. Sometimes pride, respect for the play, loyalty to his partners are enough to make him want to improve. The stimulus must be chosen to fit the actor. Whatever the means, whatever the temporary cost to the young actor emotionally, he must be lured to cooperate in his own improvement because his only implements for conveying the play to the audience are his voice and his body.

Once an actor decides to improve, it is not overwhelmingly difficult to help him, for good habits, once acquired, are actually more comfortable than bad ones.

The Actor's Body

The director in rehearsal is not a dancing master and cannot hope to give the actors the skill and agility and complete expressiveness that they would gain from a good course in modern dance. He can, however, help them to gain general bodily efficiency — freedom from useless and inhibiting tensions, accuracy, and nimbleness in conveying what the character must convey. All serious actors must, of course, take as much training in modern dance as they possibly can, just as they must study singing to strengthen their voices.

Since the motivated body is ordinarily "right," it is not necessary in rehearsals (unless the style of the play or the character calls for it) to worry the actor with "grace." Especially in dealing with young men, the idea of grace should be avoided, for the American male associates grace with mere prettiness. One strives instead for efficiency. Grace, for the actor, may be defined as the power to perform necessary physical actions with good balance and with exactly the amount of energy needed.

One's most pressing concern is to see that the actor is relaxed. When the actor has neck tensions that make him bob and jerk his head, or when arm tensions force him to saw with his forearm or to clench and unclench his hands repeatedly, these tensions are felt by the audience and empathy is broken. The audience realizes that the actor's incompetence, not the character's emotion, is being expressed.

It does no good merely to say "don't." If concentration and right objectives, along with the relaxing effect of the scene's beats do not break the bad habit, the director must find a way to discharge the tension; for whenever there is tension, some muscular discharge is needed. He may be able to help the actor by substituting an action appropriate to the character. Here is one logical occasion for the discreet use of a mannerism. It is usually advisable to explain to the actor why the mannerism is needed and, of course, to motivate it and see that it is timed to be useful rather than distractingly overused.

Sometimes the actor's tensions can simply be transferred to the belt muscles, where they have real value in supporting the voice. In making this transfer, one must be sure that the neck muscles are relaxed, or more harm is done than good.

Every serious theatre group should have a course in modern dance for its actors because modern dance, unlike ballet, is an expression of human feelings. It is, of course, unnecessary for the average actor to gain a degree of skill as great as a concert dancer's, but he needs the understanding that dance gives of his own muscles in the act of expressing his feelings.

Whether or not the actors are given the advantage of regular dance training, a first exercise in modern dance is of great value in helping a company to relax and is inestimably useful to a hypertense actor. This is an exercise of exaggerated muscle tension to force the skeleton of the body into its most upright and noble position. It is important to remember that it is an exercise and its purpose is to teach the muscles what they need to remember when the body is at rest. Needless to say, this tension is not supposed to be present when the actor or dancer is playing a part. But only the kinaesthetic memory in the muscles themselves will make possible the controlled and efficient use of a perfectly poised and efficient and ready body.

1. Each step in the exercise is held with maximum tension until the relaxation at the end.
2. Stand, feet together, toes straight foward, weight on the balls of the feet.
3. Grab the floor with the toes as if pulling the heels forward, so that the arch of the foot is well off the floor.
4. Pull the knees upward with the thigh muscles (be sure that the knees are not forced backward or buckled forward).

5. Squeeze the inner thighs together and tighten the buttocks.

6. Push the small of the back toward the back wall, making the pelvic cradle horizontal to the floor and the ceiling.

7. With the arms a breath space from the sides, and relaxed, press the shoulders down and back, maintaining the straight back, with weight on the balls of the feet.

8. Press the back of the neck (not the back of the head) toward the back wall.

9. Increase the muscle tension built in 2 through 8 to its maximum.

10. Slowly release the tension and at the same time bend the knees slightly, drop the head forward, pull the arms forward with the backs of the elbows upward and above the back of the head.

11. Bounce the knees four times, forcing a stretching out of the muscles in back and shoulders.

12. Swing the arms down, fingers brushing the floor as they go backward with a deeper knee bend; then with another knee bend or bounce, swing the arms forward and circle to the sides.

13. Return to an easy standing position of controlled relaxation. Repeat all four times.

If a single actor or only two or three in the company seem hypertense, it is a good idea to call them to rehearsal fifteen minutes early and start the process of relaxing them with this exercise. Often, the whole company profits from taking this as a group exercise to relax them, if the play especially requires easy and relaxed playing, or if the day has been unusually difficult for a good many of the actors.

One of the most difficult tasks for an unskilled actor is learning to break his physical tension after an emotional explosion. He needs to be able to do this in order to be able to increase tension with the progress of the scene and the play. A group of exercises can be invented around emotional material other than the play on which the actor is currently working. In an emotional speech such as Capulet's tirade against Juliet, a "kill" gesture might be put in as forcibly as possible on "Or I will drag thee on a hurdle thither," after which the actor should relax as quickly and completely as possible before repeating the gesture on "Out, you greensickness carrion." Or, on Juliet's "Oh God! Oh, Nurse, how shall this be prevented?," the actress might be told to relax completely on "Oh God," clutch the Nurse with great tension on the next sentence, and then relax completely before saying, "My husband is on earth, my faith in heaven," which implies a different kind of emotion. This sort of thing should be done solely as an exercise, and never on material which the actor must perform publicly. What it accomplishes is to give the actor the experience of full and rapid release of tension through complete, appropriate muscular action and the feeling that he has the *right* to pause and gather his forces before the next outburst. If he simply understands that he need not rush and that he must complete one feeling before trying to force the next, he is more able to relax.

Finally, the actor is helped to relax by understanding that he needs only enough tension to induce an empathic tension in the audience; the purpose of his emotions is not to wear himself out, but to stir emotions in the audience. Too much tension in the actor will destroy empathy in the audience by making them aware of their own overtaut muscles.

One of the first requirements of acting is mobility, a power gained through the efficient use of the skeleton as well as the muscles involved in standing and walking. Many actors habitually stand and walk badly. An actor may sag because he is embarrassed about his height. An actress may have been taught in modeling school to walk with the pelvis forward or in ballet school to come to rest in the third position. Some actors have never used the arch of the foot and the help of the great toe for standing and walking. The great value of the skeleton is unknown. On stage, bad postures look affected at best; at worst they convey something the actor does not intend at all. Moreover, bad posture affects the voice, for a sunken chest is a regular accompaniment of the forward pelvis, and the unnecessary strain of bad posture makes the whole job of acting harder than it needs to be.

Sometimes merely drawing a stick figure in the bad posture of the actor, or asking him to watch the way his fellow actors move, will help him to see the efficiency of good posture in executing emotional tasks. But sometimes an exercise is needed to give him the actual experience of standing and moving efficiently.

Any number of fine exercises exist to improve the actor's posture and walking, and each director has certain exercises that have proven useful to him in helping the actor. The exercises which follow work, in general, provided that the actor keeps practicing them. It takes many repetitions to break a lifetime habit.

In *Building a Character,* Stanislavsky analyses walking as a series of shifts of weight and emphasizes the use of the leg joints as shock absorbers at the moment when the weight is actually transferred from one foot to the other. The following exercise helps the actor to understand exactly what he does when walking.

Grip the floor with your toes, head up, shoulders back and down, torso pulled up from the pelvic girdle.

Step forward on the left foot, straightening the left knee as the heel touches the floor, and pushing the weight forward with the arch and great toe of the right foot. Both knees are now straight.

Relax and step back to original position, and repeat with right foot forward. Alternate feet, until it is clear that the rear foot is used for propulsion. Notice that the knees alternately bend and straighten. Avoid locked knees.

Start actually walking with: Step left, replace the foot; step right, replace the foot; step left, right, left.

Repeat this across the stage several times until the actor gets the habit of using the arch and great toe of the rear foot for propulsion and the knee and ankle joints for absorbing shock.

An exercise that frequently gets good results is the "hook in the chest" walk:

Imagine a wire from a track in the grid attached by a hook to your sternum (breastbone, to which ribs are attached in front). Imagine that the line is tightened, pulling the chest higher, higher, until your heels are barely touching the floor. Be sure that the shoulders are down and back, and that arms, neck and knees are free of tension. Now the line starts moving along the track, pulling you with it.

When this exercise is successful, the actors report that they feel unaware of their legs, enjoy a sensation of lightness, ease of movement, absence of jolt. They can often be persuaded to practice this exercise walking to and from rehearsals. Later, when they sag in rehearsals, they need only be reminded of the hook in the chest in order to take a better posture immediately.

For an actor who has simply not felt the elation of rapid movement since childhood, a kind of crack-the-whip game is often helpful:

Taking the actor's hand, lead him rapidly in varied figure eights around the stage furniture, forbidding him to run.

Since the leader plans the moves, the actor must be very alert to follow, and he inevitably moves efficiently or he comes to ruin. The game has the further value of exciting him, and the increased flow of adrenin increases his energy.

If an actor does not respond to the above exercises, it is possible that he lacks the use of the arch of his feet because of what is commonly called "flat feet." In this case, which is not at all rare, he needs an exercise to strengthen his arches. The following is an exercise which dancers use:

Stand with heels together, toes very slightly apart, with the weight on the balls of the feet. (Looking at the profile, a vertical line would pass from the crown of the head through the ears, shoulder-arm-socket, hip joint, knee, and finally the balls of the feet, or just slightly back of the balls of the feet.) Only enough muscle tension should be in feet, legs, thighs, and torso to give the actor a sense of lightness and poised readiness. The aim of this exercise is to develop strength and controlled relaxation.

(1) Rise to balls of feet in eight counts and down in eight counts. Press the heels together during this time. Repeat.

(2) Rise on four counts and return on four counts. Repeat.

(3) Rise on two counts, return on two counts. Do four times.

(4) Rise on one count, return on one count. Do eight times.

(5) With heels touching floor, bend and straighten knees sixteen times. Keep these knee bends easy and without strain. The purpose of this exercise is to stretch the calf muscles and Achilles tendon and so balance the contractions used in (1), (2), (3), and (4).

(6) Jump into the air eight times. Emphasis here is on lightness, not height. Be conscious of the final thrust through the toes on leaving the floor, and cushioning the landing through the arch of the foot. It is important for the heels to touch the floor lightly at every landing, as well as for the knees to bend. As strength is gained, there should be no sound on landing.

In general, it is wise to handle these problems of physical inefficiency outside of rehearsal. Ten minutes before or after may be enough to give the actor the idea. Of course he must wish to improve and must practice constantly, not just in rehearsal. But, given a normal body and the will and effort, it is perfectly possible to improve even a very bad carriage in a week or ten days.

The Actor's Speech

In dealing with the actor's speech, the director does not function as a speech therapist. He generally has only mild functional inadequacies to deal with, and, unless he has had some clinical training, he should limit his work to the easy problems of making adequate speech excellent. In so doing, much of his attention will be devoted to the psychological condition of the actor, and any exercises that produce beneficial results will be good, even if unscientific. For example, if the actor can "throw" his voice without damaging his throat, he does not need to be made conscious of his vocal mechanism.

Standard speech in the non-commercial theatre is speech that is intelligible and acceptable to the listening community and sufficiently homogeneous within the group not to call attention to itself. This is the least that one asks of every actor, and it does not seem to be an excessive demand on people who venture to perform to an audience, even if they do not intend to go into a professional career. Yet every amateur company includes some actors who have had inferior speech influences and little or no training, who have no idea that they speak badly, and who do not want to change. Although half a chapter in a book of this kind cannot be designed to remedy all of the specific problems that arise in rehearsals, such as regional peculiarities, certain problems arise with such frequency in every area of the country that a director must be able to deal with them.

The first problem is simple intelligibility, which seems to be related primarily to rate and to the firmness with which the actor makes closure on the consonants.

The habit of rapid silent reading is reflected in the tendency of some actors to speak too rapidly for comprehension. They are unconsciously trying to speak as rapidly as they have been taught to read. When they do this, they inevitably omit a great many sounds. This habit is particularly noticeable in the speech of certain Easterners. People who speak in this way are convinced that they have said every sound in the sentence; they heard themselves say them all. The quickest way to motivate improvement is to tape their speech so that they can listen objectively to what they do. Sometimes the shock is great enough to cause instant improvement. In any case, three arguments now become helpful in persuading them to improve: that the audience can hear only sounds that the actor actually makes; that the ear is less efficient in listening than the eye in reading; and that the actor needs even more care than other public speakers because he speaks sometimes in profile and even upstage, so that the audience has no chance to read his lips.

Slowing the rate of speaking is the greatest single help toward intelligibility. Not only does it immediately make the actor's job easier by giving him time to think and feel what he says, but it also gives the audience time to absorb what it hears.

Much has been written on how to breathe; but the fact is that most people breathe well when they are relaxed. It is usually best, therefore, not to get the actor conscious of his breathing mechanism, but simply to make sure that he is breathing often enough.

Some actors become tense, feeling that they must "get through the speech," and literally forget to breathe. The first way to correct this tendency is, of course, to insist that the actor become motivated. If his psychological tensions are relieved first, so that his breathing responds to the meaning of the speech and to the character's feeling, he feels less hurried and is not afraid of the instant of silence when he takes a breath. Once in a while it is not only necessary to point out breathing spots, just as a singing teacher might have to do, but also to insist that the actor use them.

Punctuation sometimes has a bad effect on the inexperienced actor, who has a tendency to read all adjectives with their nouns, for example, and to inflect upward at every comma, downward at every period. Fortunately, many playwrights punctuate badly. They do this deliberately, to help the actors, because the speaker phrases differently from the writer. Many playwrights write as if the words were evolving from the mind of the character, who had to pause to select the adjective or the noun or the verb or to think of each element of a series. A playwright sometimes writes dashes where he thinks the actor should pause, or exclamation points to indicate a change of pitch.

That — woman!
Those poor — dear children.
We saw lakes! and trees. Boats, picknickers — lots of sunshine and the — lovely sky.

The actor, however, often ignores the playwright's punctuations, finding the breath pause that is more congenial to him, or even eliding a period, when the meaning or feeling of a sentence reinforces the sentence before it. He might say, for example:

He just withered away he fainted.

Wherever the pause comes, there is an opportunity to breathe, and the actor should use it, thereby slowing his speech in a way that makes for intelligibility to the audience and minimizes the actor's strain.

In good phrasing, the actor reduces the number of words he says per minute without becoming monotonously slow, for each phrase is said as rapidly as the emotion behind it dictates, and the moment of pause also varies according to the extent of emotional or intellectual change between phrases. It is in the pause that the audience has a chance to catch up. Good phrasing has a further advantage in helping the actor to avoid pitch patterns that are almost always caused by inadequate mastery of meaning.

When the actor speaks slowly enough, phrasing intelligently, there is ordinarily improvement in his diction. However, even when he realizes that he has been speaking inefficiently, it is often hard for him to become accustomed to making consonantal sounds firmly. As with his learning of bodily behavior, he must first experience what is effective and then practice to develop muscles that will habitually perform well.

Consonant sounds are made by impeding or momentarily shutting off sound. For example, [f] and [t] are nothing more than breath escaping in a certain way. In order to make the friction or the explosion audible, a speaker must apply firm pressure at the correct point in his articulatory mechanism. Actors have to develop strong and nimble lips, tongue, and velum to do this because the firmness of the closure is more important than the amount of breath released in telling the listener what the sound is.

Making the sound forcibly enough regularly creates one minor problem that is relatively easy to overcome. The actor is embarrassed to find that when he speaks with enough energy and passion, the force he exerts on the consonants causes him to spray. This is inevitable. All good speakers spray when speaking particularly vigorous passages. One simply makes a joke of it.

In trying to correct inadequate articulation of consonants, one sometimes gets results by pointing out the emotional values of the sounds of words. Although an actor's primary concern is with meaning, he needs to love words for their own sake as well and to recognize how he can utilize mere sound in conveying emotional values. The strong repetition of [d], for example, creates a low-pitched beat in

> . . . . down the vast edges drear
> and naked shingles of the world

that sounds like doom and definitely affects the feelings of both speaker and listener. The nasal consonants in "down," "naked," "shingles" are the raw sounds by which one involuntarily expresses pain.

In asking the actor to think about the sounds of his words, it should be pointed out that there is a subtle but essential difference between enjoying the words, with their sound and meaning, and enjoying the sound of one's own voice. Narcissism is repellent in whatever form it appears.

By slowing the rate and improving the diction, one not only relieves the actor of the nervous pressure that results in throat strain, but also insures against the common cold on opening nights; for a cold may destroy resonance, but it never affects the power to use any consonants except the nasal consonants. One can be heard, if he customarily speaks with firm consonants.

This way of speaking is also indispensable in an auditorium that echoes. Contrary to untutored opinion, one must avoid talking loudly in a hall that echoes; for the loud vowel, making broad sound waves that are repeated several times, drowns the less ample waves of the consonants. In an echoing auditorium, one learns to use clear resonance, but relatively little force on the vowels, and to push the consonants as forcefully as possible, even separating the words a little. If the effect is somewhat like "the rain in Spain," the actor will not take long to recover when he has the luxury of working in a better auditorium.

A few special sounds give trouble rather regularly in all parts of the United States. These are final and medial [t], final [d], and [l], the nasal consonants and the voiceless plosives and fricatives, the ones that spray. A few exercises will at least help the poor speaker to become aware of these sounds.

1. Distinguish between [d] and [t] as you pronounce: haughty lady, a little fiddle, steady fighting, loading cattle.

2. Spit the [t] and note the angry effect in:
Here is no continuing city, here is no abiding stay,
Ill the wind, ill the time, uncertain the profit, certain the danger.
O late late late late is the time, late too late and rotten the year.
Evil the wind and bitter the sea and grey the sky, grey grey grey.
O Thomas return Archbishop; return, return to France.
Return. Quickly. Quietly. Leave us to perish in quiet.
3. Be sure to say every [l] and [d] in:
Gold! Gold! Gold! Gold!
Bright and yellow, hard and cold,
Molten, graven, hammered and rolled,
Heavy to get and light to hold,
Hoarded, bartered, squandered, doled,
Spurned by the young but hugged by the old
To the very verge of the churchyard mold,
Price of many a crime untold.
Gold! Gold! Gold! Gold!

The nasal consonants, [m], [n], [ŋ], are so valuable for emotional expression that the actor should learn to enjoy using them. They are the sounds of raw emotion, the moan of pain or delight. For example:

Mmm! That's good!
Nnn! That hurts!
Going, going, gone!
My whole being cringes.

They can be inflected, and they even tend to influence the quality of the voice and thus to affect both speaker and listener emotionally. Even though the breathstream goes into the nose in making these sounds, there is firm closure at the lips on [m], at the alveolar ridge on [n], and at the soft palate on [ŋ]. The following exercise will encourage the emotional use of nasal consonants:

We are the music makers, we are the dreamers of dreams,
Wandering by lone sea-breakers and sitting by desolate streams,
World losers and world forsakers, on whom the pale moon
    gleams,
Yet we are the movers and shakers of the world forever it
    seems.
One man with a dream at pleasure shall go forth and conquer
    a town
And three with a new song's measure can trample an empire
    down.

Anyone who frequently uses a microphone has been taught
to elide [p], [t], [k], [θ], and [s] because these sounds "blast
the mike." Film actors are, of course, careful to make them
lightly. The stage actor, however, has no artificial amplifica-
tion and must make them with great force because they make
small sound waves that get lost between the ampler waves of
the vowels and the hard or voiced consonants. In the following
exercise there are many "spray" consonants:

The sea of faith
Was once, too, at the full and round earth's shore
Lay like the folds of a bright girdle furled.

Finally, any severe regional peculiarities that make the actor's speech unintelligible to audiences in his own area, or that
are so strikingly different from the other actors in the company
as to distract, must be remedied, even if the actor does not
intend to be in another play. In every region of the country,
the speech of the inhabitants has a special flavor, the result of
climate, the uses to which the voice is put, the strong factor
of imitation during the formative years of learning to speak.
In New York itself, there are several "native" dialects, from
that of the Latin Americans in north Manhattan to the "goil"
on the subway and the Yiddish of Delancey Street. In any
region, a newcomer can easily distinguish differences, but a
"native" who is not speech conscious will not realize that his

English differs from any English under the sun. The Brooklyn habit of saying [muən] for "morning" is as unconscious as the Southerner's [mounɪn]. The Southerner's [keɪnt] is no more noticeable to him than the Middle Westerner's [kɛənt] to him. If the Southerner says [lɪdl], the Easterner says [lɪʔl] with the glottal stop. It sounds as ridiculous when Eastern city people try to play *Green Grow the Lilacs* as when Southern small town people try to play *The Women*. Dentalized [t] is as much of a problem in New York as the failure to make the diphthong [ɑɪ] in the South.

In correcting regional speech it is possible to accomplish a great deal in a month by working on one sound at a time. The Southerner can master [ɑɪ] or the New Yorker the [ɔɪ] of "girl" in a couple of days, with good will and a good ear, by simply reading a newspaper aloud and emphasizing all the [ɑɪ] or [ɝ] sounds for three ten-minute periods a day and by trying to remember to make the sound correctly in his daily speech. He can then proceed to correct the flat-tongued dental [t] or the [ŋ] made with lazy palate, and so on, until his speech is standard. In working to establish new speech habits, the actor must first, of course, develop his ear. He must be able to distinguish his errors, imagine the correct sound, and then speak it.

A good drillbook for the director to own is Fairbanks's *Practical Voice Practice,* designed by a voice scientist for the improvement of slightly substandard speakers "to develop voices that are adequately audible, intelligible, undistracting, reasonably pleasant and expressive."

The Actor's Voice

Many an unskilled director has created tensions and even harmed an actor's voice by demanding that he speak "louder," when what was really needed was that he speak more accurately. Asked to speak out, the tense actor only manages to give himself a sore throat. Projection is not a matter of roaring; it is adequate resonance and the firm formation of every sound in every word to the extent that it is needed for comprehension. Of course one does not want to sound like Eliza Doolittle pronoun-cing ev-e-ry word. But to pronounce all the vowels loudly and elide half the consonants produces speech about as intelligible as the following sentences look:

> Thevic TO-rious AR-mywasonthe ROadtothe CAPital.
> Hisun SELF-ishnessen DEAR-edhimto All.

The reader can go back and study what he has missed, but the auditor has been left behind and gives up. Projection is, as much as anything, a concern for the audience, a determination to share the play.

The first help for an actor who projects feebly is to hold a conversation with him from the middle of the auditorium. Ordinarily, when he is trying to communicate, and not "acting," he is relaxed and can make himself clear quite easily. If he can, one then simply points out to him that this is the kind of voice to use in the play.

If this does not work, it will help him to witness an experiment. He stands beside one of the best speakers, up center. The other actors are asked to sit in the auditorium, about two-thirds back, and listen. The good speaker is given something difficult to read, something that the others do not know (Jeffers or Eliot are useful). He reads the first four or five lines as loudly as he can (to avoid breathiness) and gradually reduces the volume until he is barely vocalizing. The company out front are instructed to put up their hands when they miss a word. When several hands go up, the speaker is stopped. It will surprise everyone, including the speaker, that before he is stopped, he is literally holding back his voice. If the poor speaker knows how to listen, he will be able to report how this was done: by slowing the rate so that there was time to pronounce all the consonants forcibly, and by lightly stressing all unaccented syllables. The poor speaker should then be asked to practice in this way with the assistance of the company, until he gets a sense of how carefully one must speak in order to be heard by "the deaf old lady in the back row."

There are two cautions in the use of this exercise. First, it makes speaking so easy that the actors may get an idea that they do not have to work to command attention and may develop a habit of speaking at a dreamily quiet level. They must be shown that there is a level of authority, a little louder than they would use for speaking in a living room. From this level, which insists upon the listeners' attention, certain scenes or speeches must be played more loudly or more quietly, according to their content. The point of the exercise is not to establish a loudness level, but to demonstrate that intelligibility is achieved by accuracy, not loudness.

The second caution is that one must work for nimbleness and variety of rate, to avoid sounding as if his own language were difficult for him. Practice, as usual, should be with material other than the play upon which the actor is working. Any material will do — a textbook or a newspaper. Especially helpful are some of the patter songs from Gilbert and Sullivan operettas.

The speaking apparatus, when properly used, is like a megaphone, narrow at the back and wider at the front. When the mouth is only half open, it is like a megaphone with the front end shut off, not very effective. Two common faults of actors are often completely eradicated by simply getting them to open their mouths. One is nasality, in which the breathstream bypasses the mouth and goes into the nose, where it is amplified. The other is "back placement," in which the attempt is to resonate on the soft palate. This is rather like playing a rubber violin. For strong vibration a hard surface is needed. The mask of the face and the front teeth seem to be the best surfaces to amplify the vibrations made by the vocal bands. Sometimes the actor can help himself by thinking of his front teeth as he exercises and by trying to direct the breathstream toward the front of his mouth. Above all, he must get the habit of opening his mouth more widely than he customarily does.

There are a few occasions when the actor is required to stress unnaturally, both for intelligibility and to gain or keep attention:

1. Verbs and nouns have to be stressed because they carry the core of meaning of the sentence.

2. The first speeches in a play or in each scene have to be spoken with particular care, and usually with some additional volume, because the audience have to be jolted from a relaxed or partly relaxed state into full attention.

3. An actor's first speeches on his entrance must be spoken with great clarity because the audience are getting accustomed to his appearance as well as to his speech, and he must make himself heard and understood. He is competing with his visual self.

4. In picking up cues, the first word of a speech is slightly emphasized, even if it is "the" or "a" (although the [ə] sound of the article is given as in ordinary speech). The clean attack on a speech lets the audience know at once who is speaking and spares them a moment of confusion.

5. Unaccented syllables need light stress at all times on the stage. "If" and the prefix "un-" need a good bit of stress because, if they are lost, the audience understands the reverse of what the speech really means.

6. Unfamiliar words and proper names must be made entirely clear. The audience may not recognize them, but at least they are sure they heard and do not become discouraged or interrupt their neighbors' listening by asking, "What did he say?"

7. Of course any speech directed upstage or out of a door into the backstage space must be projected very carefully.

"Drunk" speeches present particular problems. The speech of a drunken person is actually very weak in consonants, strong in elisions. To play a scene like this would render it completely unintelligible. An illusion of drunkenness is given by selecting other characteristics of drunken speech, the tendencies to pitch monotony and denasality. Selected elisions are used, but words that convey essential meaning must be pronounced to be understood. Tom's drunken speech in *The Glass Menagerie,* Scene 4, might read:

> The'wsa a big stashow. The headlineron this stashow ws Malvolio the mgishn. Heee pformed wonerfltricks, many ofem, shush as porng wader baknfoth btween pishers. First, turn twine, nen turn tbeer, nen turn twiskee. I know twas wiskeet finly turned into becausee needesomebody tcomeup outa thaudience telpim, an I cameup — boshows! Was Kntucky Stray Bourbon.

If every sound left in this speech is pronounced, the speech is intelligible.

Laughing and sobbing present quite difficult problems of projection. An actor who habitually laughs aloud will find it easy to inject a chuckle or giggle or a few honest "ha's" in appropriate places. If he does not habitually laugh, some exercise may help him to acquire this useful habit:

1. Pushing convulsively from the belt muscles, expel all breath on the syllable "ha." Relax. (Without thinking of it, you will take a breath.)
2. Repeat, using two "ha's." Relax and breathe. Then three "ha's" and breathe.
3. Try three "ha's" and breathe three successive times.
4. Vary the number of "ha's," breathing after three, then four, then five, and repeating.
5. Vary the vowel, using Hee, ho, haw, and others.
6. Vary the pitch, using suddenly higher pitch after a breath. Try a series of "ha's" on a descending scale.
7. Try varying the pitch and the vowel.
8. Study and imitate people actually laughing.

The trick is always to take a breath when it is needed, as people do when they are really laughing, and to push the air out by means of the belt muscles. It is useful to note, too, that real laughter does not create facial tensions. True, if one laughs for a long time, his facial muscles become tired from the unaccustomed position; but if in feigning laughter one strains to widen the mouth, he not only looks false, but also finds that he does not feel like laughing. Laughter relaxes.

If an actor is to laugh during a speech, he must be careful to laugh between words, and he may even use the laugh syllable to create emphasis, as in the following exercise:

Ho ha ha ha ha ha (Breathe) I thought I would ha ha die. Mary oh ha ha ha (Breathe) ha ha ha (Breathe) Oh ha ha ha ha Mary came in with a ha ha ha (Breathe) Oh ha ha ha ha a feather on her hat that was (Breathe) ha ha ha O ha ha ha ha ha (Breathe) a feather that was (Breathe) Ah ha ha (Breathe) it was ha ha ha ha (Breathe) a yard long.

The laughing actor must be particularly careful to enunciate each word clearly with special emphasis on the consonants. The same is true of vocal sobbing.

By the way, the audience can almost be counted on not to laugh when an actor laughs audibly, even if he does it well. Chuckles and suppressed laughter make them want to laugh, just as suppressed tears and sobs make them want to cry. From this one might formulate a kind of rule that the actor should generally stay a step behind the audience in expressing extremes of emotion, breaking into full expression only after the audience is ready for it.

Most of the speech problems that can be dealt with in rehearsal are related to diction. Vocal problems are much less susceptible of rapid treatment and generally should be turned over to a specialist. But a few such problems can be solved merely by releasing the actor's latent capacities.

THE DIRECTOR IN THE THEATRE

A good actor can usually command a speaking pitch range of at least two octaves. However, some inexperienced actors use a very narrow pitch range. There are various possible causes. The undergraduate male may simply be having a hangover from his voice-changing period. Afraid of embarrassing cracks in his voice, he has unconsciously limited his speaking range to three to five tones, though often he is able to use a much wider range in singing. Sometimes merely calling his attention to this will help. In any case, if he has the singing range, he can learn to use this range in speech once he begins to work on the problem.

Some girls use a monotone because they are pitching too low, hoping to acquire a "sexy" voice like certain screen actresses. Sometimes they can be teased out of it. Some people use a narrow pitch range for the same reason that they have bad posture — because they fear any appearance of superiority. These people often declare they are tone deaf, but there are not very many tone deaf people. One can almost always get them to distinguish and to make differences of pitch by taking them to the piano. By emphasizing their right to distinction by virtue of whatever charm or talent they may possess, one can sometimes free their emotions, and their voices may follow suit.

In stubborn cases of too high, too low, or monotonous pitch, it is best to send the actor to an otolaryngologist to see if there is anything wrong with his vocal bands. If there is not, he may be helped to improve through long practice at the piano; but any attempt to change actual pitch range rapidly is useless and often damaging to the actor's vocal bands.

The following exercise from "The Congo" is useful in teaching the actor to utilize his full pitch range and incidentally helps develop breathing control. The base line represents the speaker's optimum pitch (see Fairbanks, *op. cit.*, p. 63). As the words go up, the pitch should go up, and vice versa. "Bing" slides two octaves or the whole range of the speaker's voice, and the last "boom" is said on the lowest note he can vocalize.

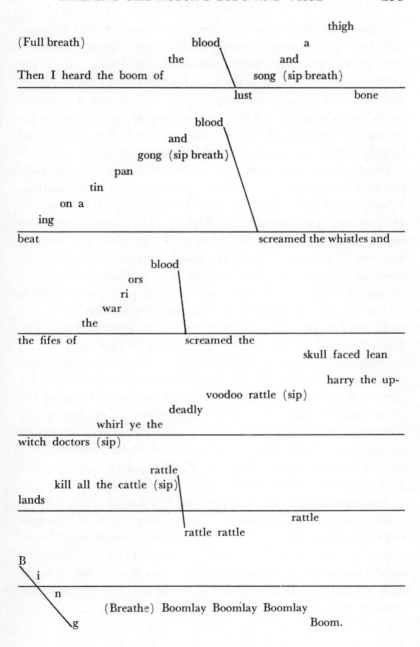

```
                                                    thigh
(Full breath)                    blood            a
                           the                and
Then I heard the boom of            song (sip breath)
                                  lust              bone

                            blood
                       and
                 gong (sip breath)
            pan
         tin
      on a
   ing
beat                              screamed the whistles and

                       blood
              ors
             ri
          war
        the
the fifes of              screamed the
                                    skull faced lean

                                         harry the up-
                          voodoo rattle (sip)
                      deadly
             whirl ye the
witch doctors (sip)

                    rattle
       kill all the cattle (sip)
lands
                                         rattle
                          rattle rattle

B
  i
    n
         (Breathe) Boomlay Boomlay Boomlay
    g                          Boom.
```

Good vocal quality is the best tone the actor can produce with free throat, proper breath support, and resonance on the hard palate with the mouth sufficiently open. But all of the qualities are useful. The actor with peculiarities of vocal quality may be valuable in character parts, for the voice is a powerful factor in creating the illusion of a character, as well as in inducing the emotions of the audience. It is only fair to add that history records faults of vocal quality in some great actors.

Many actors find it difficult or impossible to change their personal voice qualities by technical means; yet a relaxed actor's voice changes spontaneously under stress of emotion. A happy voice, for example, is "bright," that is, with resonance on the hard palate and the front teeth. In tears, the voice is likely to be denasal because the nasal passages are blocked by fluid. If the actor is sad or lazy, he may resonate inadequately on the soft palate. If he is nervous, he may have tensions within the speech mechanism that produce nasality or a metallic quality. An angry or surly person may speak gutturally. The voice of a motivated actor reflects his feelings.

With training it is possible to acquire any voice quality and use it steadily throughout a long role without voice strain, for none depends on tension of the vocal bands. But unless the voice reflects character and emotion truly, it is disgustingly "phoney." Nothing is worse than vocal clichés, such as playing an old man with a high-pitched, cracked voice. Actually, with the calcification of the aorta and vocal bands in age, the voice is likely to go down in pitch and to become husky.

Adequate diction can be taught in three weeks to a month; it takes years to extend the pitch range very much and to gain technical control in the use of the various qualities. Yet any actor who can command his feelings may find himself inadvertently using a variety of vocal qualities and a wider pitch range than he customarily uses in daily speech, or than he can command technically.

The problems of changing the actors' bodily behavior and speech habits must be accomplished without forfeiting more than a minimum of rehearsal time or interfering with the planned objectives of rehearsals, except in rare cases, or in cases when several actors are helped by one exercise. In difficult cases, the director should work privately with the actor. In rehearsal he can do little more than use the actors he has cast to the best advantage and point the way toward the acquisition of greater skills. Most of his exercises will be in the nature of changing the actor's mind as much as his speech.

But speech and bodily behavior must be dealt with at the earliest moment, for it takes time to remove ingrained habits. Later, when the actor is working toward concentration in the emotional building of the play, it is undesirable to interrupt the company for these elementary matters. Yet it may be just because of speech and behavioral difficulties that an actor is unable to fulfil the emotional requirements of a scene.

Assignments

1. Find examples of people who move badly. Determine exactly what they do that is wrong, why they do it, what motivation could be used to encourage improvement. Invent exercises that would help them.
2. Using a member of the theatre group with whom you are working, try as an experiment the correction of some inefficient bodily behavior.
3. Using lines from plays, submit a set of exercises based on the emotional motivations and basic bodily patterns as suggested on page 276 f.
4. Study the effects of tension on the bodily action of some actor in rehearsal and see if you can devise a mannerism appropriate to the character to relieve the tension. *Do not tell this to the actor.* Think it over, and then you may want to suggest it to

the director, outside of rehearsal. If he uses it or adapts it, report on its effectiveness in relieving the tension.

5. Study the exercises given by Aubert and Alberti and decide what is the difference between the method of the elocutionist and that of Stanislavsky in getting actors to "express" emotion.

6. Study the speech of your associates and list their faults of diction. Find exercises that would help them to improve.

7. Tape your own reading of a speech from Shakespeare and then compare it with the recording of the Shakespeare Recording Society or some other good recording for: (a) location and timing of pauses (phrasing), (b) use of pitch, (c) energy, (d) voice qualities, (e) diction, (f) words per minute.

8. Find exercises that would help you to improve.

9. Try to improve your resonance by talking across the street to a friend, without shouting. Try this across a large gymnasium and across a larger outdoor area. Do not shout or strain the vocal bands. Use better resonance, firmer consonants, and abdominal support, but not more breath. If your throat feels tired, stop.

10. In a newspaper article underline all negative prefixes and "if's." Practice reading with a slight stress on all underlined syllables.

11. With a partner, practice picking up cues, accenting the first syllable of each speech.

12. Write off phonetically the way you would direct an actor to read Michael James's first speech in Act III.

13. Practice the laughing exercise on page 293 until you feel like laughing as you do it. Select or make up a speech that might set you laughing and say it, making sure you pronounce all the words carefully while laughing between them.

14. Find a speech that might be said between sobs — Romeo's scene at Lawrence's cell, the Nurse discovering Juliet "dead" — and practice it until the words are clear between believable sobs.

15. Using Fairbanks, page 63, find your own optimum pitch. If you are not pitching correctly, use his exercises to correct your fault.

Reading List

Alberti, Mme. Eva Allen. *A Handbook of Acting, Based on The New Pantomime.* New York: Samuel French, 1932.

Anderson, Virgil A. *Training the Speaking Voice.* New York: Oxford University Press, 1942, revised, 1961.

Aubert, Charles. *The Art of Pantomime.* (Translated, Edith Sears.) New York: Henry Holt, 1927.

Clark, S. H. and Maud May Babcock. *Interpretation of the Printed Page.* Englewood Cliffs, N. J.: Prentice-Hall, 1940.

Ecroyd, Donald. *Speech in the Classroom.* Englewood Cliffs, N. J.: Prentice-Hall, 1960.

Fairbanks, Grant. *Practical Speech Practice.* New York: Harper and Bros., 1944.

H'Doubler, Margaret N. *Dance: A Creative Art Experience.* New York: F. S. Crofts, 1940.

Herman, Lewis and Margarite S. Herman. *Manual of Foreign Dialects.* New York: Ziff-Davis Publishing Co., 1943.

Laban, Rudolph von. *The Mastery of Movement on the Stage.* London: Macdonald and Evans, 1950.

Morgan, William R. "Experimental Studies in the Aesthetics of the Theatre II. Comparison of Facial Expressions of Ten Student Actors in Simulated Laughter and Genuine Laughter." Master's thesis (State University of Iowa, 1948).

Stanislavsky, Constantin. *Building a Character.* New York: Theatre Arts, Inc., 1949.

Thompson, Betty Lynd. *Fundamentals of Rhythm and Dance.* New York: A. S. Barnes, 1933.

Chapter 14

Detail Rehearsals

In the first week of rehearsals, the actors have been externalizing all that the director already knows about the play. They have learned their basic crosses and major business. They *understand* the play. But as the director watched the continuity rehearsal, some of his notes probably were, "cold," "no energy," "don't seem to know each other." The director has at least partially analyzed the problems he will have in getting the actors to "live the play." He has also seen in the continuity rehearsal many connections in the script that he missed in his prerehearsal study and planning. Now he and the actors must learn more about the play together.

The middle period, two weeks or more, is the time of enriching the play, of studying it more deeply so that every connection will be recognized and made clear. In this period, the play must become meaningful at every instant and must flow through the bodies of these actors and in their voices, as desire, conflict, tension, and release. Since the director never forgets that it must also flow through the nervous system of the audience, everything that is found to be right must be drilled until it can be done accurately at every performance, no matter what the mental or physical condition of the actors. As first rehearsals were directed primarily at the actors' understanding, because it would be impossible for them to play truly unless they understood, the detail rehearsals are directed toward their emotions.

It is in these middle rehearsals that the director's greatest concentration is needed, for he must recognize the bare spots — moments when a too rapid reply, a pitch pattern, a failure to use a property spontaneously, or unseeing eyes reveal that an actor does not know what he is doing. He must keep his own imagination alert for ways of expressing feelings that he senses in the actor, so that the actor's work will become easier as his mind and feelings begin to cooperate in a scene. He must know the moment when a direction will be helpful and when to let the actor find his own way. He must solve the difficult problems of cohesiveness still remaining in some members of the company.

This is also a period of busywork for many directors, getting publicity taken care of (and sometimes writing it himself), settling minutiae of scenery (and sometimes building it himself), helping the property people to find the right things, working with the light and sound and costume people — in fact, the whole production is under way.

Under so many pressures it is easy to allow oneself to be absorbed each moment of the day in pressing problems related to the externals of the play and to arrive at rehearsals tired and unprepared. But before these middle rehearsals it is essential that the director find some time to slough off the hundred demands of the day, read through the scenes that are to be rehearsed in the evening, and give thought to the needs of the actors. The most magnificently successful publicity that brings a large audience to see excellent scenery and costumes on opening night will not fill the house for a week. Only the actors can do that.

It is almost impossible to outline a procedure for these re-hearsals. They move as slowly as the blocking rehearsals did. A visitor who drops in for part of a rehearsal one or two evenings can hardly tell what is being accomplished as a single scene is built by many details for perhaps half an hour and then left unfinished to give the actors time to digest what they have learned. As a rule, the director sits beside the prompter on the apron or in the pit and deals with the actors quietly, trying to think with and for them, to seem to them almost part of their own minds. Sometimes he moves into the stage to "show" a point of technique, trying not to break the established rapport. Sometimes, to reach an intimate or painful memory for the actor, or to give him a stimulating response that will surprise and vitalize his partner, he leads the actor out of the group for a moment's talk. Since the objective is always to deepen rapport and concentration, there are few evidences of friction or displays of "temperament" on either side of the footlights. And the rehearsal goes as it may, with everyone trying to fill the bare spots with meaning.

Characterizations

This is also the time when the actors begin to see that the concept of character is far deeper than externals and that "characterization" is a matter of seeing what the character really sees, accepting his values and his desires, and utilizing the means that the playwright has given him. Michael James, a "character man" in the terms of the theatre, finds that he would like to be a father to Pegeen Mike, but that this is rather like nursing a nest of wildcats; it is very uncomfortable. As she is an efficient manager, he has adopted a technique of doing whatever she demands, whenever this does not interfere with his own comfort. In this way he is able to think of himself as the boss in his own shebeen. This becomes the key to his scene with Christy in Act III. He is most comfortable away from home or with friends as a barrier to Pegeen's acerbity. His most effective act as a father, and one for which he expects praise, is having found a husband to take her off his hands. When the actor is filled with these relationships, so that his moves toward Jimmy and Philly tend to gather them in, his moves toward Shawn grasp and possess, his moves toward Pegeen soothe and flee, then the actor is moving and speaking like Michael James. For externals, if the actor is a little stout, he may walk and sit with feet a little apart, but this is the result of his stoutness. His wish to be comfortable might inspire him occasionally to hang his thumbs in his vest pockets or fold his hands on his stomach or tend to reach for chairs with the appropriate part of his anatomy. But at this stage of rehearsal, the dynamic uses for his body take his full attention and create enough externals to make his playing credible and moving to him. Meanwhile, if he has any intellectual curiosity and independence, he has been studying dozens of pictures of Irish peasants and has an image of how he looks in costume and makeup. He may be rather florid, because he drinks a good bit and may have high blood pressure; he may or may not start growing sideburns, after studying his face in relation to the pictures. He may have found some detail of costume that appeals to him as right and imagine himself dressed in it as he rehearses. If any further "characterization" is needed, he will find this out later. The actor's job just now is to establish his own belief, relationships, and the firm course of Michael James's feelings. Meanwhile, the director will be estimating what the actor does in terms of its value to the audience.

Strong Imagery

Belief, full and complete, is essential before one can expect much emotional involvement from the actors. The actor must be aware at all times of who he is, where he his, and what he wants of the person with him. Pegeen, as she writes her letter, is the daughter of a prosperous (by her standards) shopkeeper whom she pretty successfully "runs." She is also about to be a bride. She is pleasantly important. She holds an old-fashioned wooden pen, the nib of which is a little rusty because it is not often used. As she writes, she sees the walnut wood of the table (there may be a smear from supper, which she will want to wipe off with her dishcloth later). She smells the oil of the lamp (which may need trimming). She notes as she puts up the glasses that the shelves are neat. As she throws the water out of the dishpan, she sees the gray ring around the inside and wipes it off carefully. The chest contains good wool blankets and Michael James's clean, thick underwear that smells of soap and sunshine. Outside of the door she sees the ocean gleaming in the dark or green under the morning sky. The breeze is always fresh and salty. Pegeen runs this place and knows every board and nail and bottle in it. Her costume is plain, but she has undoubtedly put some gay trimming on her apron, which she made herself. If she wears shoes, they give her a sense of superiority, for the other girls do not. The character of Pegeen will begin to affect the behavior of the actress as she gains awareness of all these details of Pegeen's environment.

It will be the same bare stage with rehearsal furniture and work lights if the play is *The Importance of Being Earnest*. But Algernon Moncrief will see an enormous apartment, the walls done in damask with stars. There is gilt on the moldings and gilt mirrors that reflect his *comme il faut* image. A fragile and expensive pair of Chinese vases flanks the gilt clock on the mantelpiece. The sofa is deep plush in a delicate yellow and the tea table a Hepplewhite antique. The Chinese rug is white and an inch and onehalf thick. The silver tea service is massive, and the cups so delicate they float in the hand. He might imagine his bedroom, offstage, with all sorts of luxurious de-

tails and an array of unguents and lotions and silver brushes on
the dressing table. Almost certainly Lane shaves him.

When he goes out, he rides in a carriage, rented (since he
lives in town) from a liveryman who serves only the best people.
Lane has to walk down the street to order it. Algernon wears
a top hat and a cape when he goes to the play, pin-striped
trousers in the morning, and he has a whole set of Bunbury
suits. The selection of a cravat is a matter of critical importance; in fact, it is almost the only thing about which he becomes really anxious. He checks his selection in every mirror he
passes. All these details of Algernon's habits and surroundings
are almost certain to make the actor adopt a straight spine,
sitting or standing, and a stifflegged walk. He wants to look
down his nose a little at everyone, including his Aunt Augusta.
He will use his hands daintily because everything he touches
is exquisite and because he has never used his hands for anything except to gesture. There will be a tendency always to
return the gesture to his own chest, for he is the center of
everything. The actor at some point may wonder if Algernon
uses a monocle; the director's answer would be "no," for it
would be completely irrelevant. Further a monocle would change
his simple and cheerful conceit into a calculated barrier to his
associates. Poor eyesight would also make him less than perfect.
In spite of his remark that he is "always immensely over-
educated," Algernon never reads anything in the whole play.
Algernon's façade must be built through his relationship to his
environment.

In *The Glass Menagerie,* the bare rehearsal stage becomes
Amanda's dim and narrow living room, where a light must burn
nearly all day. The "three chairs" represent a threadbare couch.
The wicker armchair has a faded cretonne cushion, and the pad
at the back has city dirt ground into it from Tom's shoulders
as he rests there before supper night after night. On damp
days, the pad smells of sweat — perhaps the very detail that

would inflame Tom to strike out against Amanda. The chenille portieres are dry with dust. The matting on the floor is broken at the side nearest the dining room. When the actors imagine these things clearly, they develop a kind of shame and a fighting restlessness. Amanda learns to pick up her shoulders and pretend it is not so bad. Her voice has the excessive inflections of pretense. Her worried eyes contradict her tight smile. What the actors see and touch and what they wear affect their feelings and the way their bodies behave.

The effect of fully imagining the environment is epitomized in the way the women bear their disappointments in these three plays. Pegeen throws her apron over her head and howls as she plops on the wooden bench with, "Oh, my grief, I've lost him." Gwendolyn arranges her silken skirts on the white wrought iron garden sofa as she conceals her alarm, "I'm afraid I have the prior claim." Laura sits on the worn couch, holding the broken unicorn and manages a tight-throated, "You won't — call again?"

Details of stage business are also part of the environment that have their effect on the characters. Amanda goes to the telephone full of hope and determination. The phone is brownish where the surface has been worn with years of use. What goes through her mind as she dials? The sharp hatchet face, perhaps, of Ella Cartright, who never really wants a subscription to the "Companion." A quick, defensive tension comes into Amanda as she decides to be bright ("Nothing succeeds like success"). The phone rings a long time, increasing her fear, until Ella answers. Amanda's arms relax for an instant, but the phone is quickly hoisted, the flag of her cheerful determination. As the sales talk turns into pleading, would there not be a tendency to pick up the phone and move a little away from the table (toward center)? Would she not hold the phone to her breast as she fears she has lost her customer, and would she not almost caress the phone when Ella agrees to buy? With the telephone clearly imagined, there is no trouble in punctuating the attack breaks. Without it, the actor has a tendency to fear the "long speech" and to do nothing, or far-fetched mechanical things, in order to keep the speech interesting.

What happens to Lady Bracknell as she sips Algernon's tea? The silver service is an heirloom, the cups bear the family coat of arms, and all is so gratifying that she can ignore Mr. Worthing and gossip shrewdly with her elegant nephew. The aroma of the tea is much superior to Lady Harbury's, but the tea is quite a bit too hot, even on the second sip, which shocks and offends her, and makes her angry enough to lash out at Mr. Bunbury for shilly-shallying about dying. Only when she puts her cup down can she control her irritation and deliver her ultimatum with her accustomed firm authority.

If the actors can be made to imagine their properties fully, they tend to be stimulated by them to correct relations with the other characters. Clearly imagining properties not only deepens concentration and belief, but also gives the actor a chance to time such business as eating, lighting cigarettes, mixing drinks, removing coats, so that he neither feels hurried nor omits the small things the character would logically do — such as the proper disposal of a lighted match or the handling of clothing in a way suitable to the character. From the point of view of the audience, the correctness of all these details helps to create an unbroken line of belief.

Many untrained actors, and even seasoned older ones, have to be persuaded to make the effort (for it is not easy) to imagine properties; they are sure they will handle them all right at dress rehearsal. If they are persistently unable (or unwilling), they should be given their properties for at least one early rehearsal so that they become accustomed to utilizing them; for actors have a way of behaving, on their first use of props, as if they had never before seen such a thing as a cup or a telephone or their own coats. Usually it is unnecessary to provide the real property in rehearsal more than once for the effect to be felt by the actor, who then has a recent memory of its use to carry him through to dress rehearsal without the actual article.

Relationships

After a week or so of conscientious rehearsals, the director may be shocked to realize that the actors do not yet respond to each other in terms of their relationships in character. They are merely pretending to be father and son, husband and wife, friend and enemy. They perform with cool accuracy the pattern they have been taught. The time has come for them to invest the pattern with the nuances of deep personal relationship. This is the time for a little prerehearsal talk some evening between the whole company.

The reason a person feels as he does toward another person in real life is that they have some memories in common, some experiences with or relating to each other. The director must help the actors to find the right memories. A device that often works is to put the ingenue's hand (for example) into the hand of her stage father and ask, "Who is this nice man?" "Jim," the actor's name, is not the right answer. One must help them to uncover their mutual past — the gifts, whippings, submissions, defiances, hopes, concern, pride, anger, or pleasure they have occasioned each other, most of which the director leads the actors to think up themselves. As they begin to attach their own memories and feelings to the person of their fellow actors, and to respond to each other's memories, their belief deepens and they relax physically into the physical behavior of their characters. Then their relationships become richly believable.

At some point during the middle rehearsals, each actor should be led through a thinking and remembering process with each character with whom he plays a scene. The very minor characters particularly need this help because the playwright usually has not written these characters very fully. It is delightful to see how happy the bit players are when they are expected to act as truthfully and interestingly as anyone else in the play.

The first couple of actors may find it difficult to invent or express their relations with each other as characters, but, as the director asks leading questions, the invention becomes easier. By the time he is half around the company, the actors are challenged and eager to say what they have found out, and they continue the probing process after they have left the rehearsal.

The sort of questions to be asked are: How long has Pegeen known Shawn? Were they in school together, at church meetings, picnics? What did they think of each other, do to each other at these times? Who decided they should marry? What were the deciding factors? How did Shawn propose? Did he ever think of marrying Honor or Nellie? Does she know it? If so, what would their feelings toward each other be now? What kind of woman was Shawn's mother? Who "wore the pants" in the family while Shawn was growing up? Does this tell any thing about his feelings for Pegeen? Why is he so afraid of Father Reilly? Did his father's death have anything to do with this? Did his father ever get drunk with Michael James? What have been Shawn's dealings with the Widow Quin? Have they traded, spoken after church, known each other's parents? Did he know the "late lamented" of the Widow? Did he visit in their home? Does he go there now? Does he believe she murdered her husband? Why doesn't she marry Shawn? Is he trying to get more money than it is worth for the field she wants to buy? Does this make him uncomfortable in her presence, or does he feel a kind of masculine triumph in his plan to swindle her? Is he a good business man? Where does his money come from? Why did Philly send Shawn for Michael James when he got drunk at the wake? Whose ass-cart was it that Shawn drove? What other relationships does he have with Jimmy and Philly? Is it justifiable to imagine that Philly is Shawn's godfather?

These questions have perhaps been asked by the director during his study of the play. His answers may be useful, but the questions are more so, in getting the actors to think. The actors' answers, of course, must be consistent with what the characters do in the play, but they must also be answers that appeal to the actors, answers that sharpen and color their feelings.

It is very important not to let this session become either didactic or quietly intellectual, or it will not help at all. Each actor must think up his own answers in terms of real relationships that he has experienced. Immediately upon discovering a past together, the actors should try to behave toward each other as if the imagined past were a fact, and the rehearsal must begin while they are still excited.

Listening and the Subtext

This is the time when listening becomes important. Whatever an actor hears his partner say on stage has more than a verbal meaning for him; it is an attempt of his playing partner to influence him in some way. He is influenced either in the direction his partner wishes or in some way dictated by his own objective, but the play can not logically proceed until some effect has been made on him by each attack in the scene. It is a time also to insist that each actor look for responses in his partner as he pursues his objective from attack to attack in a scene and that he select his attacks in terms of his partner's responses. This interplay is fundamental to any building of truth, and certainly to any sound building of emotions.

To the audience, the listener conveys what is happening. The most magnificent reading of the Queen Mab speech, for example, is not a dramatic event if nothing happens to Romeo, or if Romeo listens in such a way as to convey that Mercutio is boring, or if his own gloom is so deep that Mercutio's fancy has no chance to penetrate it.

It is often hard for an actor to stay in character during a "long speech" of his partner. The problem of listening is greatly reduced when both of the actors know the objective-attack pattern, for then the listener realizes that his own objectives (as the character) are being assailed and tends to react properly. He is helped by strong imagery and clear relationships. But maintaining his objectives during twenty to thirty lines of listening is also greatly aided by thinking (as accurately as he can) what his character might be thinking as he listened. The result is a series of verbal (though not spoken) answers to what his partner says — a subtext, which the listener faithfully thinks at every repetition of the speech. Here is a possible subtext for Romeo during the Queen Mab speech:

ATTACK I
MERCUTIO   ROMEO'S SUBTEXT
Oh, then I see Queen Mab hath
been with thee.   Who?
She is the fairies' midwife   Ah! This might be amusing
and she comes in shape no bigger
than an agate stone on the fore-
finger of an alderman,   I don't feel like being imaginative
drawn with a team of little atomies   tonight — My heart is heavy with
athwart men's noses as they lie   dread
asleep.   Leave my nose alone — Go away!

ATTACK II
(Mercutio sits beside Romeo)   Well, go on with your story
Her wagon spokes made of long
spinners' legs, the cover of the
wings of grasshoppers, her traces of
the moonshine's watery beams, her   This is attractive, and you're a good
whip of crickets' bone, the lash of   fellow to care whether I go to the
film, her waggoner a small gray-   party or not
coated gnat not half so big as a

round little worm pricked from the
lazy finger of a maid.
Her chariot is an empty hazel nut
made by the joiner squirrel or old
grub, time out of mind the fairies'
coachmaker.

Rosaline — she hath forsworn to
love and in that vow do I live dead
that live to tell it now — Why do I
dwell on death? Is it a premonition?

ATTACK III
And in this state
she gallops night by night through
lovers' brains and then they dream
of love.

What is it? Oh, you were saying?

You're trying to comfort me —
Thanks
Love — that's it — Not really a
premonition

ATTACK IV
O'er courtiers' knees that dream of
curtsies straight, o'er lawyers' fingers who straight dream on fees,
o'er ladies' lips who straight on
kisses dream,
which oft the angry Mab with blisters plagues because their breaths
with sweetmeats tainted are.

Rosaline's lips, so full and sweet

What a grand clown you are, Mercutio — Better listen to him than
this fear

Mercutio might also need a subtext to help him make transitions. For example:

Mercutio's first attack ends with "athwart men's noses as
they lie asleep," and the teasing gesture of running his fingers
across Romeo's nose. Romeo turns away in irritation, and Mercutio turns to Benvolio with a subtext line that completes the
attack:
"That roused him, at least. Look, Benvolio!"
But Romeo is in the doldrums again. The transitional subtext proceeds:
"Well, he wasn't roused much. But there was a moment
there when I thought he would perk up. I'll try again."

He is now ready for his next line.

Alert actors often create their subtexts spontaneously. If they do not, the director must help them, for, unless the actor is thinking and feeling in character at every instant of a scene, he will not be moved, nor will the audience be moved to the full extent that the scene could move them.

Dynamic Directions

In naming objectives and attacks, one tries all along to keep close to basic patterns of bodily action, but here and there the directions may seem to have been too temperate, too intellectual, too general. Feeble motivation becomes evident when a movement or gesture, originally ample, dwindles at each succeeding rehearsal until it is hardly more than a turn or a suggestion of the original movement. The only way the move can be restored to its original extent is by intensifying the need for the objective and sometimes overintensifying it.

At this point an actor may express his conviction that so much emotion is "ham" or "corny." Sometimes, it is easy to dispose of the problem by simply defining "ham" as expressing more than one feels, pretending, with theatrical gestures and false voice, and "corny" as cheaply sentimental. But the core of the problem seems to be that civilized living inhibits the display of emotion. Moreover, just as Pavlov's dog was taught by electric shock not to salivate when meat was presented, a little child is taught by parental disapproval or punishment not to scream for what he wants, not to cry when he bumps his head, not to make a nuisance of himself in his delight over a new toy. As he gets a little older, he actually feels his emotion less strongly, until, by the time he is adolescent, he is almost phlegmatic about many of his wishes. One job that must be done in rehearsal is to restore salivation, so to speak, — renew the actor's capacity to feel. For the most basic lure of the theatre for the audience is that it healthily reawakens the powerful feelings they may not express in their everyday life.

Another circumstance that tends to make the actors phlegmatic is that most adults in reasonably comfortable circumstances lead fairly dull lives, if only in the avoidance of great emotional crises. They actually do not recollect occasions when their own feelings were deeply stirred. Yet every normal human being has experienced such occasions, and the director must help the actor to recall them, so that the actor can approach his part with the vivid memory of his own feelings, not the second-hand feelings he has experienced in the movies.

To apply this observation: when Christy walks out to try on Shawn's suit in Act II, Shawn goes wild, but the actor does not. His stage direction is "(Walking about in desperation)". He has been given long, despairing, weak crosses, and tense, short, strong crosses as his feelings of hope and failure alternate, ending in many short and varied diagonal moves as his practical, cautious nature disintegrates in reckless attempts to bribe the Widow to help him.

What can be done, if the actor simply does not feel frantic? His body becomes tense and his character vanishes away as he attempts the very logical and theoretically effective business. He must return to his motive to find out why this moment is so shattering to Shawn.

A speech of the Widow opens up one of the wellsprings of Shawn's character: "It's true all girls are fond of courage and do hate the likes of you." Nobody likes to be hated. The truth is, Shawn holds his grip on life from the fact that he always had a little more money than his neighbors; he could weather the potato famine. This has probably set him apart since childhood. He was always better dressed than his schoolmates. They may have jeered at him and dirtied him up once in a while, but he possessed the only bicycle. As he grew into his teens, the other boys sat in their dusty boots in a shebeen at night enjoying a drink and a story together. He felt them watching him with a kind of scornful envy as he drove by in his ass-cart alone. Now again, half the boys are courting Susan or Nellie, whom Pegeen characterizes as a "pack of wild girls," or even Sara, "without a white shirt or a shift in your whole family." Shawn has purchased (with a drift of heifers and a blue bull from Sneam) the prize girl of them all and the tidy business she will inherit. As usual, he has planned to "show those fellows" who was the fool.

But now for the first time, his money has failed him, and with it, his ego totters. The ground cracks under his feet, and he clings wildly to roots and stumps to save himself from the abyss of a lifetime of sneers. Now the objective "to get Christy to leave" becomes a last-ditch battle to save his self-respect, and he is willing to sacrifice every other value for it — his dignified habit of ignoring his enemy ("I'd inform again him)", his hatred of physical violence ("I'd near have courage to — run a pike in his side"), his filial duty ("It's a hard case not to have your father, that you'd easy kill and make yourself a hero"), and finally, his main safeguard, his possessions, in a flood of promises which the Widow herself has to stem. He hardly thinks of Father Reilly. Shawn has disintegrated as if blown to bits. He cannot lose Pegeen without losing the entire structure of his ego.

The director will seek equally violent images to motivate Philly's search for liquor in the opening of Act III, if a phlegmatic actor needs them. Of course the images must be logical and consistent with the core of the role as the actor understands it, and both actor and director must work until they find something that actually does move the actor. But at this stage, one is justified in the wildest exaggeration, if through it, the actor finds the emotional energy to play the scene.

Remembering Feeling

Although it is easy to remember that one has had an emotional experience, it is sometimes difficult to recover the psychological and physiological states that accompanied the experience. One may remember that his hands were clammy, but he cannot get them clammy again. As Stanislavsky points out, it is impossible to induce changes directly in the basic symptoms of feeling — pulse, temperature, blood pressure, glandular secretion. But the changes can be induced indirectly, and sometimes rather completely.

An easy example is the scene in which the Widow, Mahon, Jimmy, and Philly watch an offstage race in Act II. It sometimes helps the actors merely to remind them of their behavior at a football game. But if they do not respond enough to make the scene spontaneous and true and exciting, they must be stimulated to a complete recall by reminding them of circumstances in which they yelled with abandon, laughed, pounded their neighbors, jumped up and down. They must tell it themselves; the director's function is only to see that they remember specific details and avoid generalities like "I was very excited." He must keep them remembering exactly what they saw and heard and did. It may go something like this:

It is the last quarter, 6 - 0, on a drizzling November afternoon. The field is wet, and by now, after every scrimmage, there is a brown spot of mud. Both teams are wet and worn out — but if the field had been dry, we would have stood a chance. The stands are absolutely quiet. The ball is deep in our territory and the game is as good as over, nothing to do but wait for the gun. It's cold. I blow in my gloves. A fellow down the aisle takes a pull at his bottle. Suddenly a big yell. They have fumbled. Number 37 picks it up — good old Joe! The cheerleaders are up, and "Go, team" supports the runner, heading across the fifty yard line, the forty-five, the forty. He stumbles. Go on, Joe! The roar. He recovers. A tackler is on his heels. He eludes him. Go Joe, Go. Megaphones are in the air as he eludes tackler after tackler and goes into the end zone standing up.

Changes will come into the actor's eyes and particularly into his voice as he remembers accurately. At least incipiently, he will make some of the moves he actually made during the game. The telling is no good at all if it is merely an intellectual description. His imagery must be extremely keen and clear and must include some spontaneous kinaesthetic memories.

In getting an actor to remember an emotion-filled incident, one must be sure he does not concentrate on how he felt, but *on the external details of the experience*. The emotional state comes unbidden with complete and clear recall. To dwell on the feeling obstructs its occurring in actuality and makes the attitude toward the experience sentimental — "corny."

Emotion is very complex and sometimes depends on unremembered details that are part of a lost experience. In a class exercise on objectives and attacks, a college student was improvising a scene in which she played a child trying to get her mother to give her a cookie. The scene went through the usual attacks — grab, flatter, bribe, wheedle — until the child snuggled along the "mother's" arm and the mother shook her off with, "Go on and play now and don't bother me." Suddenly the "child" cried, "You don't love me," and began to sob uncontrollably, while the class waited for her to quiet down. Evidently the unrehearsed line and the slight push, perhaps some quality of the "mother's" voice, perhaps even the material of the sleeve against the actor's face, were parts of a forgotten childhood pattern. The student could not explain her sobbing. She said she never cried, and she had no strong feeling of having been "rejected." The point of the illustration is that by consciously building all that one knows of an experience, he is likely to stumble on some deeply buried association that is the specific tinder for the flame of emotion.

The success of any attempts to recall the actor's feelings depends on finding an experience that has actually moved him, on finding the details that are effective in restimulating the feeling, on the director's ability to enter into the experience without coming between the actor and his memory, and on choosing the right time for the experiment. Its permanent effectiveness depends, too, on playing the scene immediately after the real outburst, so that the real feelings will become associated with the scene, like the bell with the steak. Eventually, the actor will not need the "steak."

Two cautions are obviously needed in the use of this device for recalling strong emotion. First, it probably should not be employed until the director and actor have firm rapport, so that they communicate a great deal without words. Thus, it is not necessary for the actor to tell the director his experience, unless, perhaps, the recollection fails to vitalize the scene — in which case it may be an inadequate stimulus, or the actor may need the director's help to probe it in the right way. Nothing is gained by urging the actor to unveil intimate memories — and all strongly emotional memories are intimate — before his associates, or even his best friend. All one is seeking is that the actor find a memory that works in this instance.

Second, if the memory is effective, there is a risk that the first recall will result in a relatively complete loss of control, just as when the emotion was previously experienced. This is, of course, very tiring to the actor and embarrassing to him and the rest of the company. It has its value, though, in refreshing the memory of strong emotion, in giving some of the more apathetic members of the company a notion of what strong emotion actually does to a person, and above all, in revealing the need for stringent control. For raw emotion is merely shocking to the onlooker; to be beautiful and moving, it must have form. Moreover, in yielding completely to emotion, the actor becomes himself, not the character, and is unable to continue the play. Having had this experience of loss of control, the actor can learn that there is a moment as his emotion becomes intense, when he must stand outside of himself and permit himself, with a degree of satisfaction, only the amount of expression needed to move the audience properly. He then takes deep breaths through the mouth that tend to relax him and remind him of the here and now until he can regain control.

Analogy

If all probing fails to bring up a memory similar to the emotion of the scene, the director must help the actor to find an analogous experience. How can the actor feel as Michael James feels when Pegeen declares she will marry Christy?

Human beings, though infinitely varied, have much in common. As they are alike biologically, they have many common experiences as a result of which they are much alike psychologically. Everyone has reached out and taken something with delight — if only a hamburger after a late rehearsal. Everyone has known the delight of being enfolded — if only in prayer; everyone has killed insects; everyone has fled in panic, if only from a *faux pas*. By the time one is ten, he has felt the pangs of hunger, the pleasure of eating, the bite of cold wind and the creeping warmth of the hearthside, the restless seeking and the protective care for a younger sibling or pet, the shoe that pinches, the impulse to strike out at barriers, and the exhilaration of walking barefoot and free. The specific experience differs and is felt more or less acutely according to the age and social background of the individual and according to its involvement with other needs. But in kind and degree, every normal human being, by the time he has reached the age of ten, has experienced almost every human feeling.

If an actor ever had a puppy which turned on him and bit him while he was fondling it, he knows some of the shocked resentment of Michael James. Michael James reacts by fleeing because in his social experience men settle their problems by slugging, and he has the memory of an aching jaw or a shiner. If the actor has never been forced into a fight, he may not know the panic Michael James feels on "You'd make him a son-in-law to me, when it's father-slaying he's bred to?" Perhaps the director can uncover a memory of a wreck, a fire, a tornado, to induce the terrific activity that accompanies panic. Failing here, there are other possibilities. Nearly everyone has caught a finger or a foot in something and found himself struggling apparently fruitlessly and with growing alarm. Nearly everyone has felt panic upon reaching a door and frantically searching for a key that is not in its accustomed place. Everyone has seen a bug or an animal struggle wildly when injured. Any memory of panic will serve to get the actor to redouble his internal struggles. Any real feelings, even pale, are better than mechanical acting. A good analogy is another bell that causes "salivation."

The more a director knows about an actor, the easier it is to find an analogy that will help him. But sometimes it is very difficult to discover any experience comparable to the one the actor must perform in the play, and one has to twist the meaning of either the actual experience or of the scene in order to complete the analogy.

One far-fetched analogy worked in the case of a thirteen-year-old actor who was supposed to cry when he learned that his adored (stage) sister was to have an illegitimate child. The boy, of course, had no comparable experience — not even a sister. He had no recollection of ever having cried. Upon analysis of why the boy in the play cried, a new angle developed: he had lost his sister; she would never be the same again. But the young actor declared he had never lost anything he cared enough about to cry. Although this was almost impossible, the idea was dropped and other angles were explored. Suddenly the actor recalled losing something that he cried over when he was about eight. The bond of sympathetic understanding was firmly established when the director correctly guessed that what the child had lost was a puppy. The rest was easy. The feeling came back to the young actor through a careful reconstruction of the memory — the school books on which he could not concentrate, getting up and calling into the autumn night, the cold air and the smell of leaves burning, the listening and fear, and the image of the small dog soft and dead in the road, the return to his books, and the letters that ran together. He found himself telling about it with a choked voice and tears in his eyes. Thereafter, by thinking, "She's gone; I'll never see her again," he was able to cry at the right spot.

It does not matter how far fetched the analogy is, provided the last step is taken, that is, the establishment of a logical connection between the remembered experience and the feeling needed in the play.

In using analogy, the director must not behave like a dispassionate clinician, but must himself be rather close to the emotion he is seeking to arouse, and he must probe the actor's experience with respect and sensitivity for the actor's personal feelings.

Last Resources

As detail rehearsals proceed and dress rehearsal becomes imminent, some actors may not quite be able to bring off certain scenes. The director is thrown upon his last resources. At this point he is generally worn from daily pressures and from his expenditure of nervous energy in rehearsals. He has, by now, an idea of what the play as a whole is likely to amount to, and he is about ready to give up on certain scenes or certain actors. Yet he still has a chance to get the actor's pulse beat to ac-

celerate with the character's feelings. At this time he must sum-
mon the greatest tact, insight, and determination, for his last
resources may seem to the actors insensitive, even ruthless.

He must be a magician now. Among the tricks still up his
sleeve is asking the actor to repeat an emotional scene several
times, always starting at the emotional level he reached at
the end of the end of the last repetition. The race scene in
The Playboy might profit by this treatment. The girls' entrance
in Act II may be dull because they enter "cold." To warm it
up, they may play the scene to "It's a man!" and start over,
repeating until they can enter the scene bubbling with excitement. The actor playing Romeo finds it almost impossible to
suit the action to the word on

> Then mightst thou tear thy hair
> And fall upon the ground as I do now,
> Taking the measure of an unmade grave.

It is useless to insist on the bodily behavior implied in the
script, if it destroys the actor's concentration. He must be told
to express his grief in any way he pleases, and then made to
play the scene from his entrance to this point, time after time.
At each repetition, he starts with the emotion he has built at
the end of the last repetition until, after several repetitions, he
may come to feel the kind of despair that justifies his falling
prone. In using this device, it may or may not be advisable to
let the actor know what the director is trying to do, depending
on the nature and quality of the actor's antagonism to the
particular business.

One last trick remains for inducing emotion, that of driving
the actor too hard with too many repetitions and a little jeering. In using this device, the director does not let the actor
know the technique he is using. The actor knows only that he
is working terribly hard and the director is not satisfied. His
feeling approaches rage or panic, both strong feelings, which

may be utilized toward the effect that is necessary in the scene. This is really a last resource, and the director must steel himself for possible hysteria in the actor. If the technique succeeds, the actor will be grateful, and of course one does not employ anything so drastic without enough understanding of the actor to give a reasonable prospect of success.

A scene that might be handled in this way, as a last resource, is the last speech of Pegeen in *The Playboy*. The director will have helped her to build her thought processes carefully in order to induce frustration without "needling." She has no lines from the burning of Christy's leg to the final curtain, but she must listen and react.

1. Her last action was to burn Christy's leg — an act of angry resentment that he has disappointed her and an attempt to recover her ascendancy over the neighbors.

2. Mahon enters. Now there is no need to arrest Christy. To Pegeen, it is like pulling too hard and knocking herself over. She loses ascendancy.

3. Michael apologizes. He is so stupid and ineffectual that she could hit him.

4. Mahon's "telling stories of the villainies of Mayo and the fools is here" makes her wild. Sara is laughing at her.

5. "Like a gallant captain" and Christy's pushing Mahon out of the door is like finding the rock you hold is really a diamond, just as you drop it in the creek. "Oh, my grief" begins here.

6. "Ten thousand blessings" — is there hope? He exits. None. She is smashed in the face, stunned. The world reels.

7. "Will you draw the porter, Pegeen?" brings the old *status quo* down around her ears. It is a shelter caving in. The sun has gone. Nothing will ever be the same again.

8. "Father Reilly can wed us in the end of all" pinions her to the wall. The oaf is glad! She gives him a vigorous box on the ears, with "Quit my sight!" and goes into "Oh, my grief . . ." sobbing.

If this careful listening fails to move the actress, she must repeat

from Michael's apology, with the director picking at her responses, letting her see his impatience and irritation, sympathiz-
ing with Shawn, who has to be slapped in each repetition, and
making her strike harder, until she is angry enough at the
director to break into tears, which is actually what she must
do in the scene. After this, of course, the director congratulates
her and explains that he used this device because he knew she
had the emotional power to play the scene. If the rehearsal is to
continue, this is a good time for a ten-minute break.

If the play is a joyous one, and the actors are dull, a moment
of breaking the thread, laughing and joking, running (not walking) to the water fountain, may restore vitality. If the play war-
rants it, as *The Importance of Being Earnest* might, the intermission music might be played to let the actors dance at
the rehearsal break. They come back to the play with a sense
of exhilaration that makes the rest of the rehearsal easier.
Again, the director does not explain what he has done, but congratulates them on their good spirits.

The Externals of Character

Somewhere in this second period it may become necessary to
stimulate the actor or to increase his credibility by acquiring
a few of the external signs of character. Characterization actually began at casting and was fairly explicit in the first blocking
rehearsals, growing deeper as the actor mastered motives and
attacks, his relationships with the other characters, the world
the character lives in, the clothes he wears, his tastes, and
his general social attitudes. However, if the actor's body and
voice are somewhat inflexible, his imagination dull, or his experience limited, he may be sent out to hunt for an image of
his character. He should have an idea in what places to hunt.
Prototypes for all the older *Playboy* characters might be found
in hardware or feed stores, in small bars, in a farmer's market

— where one might also find the Widow Quin. The young people might be found in a village high school yard or in the dime store. Gwendolyn might be found in the best hatshop in town. Miss Prism and Canon Chasuble might be on a high school or college faculty. If the actors have little acquaintance with the class of people they are playing, it is essential for them to seek their characters out in the world, for their imaginations will only create stereotypes if they find models in their movie-going experience. If young people are playing middle-aged characters, they need to watch long and earnestly the subtle differences in appearance and behavior that distinguish people in their forties from people in their twenties.

Sometimes all of a character's attributes cannot be found in one person but must be drawn from two or more, to get a complete pattern of appearance and behavior. Philly, for example, might be created from the laugh of one man, the wink of another, hand gestures of a third, and so on.

If an actor adopts a mannerism, he must be able to say why the character has acquired it, what caused it. And he must learn to use the mannerism for emphasis and not to distract. He must not cheapen it by overuse.

The techniques of the middle rehearsal period are directed toward laying the foundations of true and strong feelings in the actors. Their concentration has been induced by full, clear imagery. Their will has been involved by the adoption of accurate and lively objectives related to the other characters in the play, and further involved by intensifying objectives. They have recalled their own or analogous feelings as carefully as was necessary to understand their characters' various states of mind, and they have established the pattern of strain and release that permits them to increase tension as the play progresses.

By the end of the third week, the continuity rehearsals should reveal that the actors know what they are doing in relation to each other at nearly every point, even though they may not be doing it quite successfully — yet. There are probably ragged or weak spots, and the play is slow, possibly thirty minutes too long. But it is sound. From this point on, the actors can enjoy the flowering of their long and patient work.

Assignments

1. Write Juliet's subtext as she listens to Capulet's tirade.
2. What details of Michael James's shebeen would Christy see on his first entrance that would help him say, "God save all here?" What details would help Shawn say, "Where's himself?"
3. How could awareness of the place help Mercutio play the opening scene of Act III, Sc. 1? What details of the tomb scene would help Romeo between the slaying of Paris and his turn to Juliet on "How oft when men are at the point of death"?
4. Study a costume play in rehearsal and report how imagining the costume changes the actors' mental processes.
5. Report on an actor's use of properties to motivate his feelings during rehearsals. When does he begin to use properties for punctuation? To what extent does the director coach him in his use of imaginary properties?
6. Suggest some analogies you might use in motivating Capulet's tirade against Juliet. Intensify the statement of his objective by finding out why he holds this objective.
7. Invent an appropriate past between Juliet and Paris to warm up their brief scene at Friar Lawrence's cell.
8. Find a statement of motive that will intensify Philly's search for liquor in *The Playboy*, Act III.
9. Try to recall a deeply emotional experience of your own so vividly that you can recreate the emotions in yourself. Can you tell what detail of your memory brought the emotion back?
10. Find an analogy for Amanda's feeling when she learns that the Gentleman Caller is engaged.

11. Study people to find external characteristics of Canon Chasuble, Tybalt, Lady Bracknell, Laura.
12. Study ten young men in their early twenty's and ten men between forty and fifty and see if you can discover concrete differences in behavior which you could point out in helping a young actor play a middle-aged part.
13. Study Houghton's chapter on Meyerhold's directing and see if you can find any traces of Meyerhold's apprenticeship with Stanislavsky.
14. Keep a diary on the development of a "character man" throughout his rehearsals of a play.

Reading List

Chekov, Michael. *To the Actor.* New York: Harper and Bros., 1953.
Cole, Toby. *Acting: A Handbook of the Stanislavsky Method.* New York: Lear Publishers, 1947.
Gorchakov, Nikolai. *Stanislavsky Directs.* New York: Funk and Wagnalls, 1954.
Hall, Calvin S. and Gardner Lindzey. *Theories of Personality.* New York: John Wiley, 1957.
Houghton, Norris. *Moscow Rehearsals.* New York: Harcourt, Brace, 1936.
Komisarjevsky, Theodore. *Myself and the Theatre.* London: William Heineman, 1929.
Lewis, Robert. *Method or Madness.* New York: Samuel French, 1958.
Strickland, F. Cowles. *The Technique of Acting.* New York: McGraw-Hill, 1956.
Stanislavsky, Constantin. *An Actor Prepares.* New York: Theatre Arts, Inc., 1936.
Stanislavsky, Constantin. *Building a Character.* New York: Theatre Arts, Inc., 1949.

Chapter 15

Last Rehearsals

The last period in the preparation of a play has as its overall objectives: (1) weaning the actors from their dependence on the director by means of as many run-throughs as possible; (2) the coordination of their work with all of the technical elements of the production; (3) and the final synthesis of dress rehearsals.

Turning the Play Over to the Actors

Three weeks or more of picking the play to pieces has had, of course, important good effects, but also some bad ones. First, although the play as a whole has been in everyone's *mind* since the beginning and more and more connections have been established in the later rehearsals, the continuity has not been *experienced*. Christy may not have experienced his release to manhood. Pegeen may not have felt Christy's final snub as the unbearable rupture in the fabric of her pretensions. Michael James has not felt the happy return to normalcy on "Will you draw the porter, Pegeen?" The flow of feeling as a continuum from the starting *status quo* to the climax must become for the actors firmly habitual and satisfying.

It is therefore good for the actors to begin their final push with a series of continuity rehearsals, so that they can assimilate what they have learned before starting technical rehearsals.

The play may be harmed at this crucial point by the fact that the director is mentally tired. He has worked so hard getting each part of the play accurate, that he knows by heart every inflection, every move the actors make. He even knows to what extent each moment will be done well or badly. He, too, has lost the sense of the whole. He feels sure the production will be moving, but he is not moved. He must recover the delight which prompted him to choose the play.

On the other hand, because he has come to know the actors too well, he may substitute his appreciation of honest hard work for critical evaluation. The audience will not be moved to sympathy for work they never saw the actors do, and cannot even imagine; they will be moved only by a competent performance. The director must recover the impersonal attitude he brought to the first rehearsals.

In other words, the director, up to this time, has been working with actors in a play; now he must work to make theatre for the audience.

At this piont it seems necessary to point out again the importance of being rested, for here the sharpest mental work is to be done. The play has been refined and refined almost to the limit of the director's ability; it is easy to let the actors take over before they are solidly ready and before the last polishing makes an excellent job of a merely good job.

Only a very alert director can find, among the remaining flaws in the play, the ones which matter now to the play as a whole. It may be a good idea to declare a weekend holiday before starting continuity rehearsals. The surprise and delight of the actors will be almost sufficient justification. But a Sunday morning in bed or out-of-doors or even catching up on his reading or correspondence will help the director regain the physical alertness and sense of detachment he needs in order to continue his contributions to the play.

Continuity rehearsals are generally divided into two parts, an uninterrupted run-through, followed by a session of criticism and spot-rehearsal of weak passages.

At the run-through, the director's place is "out front," well back in the auditorium. He takes notes, interrupting the actors for only three reasons: they lack concentration; they are unintelligible; or someone misses an entrance. The value of these interruptions is obvious. If the actors are not concentrating at the start, they do not experience the importance of the exposition in starting the whole action and later will try to build main crises on incompletely felt motives. A shallow opening can yield nothing but strain and falseness. If actors lapse into slovenly speech, it is apparent that they think their job easier than it is and undervalue their responsibility to the play. If an entrance is missed, the actors on stage lose continuity, which is the main purpose of the rehearsal. A late entrance is an occasion for the most scathing (but brief) reprimand. Many things may go wrong that are unavoidable, but anyone who commits an avoidable error reveals selfish disregard for the work of the whole company. Of course this dressing down is painful to the remiss actor, but the electric shock of the director's reproach followed by his brief, "I'm sorry," to the company and "Cue them in, please," to the prompter, has the effect of suddenly creating a professional cohesiveness, dignity, and heightened emotion in the actors who have been interrupted. And no one misses an entrance again.

The director's move to the auditorium is a kind of symbol which the actors sense. He has now become their first audience and is more demanding than the audience. If they can reach across the lighted auditorium and across the weeks of detail and frustration and personal understanding in the actor-director relationship, if their performance can draw tears or a hearty laugh or only a look of satisfaction from the director, they know they are doing well. And the director knows it, too.

He sits in the auditorium with his clipboard, pretending as nearly as he can that he has never seen the play before, willing to be moved, yet alert to the moments that jar or bore or disappoint him. What exactly must be done at each rehearsal no one can predict, but at the end of the rehearsal he must know everything that was wrong, and how important each error is, or how unimportant. Still with tact and understanding, he must find ways to help the actors make the play move truly and interestingly from the opening to the closing curtain.

Of the greatest help in these last continuity rehearsals is a visitor or two seeing the play for the first time. The mere presence of a relative or "date" of one of the actors, even if the visitor knows little or nothing about theatre, makes the director more alert to inept or tiresome passages. The response or lack of response of a visitor brings the director back to the sense of crisis with which he came to cast the play several weeks before. It is supremely important to him that this single casual visitor like the play.

At the beginning of this period, one of the director's most difficult problems may be his own state of mind. He always wishes that each act could be rehearsed separately at least once more. His sense of responsibility overwhelms him. His faith in his directing principles wavers. He doubts the capacity of the actors to fuse the almost perfect parts into a whole. One might say that the continuity rehearsals serve to wean the director from the actors quite as much as to free the actors of the director. To prevent the director from yielding to his anguish and defeating his own purpose by rehearsing the inadequacies of Act I until time to go home, he might establish a policy for these continuity rehearsals. He might take notes on the whole play, but in the spot-rehearsal following the run-through, emphasize Act III, and unless this act is in perfect shape, rehearse nothing in the other acts that takes over fifteen minutes. The next rehearsal might emphasize Act II, and the following rehearsal Act I. If the director will follow some such policy as this, he can allow the actors to get through their rehearsal and go home to sleep.

One cannot tell what will be on the director's clipboard as the run-through ends and the actors are called for the spot-rehearsal. "Slow" is a frequent note. First continuity rehearsals often run twenty to thirty minutes longer than performance time will be. This is in part the result of insisting on careful listening and motivation, but, on the other hand, it reveals that listening has not been alert enough or motivation acute enough to create a sufficiently energetic pace for certain scenes. The task is to get the actors who now perform accurately to perform nimbly.

"Pace" is not something to put on a play like veneer at the last rehearsals. It is the ebb and flow of energy as the characters wish and fail or wish and achieve. It has been built into the play from the first rehearsal, through a careful mastery of objectives and attacks. Pace is not to be recognized by speed, but by nimbleness, not only the measured burst of energy, but also the sensitively timed pause. This is what the director has been teaching from the start. Now he may have to resort to a purely technical device, picking up cues. If an actor has been listening well, he has found a "response word" near the end of his partner's speech, which stimulates his reaction and from which he takes his cue. The words underlined in the speeches below are response words:

SHAWN
I *didn't see* him on the road.
PEGEEN
How would you see him . . .
PEGEEN
. . . *Where will you find the like* of them, I'm saying?

SHAWN
If you don't, it's a good job, maybe.
PEGEEN
. . . if they find his *corpse* stretched above in the dews of
dawn, *what'll you say then to the peelers* or the justice of the
peace?
SHAWN
I wasn't thinking of that.

A good listener automatically takes his breath on the response word so that he is ready to pounce on the cue, sometimes even overlapping his partner's last word, and speaking
the first word of his own speech forcibly enough to command
attention. All actors must be taught not to wait merely for
cues, but to respond when they hear something that induces
response. This is particularly true of monosyllabic responses,
and of monosyllabic cues. If necessary, an actor will learn two
speeches together and "ride" the monosyllabic response. The re-
sponder will then learn to bring in his "oh" or "yes" promptly.

Part of the technique of inducing suspense in the audience
is keeping them listening and watching alertly and then making them wait. Suspense during a scene begins with recognition
of what the characters are trying to accomplish, is intensified as
each attack reaches its crisis, and ends with the objective still
uncompleted. The moment of tension during the attack, induced
by the unswerving drive of the actors, is the essential prelude
to the moment of waiting between attacks. In very tense scenes,
if the cues are picked up nimbly within attacks, the slightest
pause between attacks becomes adequate punctuation to secure
clarity and still maintain suspense.

If the actors have not learned to pick up their cues through
concentration, good listening, and vivid objectives, they must
learn it now mechanically. But even if it must be achieved in
this way, the result is often heightened alertness and energy.

Another common note on the director's pad is "Lines," the

failure of an actor to memorize, in a few instances, to a degree that necessitates the intervention of the prompter. At this stage, given normally intelligent actors, there may be a variety of causes of lapses of memory: (1) the actor may be overtired or ill. The remedy is rest or prompt medical care. (2) He may be tense from something that happened before or during rehearsal (a director can usually anticipate a memory lapse from this cause). The remedy depends on the cause and the actor, but more complete concentration is in order, for the personal concerns of the actor do not belong to the character. (3) He may still lack some fragment of meaning to help him over transitions. One must go over the scene with him to find out where the connection is missing and help him to make it. (4) He may have been blocked badly. Merely to change him from right to left of his partner may put him in a position to see a stimulus that is essential for his memory process. The reblocking of the scene will, of course, entail going back to the point in the script where he got into the bad position and correcting him from there. (5) There may be a confusing similarity of cue, line, and business in two scenes. The remedy is to change one or all of the confusing elements.

Serious attention must be given to any failure to bring off a crisis effectively. In such a case, concentration and understanding may seem to be complete, but energy is lacking. This, too, may stem from fatigue or some physiological condition. It may, on the other hand, derive from mere lack of nimbleness caused by too many slow and painstakingly accurate rehearsals of the scene. It may help merely to repeat the scene with quick pick-up of cues, while prompter or director drives the actors by feeding speeches a little faster than the actors are accustomed to, or snapping fingers to demand quicker reaction. The integrity of the scene must not be allowed to suffer, but sometimes the extra alertness needed to play the scene at this induced speed may put the necessary edge of energy on the scene.

If the actors do not succeed in sharpening the crisis in the next rehearsal, there may be something wrong earlier in the play — lack of clarity in exposition, inadequate values attached to main objectives, failure of the right characters to engender sympathy, a winning actor gaining sympathy unjustifiably for an unsympathetic character, a disproportionate emphasis on a minor character or incident, too much crisis-tension too soon — or something else. The director must once more study the whole play, visualizing all of it, to determine what is wrong and how to fix it. This is a dangerous situation and needs the best skills of the director, both of analysis and of execution.

If the actors start "down," that is, at too low an emotional level, this may be a sign of pernicious staleness. If it is, the director needs every persuasive or challenging device, including stretching his imagination for more "given circumstances"; for the audience must be caught at the beginning of the play by the strong will, decisive action, and emphatic speech of the actors. On the other hand, it is important to save something for the highest moments of the play. If the actors start at too high an energy level, neither they nor the audience will be able to maintain and increase their tensions steadily to the main crisis.

If it happens that the script calls for starting at a high emotional level, as *Romeo and Juliet* and many comedies and thrillers do, there is an exact spot at which the actors can come back to an emotional base line. The exit of the Duke in the first scene of *Romeo and Juliet* is such a moment. *The Playboy* starts at a rather high level and quickly builds to Shawn's flight and the mild suspense about "the queer dying fellow"; Christy's entrance is the momentary letdown.

Sometimes, watching the actors in their late run-throughs, the director sees wonderful new things they could do. The question arises, "When is the last time for changes?" The answer depends, of course, on what the change is, on the way the company have rehearsed, and on how they have responded to training. If their training habits are shallow and they depend solely on their brains to tell them all they have to do and say, they are under great personal tension toward dress rehearsal and dread change. If, on the other hand, they have learned kinaesthetically and emotionally, their whole selves are involved more and more in each moment, and anything is acceptable that makes motivation more complete or expression clearer and easier. Well-motivated actors welcome change of this kind, even after last dress rehearsal.

If the play is a comedy and visitors come to the rehearsal, the director is sure to have several notes, "Holding laughs." In the detail rehearsals, the actors have recognized where to anticipate the audience's laughter and have been not only told what to do, but in some instances, have been given business to cover a prolonged or delayed audience response. With someone actually laughing, an unskilled actor may "break up"; that is, laugh himself, an unpardonable lapse of concentration. The general tendency of inexperienced actors, however, is to "ride laughs," to go on speaking as if the audience had not responded. The effect of this in performance is that the audience will be deterred from laughing in order to hear what is said and eventually will refrain from laughing at all. With a very little practice (if no one else is there, the director himself may laugh loudly) the actors can learn: (1) to stop speaking immediately upon the beginning of the laugh, but stay in character and in relationship; (2) to break the laugh just after its crest with a strong voice and perhaps a commanding gesture, or even a cross if the laugh is persistent; (3) to start over any speech that was mistakenly begun just after the laugh began. These directions do not seem so mechanical, if the actors will recall what they actually do when a train or a jet roars by during a conversation.

No director can tell absolutely when a given audience will laugh, though if the play is well done, the laugh will come three out of four times where is is anticipated. The main reason for laughter not occurring where it is expected is that some element of preparation for it is incomplete; most frequently, the audience has not heard the preparatory lines. The conditions for getting the laugh are the same (though more subtle) as in the old Mack Sennett silent movies. With all connections clear and energy level high, the blow is withheld until the audience is aware that it is going to be delivered. The pie-thrower rears back and winds up before throwing the pie; the pratfaller loses his balance quite obviously and then falls, or he behaves with dignity while someone else shows the audience the banana peel ahead. Even wit is prepared more or less in this way. In Algernon's line, "If I am sometimes a little over-dressed, I am always enormously over-educated," the actor would stress "little" and "dressed", and draw out "always enormously over-"; and a pompous and unskilled actor might take a pause and even a gesture before "educated." He wants the audience to wait for the laugh word, then laugh. And they do it. A more subtle actor lets the audience know by a gleam in his eye and a minute pause or gesture that he is going to say something funny. The "set" for the comic moment is less obvious, but it is made with the greatest precision.

Another source of difficulty in getting laughter is that the joke is a little too difficult for the audience, and by the time they have caught it and are ready to laugh, the play has already gone ahead, and they repress their laughter because they want to hear. One often does not estimate these moments correctly before submitting them to the responses of several audiences, but one should try to anticipate them by giving the actors something to do after the speech in an instant of silence. Usually a weak move such as picking up something, turning away, crossing up or out of center will give the audience time to catch up with the meaning and laugh. Of course the move must be appropriate to the character in the situation. If the laughter is cumulative, the return from the weak move is helpful in regaining control of the audience.

By now the actors have been learning their faults for several weeks and have worked sincerely to correct them. If rehearsals have been stimulating, the actors probably went home from them sufficiently motivated and inspired to believe they could improve. There has been little time to praise them and really not much need for it, since determination and hope were always there. Now they are tired. Most of them have never made such stringent demands on themselves in a role before. Moreover, the moment of testing confronts them. They now need praise to keep them in a state of hope and determination.

Since the actors have come to know something about the director while he was studying them, they will recognize any insincerity in his praise and become discouraged by it. Accordingly, it is essential for the director to be both plausible and specific in his praise. A note of approval taken during rehearsal will remind him of particular praiseworthy moments. The company as a whole generally warms to praise given a single member, but in the course of these final run-throughs it will surely be possible to find some commendation for each actor.

In general it is wise not to prolong the run-throughs beyond about three hours, for rest and good spirits are essential, and the technical rehearsals ahead tend to be slow and wearing. At the last run-through, the actors should be advised what procedures will be followed in technical rehearsals so that they can save their energies without detriment to the play.

This is a time to forestall any silly remarks about technical matters from actors who do not know the standards of the theatre. Nothing is so exasperating to the tired technical director as an actor's shocked, "Is that the color of the set?" when the crew has not yet had time to paint it. The actors must learn to respect the intelligence and hard work and artistic integrity of the technical people; and they might be encouraged, if they particularly like anything, to say so to the crew member who made it.

The night before actors and crews begin to work together is also the time to insure good relations by introducing the stage manager and the crew heads to the company and asking each to explain his functions to the actors and to tell how the actors can help them to function well. The crews will work with more good will and resourcefulness if their status is recognized as well as that of the actors.

Technical Rehearsals

In the professional theatre, in drama schools and in colleges where theatre teaching is professionally oriented, it is to be expected that all technical people will be highly competent and efficient. They have been or are being professionally trained, and the least they hope for in doing a theatre task well is a letter of commendation that may help them get a job. In the community theatre and in schools where the theatre is still regarded as an "activity," the technical crews function either because they are interested in technical work or because they have been coralled into it by some more strongly motivated worker. Moreover, they are often cramped by lack of money or facilities, and, in many parts of the United States, like the actors, they are limited by not having seen excellent productions. Their standards are necessarily based on their own meager theatrical experience.

In teaching them, therefore, the director must often draw on his greatest skills in dealing with people. Most of the technical workers have not been to many rehearsals as a rule, but it is essential to remember that they have been working and that they will not receive acclaim for their work from the audience — but only rebuffs from the staff if they do not produce results.

However unsuccessful the technical crews may be at their first rehearsal, the director must remember that to appreciate their efforts is the first and essential step toward motivating greater and more productive efforts in later rehearsals. The director's responsibility is not only to help them to know what is right, but also to see that they have ample opportunity to do it right.

Dates and procedures of technical rehearsals are planned well in advance. How many there will be and what must be accomplished at them depends on the number and complexity of details to be tied into the performance and on the skill of the operators. The light and property crews always need to rehearse. Usually costume changes must be rehearsed, sometimes sound cues and shifts of scene as well. In some plays there are special effects like smoke or fire or something collapsing or disappearing; if so, these must be drilled, for unless they can be done smoothly, on cue, with the exact degree of emphasis they deserve in context, they distract, however excellent they may be in themselves.

At technical rehearsals, the plans may be ever so perfect, but tension inevitably arises, which, between people who understand each other, only actuates greater effort to whip into shape the hundreds of uncoordinated details. The play as a whole is temporarily in abeyance again, as it was during earlier rehearsals. A visitor at these rehearsals could only interpret the condition of the play as "terrible" and the tension as antagonism within the company. For this reason it is sensible to put the "No Visitors" sign up at technical rehearsals.

A stage carpenter in the non-commercial theatre often uses short cuts and simplifications. Usually these are agreed upon in advance with the director. But in the technical director's rush period just before dress rehearsals, some new problems may come up that he has to solve without consulting the director. When the setting is first put on the stage, the actors must become acquainted with these deviations. If, for example, a door is made to close by means of a catch instead of a lock, any actor who uses the door must practice opening and closing it until he can do so without breaking the door from its hinges or shaking the set, allowing the door to fall open or shut without human intervention after he has left it, or interfering with planned timing of his entrance or exit. Any windows that must be opened or shut, or drapes that must be pulled, must be operated in the manner demanded by the way in which the designer installed them.

The actors must also learn any hazards due to the scenery, such as small differences in the risers of a long flight of steps made from two smaller flights that were in stock, the pitch of take-off steps, the location of stage braces, or paths to be negotiated in the dark. They must also be carefully instructed where to go on their exits in order to keep out of sightlines. If the play requires an "effect," the actors must be drilled in any part they must play in its operation. This is particularly essential if the effect has live fire as one of its elements.

Properties must be assembled and checked for size and apperance. The property table should be placed where the actors can conveniently pick up their properties before entering the set, and properties should be arranged in the order of their use and put away as soon as they are no longer needed, to avoid loss. The crew head must know to the inch where each piece of furniture goes and tape its exact location on the floor. All properties "on at rise" must be exactly where the actors are accustomed to finding them in their earlier pantomime, or the actors must be shown any essential variation before the rehearsal starts. Hand properties carried on must be appropriate and practicable. If objects are to be found in a purse, for example, they must be easy to extract, even if the character is supposed to have difficulty finding them, for the actor can pantomime the difficulty as he has done in rehearsals; but real inability to find the article may seriously interfere with his playing of the scene.

Methods of opening suitcases, typewriters, etc., must be shown the actor in advance of their use, lest he be awkward and break the mechanism in his panic.

Anything edible or drinkable must be carefully planned in advance of technical rehearsals. All beverages are made from a soft drink diluted to the proper color. Sometimes an exact number of drinks has to be in a bottle so that it will be empty when a line refers to it as empty. If the property man has not counted, the director must. To be eaten on the stage, food must be moist and soft enough to swallow easily in small bites, but not so soft as to disintegrate in the actors' hands. Very fresh bread spread with mayonnaise or soft cheese will serve many purposes and can be colored with vegetable dyes if necessary. If meat must be served on the stage, a mold of the roast or fowl may be made of papier maché, and a few thin slices of luncheon meat cut to the proper shape can be laid on the upstage side for the actor to serve, or a moist meat loaf may be made in a mold to represent the roast or fowl called for. The actor has been pantomiming carving during rehearsals, but no actor is proof against a real fowl flying away under carving conditions. Of course the problem of refrigeration must be solved for any food that must be kept from one performance to the next. And once in a while someone's allergy must be taken into account. Unfortunately, even in an adult company, some actors may need to be reminded that stage food is not to be consumed before it reaches the stage.

The eating and drinking of stage food must be well rehearsed. The actor learns to take small bites or sips at the ends of his own speeches, in order to persuade the audience that he is really eating and yet have his mouth clear by the time he must speak again. He must also learn to think of stage food as what it is supposed to be, so that his behavior will reinforce the audience's visual impression of flavor and texture.

Actors must be reminded to observe the old rule never to stand on, sit on, or in any way use properties except for stage business. Properties in the non-commercial theatre are often borrowed and extemely valuable. Any unplanned use may damage them. Even if insurance has been taken, as it should be, no money can replace a precious antique or any other property to which the owner may attach real or sentimental value. Besides, a reputation for carelessness will rapidly destroy the theatre's chances to borrow good properties.

Usually actors must be forcibly reminded to return to the prop table any articles which they carry offstage.

Properties, the use of which must be timed, such as making a bed or setting a table, must be rehearsed to be neatly accomplished with the lines. If with the utmost skill and economy, the action cannot be complete at the proper time, it may be a sign that the dialogue is going too rapidly. If the actors relax and speak conversationally, they can sometimes make the difficult business quite easy.

Guns that have to be fired must now be used until everyone has confidence that they will work. Some directors insist that a gun on stage must be "covered" by an offstage gun, in case the gun on stage fails to go off. But this never really covers. Once the effective instant for the firing of the gun is past, the scene is ruined by a split-second wait for the offstage gun. The onstage gun must be dependable.

It is during first tech rehearsals that the actor will drop something or accidentally get something out of place; now the director can let him know what to do about it. Actors, even intelligent and well motivated actors, seem to regard props as hostile agents and behave as if they had never seen the most everyday objects. The actor who "lives" in the house which the set represents will not think to straighten the sofa pillows or pick up a note that has accidentally fallen to the floor. If props are rehearsed for a week, probably by opening night the actors will have had all the accidents likely to occur and will know how to deal with them in character or to avoid them. They must learn that a rug turned back, a bit of paper on the floor, an untouched drink, keeps the audience wondering when it is to be put right, instead of listening to the play.

Any quick changes of costume must be planned for the convenience of the actor. If, with a little practice, he is unable to make the change in the time given by the playwright, one of several things may be done. A helper may be detailed to aid him in the change. Or a fastening may have to be made more convenient. Or parts of a costume may be eliminated, or sewn together for easier assemblage, or put on (a coat or a stole) after the actor has returned to the stage. One costume may be worn under the other, if this is feasible. Or the actors on stage may take their dialogue a little more slowly. The actor's panic is quickly relieved if the director knows a handful of possible solutions. In any case, if the dressing rooms are far from the actor's point of entrance, it may be necessary to rig a space on stage to which the actor is responsible for bringing his costume before the performance, and from which he must remove it to the dressing room after the performance is over. All actors have to be instructed how to care for their costumes properly, where to lock them for safekeeping between performances and to whom to report damages.

Sound is perhaps the least dependable element of a play, primarily because it is extremely difficult to find good recordings of such things as "car arriving with screech of brakes," "thunder and wind," "horse whinnying." Some of the well-advertised companies that make sound effects send impressions made from old recordings with so much surface noise that is is impossible to get an instant of usable sound from them. It is actually better to let the actors pantomime hearing some sounds than to shock the audience with a bad recording. Appropriate and well-recorded music is somewhat more dependable. However, if music is to be used on any kind of amplifying system, especially if the speakers are not excellent, it is wise to select something which does not have striking differences in volume level, either for intermissions or during a scene; for the quiet passages tend to fade out completely against the speaking of audience on actors, while the loud passages come in with blare. Music used as background should generally not be too melodious, or it will distract.

A serious problem in many theatres is a lack of adequate equipment for amplifying. A good tape recorder and good speakers are almost essential items of theatre equipment, but they are very expensive. Needless to say, there must be outlets for speakers wherever the sound is supposed to be originating.

If possible, the operator should be installed in a place from which he can see and hear the actors who give him his cues. Cueing sound in requires skill acquired by practice, and one of the time-consuming jobs of technical rehearsals is to drill the sound operator with the actors until they synchronize. If there are many cues, especially if the actors must speak against musical backgrounds, the sound operator must have his own script and must begin to practice during detail rehearsals. It may be advisable to hold special sound rehearsals in which the actors will play only the parts which cue in, use, and cut the sound. In some cases it is even necessary for the sound operator to rehearse along with the company from the beginning. Usually it will take a skillful sound operator a rehearsal or two to get his tape edited, spliced, and cued up for use. After this, things generally go smoothly.

In most new theatres the operators of both sound and lighting equipment are in a position behind the audience where they can see and hear what is happening on the stage. The light man particularly needs this location, for there are innumerable plays in which, even if there are no other light problems, some actor has to turn stage lights off or on. No matter how poor the equipment, this kind of cue will be attempted. If the operator cannot see the actor, the director must give the actor who touches the switch some cue audible to the operator and teach him to keep his hand on the switch until the light change has occurred.

With careful planning and a resourceful and alert light crew, much more can be done, even with very scanty equipment. For example, a "dim out" can be achieved even if there is no master dimmer, by unobtrusively reducing the number of areas used by the actors and dimming out each area as it becomes empty, until only one or two are in use. These last areas can then be dimmed out by one operator.

The more complete the lighting system, the more lighting cues are utilized to make subtle emphases as well as changes of mood and changes which indicate the passing of time. In a theatre with a really excellent lighting system, often the operator plays the control board like an organ, gaining subtle emphases by slight increases in the amount of light on the speaker, changing mood by cross-fading one color of light with another, and carrying out realistic directions like the fading of afternoon to evening with accompanying sunset changes on the cyclorama. When the light plot is highly elaborate, the operator needs his own copy of the script, well cued, a helper or two, and a good many rehearsals. It may be wise to have him start coming to rehearsals as soon as his instruments are ready to work with, or to plan a separate rehearsal for him, if necessary.

The director's function at light rehearsals is to make sure that the operator puts enough light of the right color where it will create the desired emphasis and mood at every moment of the play, to the limit of the existing equipment. When a scene must be played in dim light, for example, the operator must follow the actors' crosses subtly, but often very rapidly, so that the actor will be visible at all times without eyestrain to the audience. Sometimes the illusion of darkness can be created by starting the scene quite dim and very slowly sneaking in enough light for visibility. Any changes in the lighting of the cyclorama must be accomplished without any jumps at all. If a sunset must take ten minutes in order to be done smoothly, the actors must rehearse that ten minutes until the lighting operator can do it well, or, at a tender moment in the play, the audience will disintegrate in the realization that the effect is not heavenly but human.

It is a general rule to "burn up the stage" with all available light for a very lively comedy. A watery pink and daylight blue or thin lavender mediums in the lights are cheerful and kindest to colors in the settings and costumes, as well as to the actors' faces. For deeply serious or romantic scenes, dimmer light and cooler colors seem to create a solemn and quiet mood in the audience. Whenever possible, scenes of violence and cruelty — especially if there is blood (bought, as everyone knows, by the pint at makeup houses) — should be played in dim light to seem credible. The Greeks knew what they were doing with their rule of "No violence on stage." The more realistic the effect, the more likely it is to get undesired laughter from the audience.

In their first light rehearsals, actors often seem to get nervous, as if they were realizing for the first time that they are on stage and about to face an audience. They are actually helped over this initiatory moment by not being expected to concentrate at the first light rehearsal. Instead, they must learn how to cooperate with the light crew by varying established patterns just enough to utilize the lights provided.

If a scene must be shifted, the stage manager lists on paper, act by act, every article to be removed from and placed on the stage, with the name of the crew member responsible for each article and the exact order in which they are to work in order to avoid traffic jams. Ten to twelve minutes is the maximum intermission that the audience needs to relax. If the shift takes longer, their irritation must be conquered when the curtain goes up before empathy can be reestablished. Within an act, with the house lights up perhaps one-third, any shift longer than one minute is too long. This must be considered, of course, in planning the scenery. But a well-organized and well-drilled crew can be taught to move any well-designed scenery within an acceptable time. In drilling scene shifts, it is a good plan to have the crew rehearse for half an hour or so while the company are making up, so that the rehearsal will not need to be stopped for the crew rehearsal. The stage manager should watch crew rehearsals carefully for any particular difficulties or time lags, and plan to alleviate them.

With the whole production being brought together in two or three rehearsals, the number of details which must be coordinated simultaneously is incredible to anyone who has not experienced the situation. Here, however perfect the planning, is where innumerable moments of minor (sometimes major) friction must end in mutual give and take to gain a smooth performance. The director who understands the work of his technical people will never make unreasonable demands, but, on a reasonable demand, he will never yield to personal feelings of sympathy for the invariably exhausted technical crews. Whatever can be done must be done to make the production wholly convincing and pleasing.

Among the few things still to be learned by some of the actors is makeup. Doubtless there are still theatre groups who bring a "makeup artist" in to do the makeups; but this is a pernicious custom on several grounds. In the first place, the so-called makeup artist usually does not attend enough rehearsals to know the play and has no idea of the nuances the actors can create merely with their own faces. His one question often is, "How old are you supposed to be?" And then he gets to work, covering up the actor's most expressive instrument, his face. Second, when the actors do their own makeup, there is a professional attitude in the dressing rooms. It is seldom necessary to put a stop to loud singing, laughter, and the numerous ways in which high-spirited young people can manage to dissipate their energy before a performance. If each actor has the responsibility of his own makeup, he will be quietly thinking about his character the hour before curtain time.

There are several excellent books on makeup, and anyone can give himself a thorough course in the art by studying the books and people's faces, and practicing with the materials. A director in the non-commercial theatre should certainly know how to use makeup. Assuming that he does, the best way of getting inexperienced actors to learn quickly is to make up one side of the actor's face, personally explaining each step of the process, and then leave the actor to copy it on the other side. He will be awkward the first couple of times; but on his own, with a performance to face, he will learn. In turning his own makeup over to a novice, three cautions seem to be most frequently needed: keep the makup so thin that the actor's skin can be seen through it (this also minimizes damage to the costume); keep his fingers absolutely clean as he applies the various colors (or his half of the face will look like nothing but mud); and see that tops are replaced on tubes and bottles and the whole set of supplies returned to the cupboard after the play.

Actors who must wear beards often prefer to grow them because removing a false beard night after night is hard on the skin. If they do not wish to grow beards, they must start their makeup lessons earlier than the other actors because applying false hair requires the skill derived from practice if it is to look real and feel dependable.

Dress Rehearsals

Technical rehearsals are usually somewhat disintegrating to the actors. Sometimes they must go through two whole nights of partial rehearsals instead of going through the whole play. Moreover, since the director has confidence in them by now, he has turned his attention to more obviously pressing needs. Sometimes he is embarrassed to have no comment when an actor earnestly asks, "Did I do that scene better tonight?" The director has not seen the scene in question. His mind was on the operator of the lights or an obtrusive property or a bad makeup. The actor is pardonably hurt.

The purpose of dress rehearsals is to allow the actors to get the play back again. Ideally, all production problems have been solved, all accidents have occurred that are likely to occur, and the dress rehearsals will be as smooth as a performance. There is very little more a director can do, but sometimes this little is the shrewd word that stimulates everyone to optimum performance. His concern now is still for details, but more important is his renewed study of the actors.

The first dress rehearsal is often a little disheartening for both director and actors. But the wellformed habits of both thought and behavior are there, and the actor is more aware than the director when he breaks these habits in dress rehearsal. In the two or three nights of smooth rehearsal with the help of the production, the full pattern will be restored and amplified. At the end of the first dress rehearsal, it is extremely important that the director, whether or not he is fully satisfied, show in some way, perhaps not verbally, his approval of everyone's work.

The company should not be kept for notes after dress rehearsals. If a scene is far behind the rest of the play, the actors involved in it may be called for a brief afternoon rehearsal; but generally such few notes as may be given after dress rehearsals are better left to be mentioned before the actors go on stage the following night. The notes may be given while the actors are making up, or, for a change and to give the communication more emphasis, they may be delivered in writing as the actors enter the theatre. Or a "jam" session may be called just before the actors go on stage. Some actors and some situations profit by one technique, some by another. There is definite value in bringing the whole company, crews and all, together just before a performance, for the mere act of coming together physically tends to draw them together psychologically into a team. It is extremely important that any comments the director makes at this point be pertinent, brief, and confident. The company are keyed high; the director had better say nothing but "Godspeed" rather than run the risk of taking the edge off their spirits with insincere or banal talk.

Each situation will determine whether or not there is a curtain call. Often actors hate them, but the audience generally seems to want to express thanks to the actors for their entertainment. The people who object to curtain calls on the ground that the stage crew never takes a bow have never watched the shining faces of stage crew members as their friends, the actors, get two and three calls. In directing the call, however, it seems wise to face the fact that these honest and able young actors are more capable of moving the friendly thanks of the spectators than the deep artistic appreciation that a fabulously great company could evoke. It is therefore tasteless to "milk" the call, that is, to keep the house lights down and keep opening the curtain until the audience are tired of applauding. If there is to be a call, it must be rehearsed, and the stage manager must be told exactly how rapidly and how often to open and close the curtain. A part of any curtain call should be the acknowledgement of the company to each other for the pleasure of playing together.

Sometimes good will can be served by using the last dress rehearsal as a preview for an invited small audience. When this is done, the invited audience gets a feeling of being "in" on the play if the rehearsal of the curtain call is delayed until they are in their seats and called just before the play starts.

Certain plays, of course, would not lend themselves to this plan; and in any case, the actors should be consulted before it is carried out. If it is done, the actors must be allowed a moment or two between the rehearsal of the call and the beginning of the play, so that they will have time to concentrate on their opening scenes.

Performance and After

At performance, the director's place is "out front." Everything backstage has been assigned and rehearsed and will be accomplished by someone who can do it better than the director. It is startling to realize that no one depends on him now for anything except a good word before the curtain goes up. There is no sense in straining for the word that will stimulate the company to their best performance. Sometimes one has it, or thinks he does; sometimes one can only, in all friendliness, say thanks, then go out front, and stay there until the play is over.

In the lobby are gathering the individuals who are already moving toward the auditorium in the first step that welds them into an audience. There are old and faithful friends whose anticipation becomes more keen as they shake hands with a confident and gracious director. There are new customers, whose names it is both pleasant and expedient to learn, for in the non-commercial theatre, the more everyone feels at home, the more receptive the audience is to the play.

Before the curtain goes up, the director tries to determine what kind of audience is in the house. A rapid, high-pitched buzz of conversation seems to augur well for the play. During the performance, the director watches the play, of course, but he also watches the audience. If the first laugh does not come as rapidly or as heartily as he expected, his mind goes in two directions: do they look as if they are enjoying it or are they bored? And what was wrong on stage — nervousness, low vitality, trying too hard, wrong lights, weak preparation, anything that can be straightened out before tomorrow's performance?

At the intermissions and again after the play, the director learns to listen with grace to the pleasant things friends in the audience say to him. But equally he watches people as they leave the theatre, for it is the light in their eyes that most truly indicates their response.

Whether the play went well or badly, the director is often the prey of depression the morning after opening night. In this he probably joins the ranks of every artist whose work must be executed by someone else. It was not quite all he envisioned. Its faults are all his faults — poor selection, interpretative points missed, wrong blocking, failure really to get under the skin of some actor — whatever the faults were. This is probably a salubrious attitude, for being hypercritical of one's own work will prevent him from catching the much deadlier malady of smugness.

The reviews usually come out before the second performance. The director must deal with their effect on the actors. In general, outside of big cities, amateur critics are of three kinds: the sharp young man who has seen few if any professional plays and who thinks that criticism means only faultfinding; the "literary" critic who may or may not think of a play as a play but is well equipped to damn it as literature and regularly ignores any evidence there may have been of the audience's delight; and the negligible "gush" reviewer, whose writing nobody believes except the hard-working actors hungry for approval. Some communities, on the other hand, are lucky enough to provide a critic who understands literature, the theatre, and the potential worth of amateur performances. Usually, it would be best if the actors did not see the reviews, but they do get hold of them. The ones who are praised are happy and the ones who are "panned" or left out are unhappy, and it matters little to them if the critic is right or not. The director has to help the actors find their balance before the second performance. The ones who have been unjustifiably praised must be given something special to work on in the evening's performance; the others have to be given a plausible compliment; and all of them have to be reminded that tonight's audience will be different from last night's and that, if they are alert, they will learn something tonight that they did not know last night.

The number of performances is usually determined by the size of the auditorium in relation to the number of people who may be expected to attend. But nothing is more wasteful than a single performance, and three or four should be regarded as a minimum, if full training value is to be garnered from the time spent in rehearsal. Opening night, the actors are often too excited to be fully aware of what is happening out front; in the second performance they are experimenting, and after that they begin to know what to do. Only by working with audiences can the i's be dotted, the t's crossed, and the period put on the many techniques director and actors have worked with in rehearsal. Only the audience can indicate if these techniques are valid or not.

Two more tasks remain for the director: his bookkeeping and the routine checkup after the play to see that all borrowed articles have been returned.

After the last performance the actors may join the stage crew in the masochistic pleasure of striking the set. The director usually does not appear on this occasion, for he is trying to get his promptbook ready for the next play.

Assignments

1.   Study actors over two or three rehearsals of a scene and see if you can tell the difference between their understanding the scene and really feeling it.

2. Report on how the director's apparent state of mind at the beginning of a rehearsal affects the actors.

3. What is the evidence of a rehearsal starting "down"? Can you state the cause or causes? Was there a point at which the actors seemed to recover vitality? How was this brought about?

4. Can you note any evidence of change in the director when visitors are present at rehearsal?

5. Practice, without haste, reading a scene with a partner until you can take a breath on the response word and speak promptly on cue.

6. Outline the work of the sound crew, both in and out of rehearsal.

7. Diagram the location of all lighting instruments used in two plays. Why do these light plots differ?

8. Study the lighting operator's cues. Why are there more in the book than there seem to be as you watch the play?

9. Make notes on the work of the lighting operator. When does he begin working with the company? What does he do before rehearsals start? What does he do in rehearsal?

10. Note some errors made by actors in their first rehearsals with properties.

11. Who selects the music for a play, and how does he select it?

12. Describe the system your theatre has for amplifying sound.

13. Listen to sound effects records from several different companies and discuss their merits and demerits.

14. Make a complete sound plot for *The Glass Menagerie*.

15. Make a complete sound plot for *Romeo and Juliet*.

16. Watch a rehearsal of a scene shift and describe each change in procedure that makes the shift more efficient.

17. Watch an actor make up, and then practice until you can present a demonstration for the class.

18. Make notes on audience behavior during a play — when they seem absorbed, when they seem restless or bored, what they do after laughing, when they communicate with each other, whether this breaks empathy, or any other behavior that you notice.

19. Take notes on what you hear in the lobby during intermissions and after the play.

356 THE DIRECTOR IN THE THEATRE

20. Discuss the performance in terms of what was stressed in rehearsals.
21. Study the reviews of a play you see. Are they pertinent? Did they discuss essentials? Were they right or wrong?
22. Note as many evidences as you can of an actor's growth from first to last performance.

Reading List

Burris-Meyer, Harold and Edward C. Cole. *Scenery for the Theatre.* Boston: Little, Brown, 1941, pp. 424-441.

Dietrich, John. *Play Direction.* Englewood Cliffs, N. J.: Prentice-Hall, 1953, pp. 264-283.

Gassner, John. *Producing the Play.* New York: Dryden Press, revised edition, 1953, pp. 672-878.

Gillette, Arnold. *Stage Scenery: Its Construction and Rigging.* New York: Harper and Bros., 1959, pp. 275-293.

Heffner, Hubert C., Samuel Selden, and Hunton D. Sellman. *Modern Theatre Practice.* New York: Appleton-Century-Crofts, fourth edition, 1959, pp. 435-557.

Liszt, Rudolph. *The Last Word in Makeup.* New York: Dramatists Play Service, 1942.

Nelms, Henning. *Play Production.* New York: Barnes and Noble, 1950, pp. 271-280.

Strenkovsky, Serge. *The Art of Makeup.* New York: E. P. Dutton, 1937.

Chapter 16

The Director
Replenishes Himself

After the play, many directors report themselves depressed. The performance has gone fairly well, though never well enough. There have been the usual compliments, perhaps even more dependable signs that the audience was pleased. But, thinking about the play and its results upon performers and audience, the director is likely to feel defeated and to wonder where is is to find the enthusiasm to undertake, perhaps immediately, the next play.

Two reasons for this feeling of depression are common. In the first place, any serious artist recognizes the limitations of form in externalizing his dream. In the complex form of the theatre, the real setting — however thrillingly lighted; the real actors — however fluent and sincere; the real audience — however caught beyond its real cares — achieve at best only an approximation of the idea that initiated the production. Second, no technique has yet been found to measure the amount of energy spent by the director in developing all the participants to the point of skill and confidence that enables them to hold their audience for the two-hour duration of the performance. The

director has spent an enormous amount of energy and is simply
and quite understandably tired.

To replenish himself, he needs more than merely a little physical exercise, and day's or a week's release from rehearsals. He
faces the job ahead by going back to the roots of his faith in
the theatre, all it has meant and still can mean in man's life.

Many of his strongest roots are to be found in anthropology,
the study of primitive people and the beginnings of human institutions. Before Thespis was reprimanded for impersonating
a god, back in the days when language was still too poor to
describe all the events that occurred in man's life in forest and
cave, perhaps a father, waiting at the end of winter for the
first reindeer to replenish his food supply, etched upon the wall
of the cave his image of the creature that would assuage his
hunger. Some of the earliest drawings made by man seem to
indicate that art came about as an externalization of man's most
basic need, food for survival.

Perhaps a hunter, torn by a strange animal, ran screaming
back into the tribal enclosure and tried to explain what happened
to him, eking out his words with actions — what he saw, what
he did, what the strange animal did. When his wounds were
dressed and the spirit of the animal propitiated, the excited
tribesmen gathered and asked him to tell again what happened,
enjoying the delicious playing at fear. Or, if a stranger came
into the tribe, someone asked the hunter to retell his story —
words and actions — for the entertainment of the stranger.
Thus the primitive delight of performer and onlookers in the
story-acted-out created a kind of simple play, rooted in man's
basic need to communicate — a need older by far than Aeschylus, older than writing.

The shaman put on the mask, bones, feathers, fur that gave
him power over the creatures from whom they were taken and
over their gods. As he performed the age-old actions and uttered
the traditional words to bind the awful unknown to the service

of the tribe, he put off his humanity; in an inevitable empathic response, the priest became god during the magic ceremonials. The history of this metamorphosis, which every actor experiences in the donning of his costume and makeup, was forgotten even before Thespis travelled with his small company, imitating the agony and resurrection of Dionysus. But the medieval church gives us a clue to what must have happened. A tenth-century Concordia Regularis of St. Ethelwold contains the first modern stage directions. During the Easter mass, two priests representing the Marys at the tomb of Jesus were directed to proceed down the aisle "as if seeking." Step by step, we have the changes in the Easter and then the Christmas mass that produced the great cycles of biblical plays which eventuated in the Corpus Christi festival in England and the professional theatre in France. Nearly a thousand years later, Stanislavsky pointed out the power of "if" to stimulate the actor and thus intensified the meaning of the textbook statement that drama began in primitive ritual.

Reinforcement of one's devotion to the theatre comes from many investigations of the imitative behavior of children and animals, their power to behave "as if."

An infant imitates a smile, a cough, pat-a-cake, bye-bye — whatever his muscles are sufficiently developed to imitate. The toddler plays house, plays doctor, answers imaginary telephones, screams with panic and delight in scare and fight games. By the time the child is six years old, he carries out long and complex make believes, composed of many images which he has stored in his memory. Nearly everything one knows at this age was learned by imitation of someone or something in his environment. Kamala, a child stolen in infancy from the rice fields of India and reared by wolves, learned to walk on all-fours and howled in the husky language of the pack. Spoken language can be learned only by imitation. The lower animals, too, imitate each other and human beings. Lions and apes make believe to fight and run away. The possum "plays dead" and the salamander behaves "as if" he were not there — not really acting, of course, but capable of rudimentary "as if" behavior, the essence of acting. Thus the evidence of psychology reinforces one's conviction that the theatre satisfies a universal tendency of living creatures.

If, as Aristotle says, drama is an imitation of an action, a glance at the nature of the action will reinforce the feeling that drama is a deeply human institution. For, from Sophocles to Arthur Miller, man has built his greatest dramas on the precariousness of human life, on the element of crisis, the potentiality for change that exists in every human situation.

Thus, not only the actors, but the play itself comes from the roots of human life, from man's need to control his environment, his need to communicate, his delight in play, and his mature wish to understand his own problems.

The written history of the theatre affirms its value in the life of mankind. Hardly had drama acquired rudimentary form when it was put to use for the good of society. Egyptians and Greeks used it to teach great national and religious myths and to instill ethical principles. It was used for these purposes by the medieval church, and we have written records of its success in bringing people into church for the edification and delight of the spectacles. It was used to teach Latin, the "universal language," before Nicolas Udall wrote *Ralph Roister Doister* in Eton, before Hrotsvitha purged her own guilty thoughts by writing plays about the wages of sin and the blessing of redemption.

In recent times, too, plays have changed the thoughts of men. Beaumarchais's *Le Mariage de Figaro* gave the common man words and a song which inflamed his confidence in his own worth and thus precipitated the French Revolution. England understood the homespun American better after Joseph Jefferson brought *Our American Cousin* to London. Ibsen's *Pillars of Society,* following upon shipping scandals and reforms in England, called attention to Norway's need of laws to enforce proper inspection of sea-going vessels. From Aristophanes to *La Plume de ma Tante* and *The Premise,* satiric comedy has been a chastisement of human follies. Serious plays also open discussion of taboo subjects. Plays have helped the layman to think and behave rationally about the "fallen woman" (*The Second Mrs. Tanqueray*), divorce (*A Doll's House*), pregnancy (*Claudia*), homosexuality (*Tea and Sympathy*), the use of narcotics (*A Hatful of Rain*), the horror of bigotry (*the Crucible*). The Russians, ever since the revolution of 1918, have used the theatre as a means of instilling the principles and goals of their government in their people. France supports several theatres in Paris "to enlighten and educate." Indeed, nearly every country of Europe supports more than one state theatre.

It has been frequently contended that the spread of vice and crime and the increase of juvenile delinquency may be attributed at least in part to the emphasis on sex and violence in contemporary movies and television. Avowedly to combat the influence of the movies and to provide wholesome leisure occupation for underprivileged children, Hull house in Chicago initiated the presentation of plays, and the Neighborhood Playhouse of New York also began to provide plays as a constructive form of recreation for the young people of lower Manhattan. Churches, too, recognize the strong impact of dramatic presentation, and many churches include plays in their recreational programs for the express purpose of helping their congregations to think about important social and ethical problems. Union Theological Seminary offers a complete theatre program in its curriculum.

One's faith in the worth of presenting plays is increased by understanding the condition of the theatre in America. If the Broadway theatre, burdened by taxes, unions, and venality has dwindled to about thirty open theatres, a whole new settlement

of theatres has bloomed off-Broadway, with talent and courage
to try any play their instigators believe in. And just north of
the mid-Manhattan theatre area is springing up the Lincoln
Center, largest center of the performing arts in the world. In
the summer, professional theatres multiply all over the nation,
from Boston to San Diego, from Michigan to Miami.

Most significant is the mushrooming and the maturing of
community theatres, a movement that began in 1915 and that
has grown until it numbers its member organizations in thousands, with state and national organizations. These theatres
range from small, struggling groups with neither director nor
place to work, to sturdy civic institutions with trained staffs
and with facilities both more attractive and more efficient than
the old Broadway theatres. Scattered from east to west are a
dozen or more professional or semiprofessional theatres which
hire a resident staff and company on a yearly contract. Latest
addition to this group is Tyrone Guthrie's new professional
theatre in Minneapolis.

Modern colleges began to think with reluctance of theatre as
an academic discipline when George Pierce Baker introduced
his famous course in playwriting into the curriculum of Harvard early in this century. Now nearly every college in the
nation not only produces from one to ten plays a year, but also
offers some instruction in the elements of stage production;
several even offer the doctoral degree in theater. So generally
acceptable has theatre become in the schools that the teaching
of play production has been introduced into high schools, and
they have their own national dramatics society, the Thespians.
The American Educational Theatre Association, official organization for all this activity, even includes the Children's Theatre
Conference, which also has The Children's Theatre Press to
publish plays specifically for children.

Theatre is used to dramatize or to vitalize all kinds of civic
undertakings, from the "Maid of Cotton" festival to the Com-

munity Chest kickoff. It is used by industry to excite consumers about products and in the recreational programs that industrial plants develop for their employees.

Since 1934, the date of the founding of ANTA (American National Theatre and Academy), efforts have been made in Congress to secure subsidy for the arts from the United States government. In a recent forceful article in *The New York Times,* Secretary of Labor, Arthur J. Goldberg, urged that the United States take its cultural place among the nations of Europe in providing financial support for a national theatre as well as for our great national parks and museums. In spite of the failure of these efforts to secure formal subsidies, a great deal of money is spent by the government annually to support the theatre. Professional theatre artists are transported all over the world to play to United States troops. The United States government annually sends to American soldiers, abroad in various parts of the world, troupes trained in American colleges. Nearly every army post has its post theatre, the facility and personnel supplied by United States Army Special Services.

Through its membership in UNESCO, the United States supports International Theatre Institute, with theatre scholar Rosamund Gilder heading the American office in Paris, to improve American cultural relations abroad. Most recently, the United States government sent a brilliant company abroad in three famous American plays. Of this company, Secretary of State Dean Rusk said, "This is an extraordinary effort to strengthen the infinity of threads which bind peace together among the peoples of the world."

To all this evidence of the basic nature of the theatre and of its utility in human life, one more point remains to be added.

Ever since mass education became a dream of our democracy, the dependable bait to lure young people to college and fathers to foot the bill has been "better jobs, more money."

THE DIRECTOR IN THE THEATRE

Since the arts presented only dubious means of earning a liveli-
hood, many a young man has turned from the career he yearned
for and accepted a second best life in order to support his family
in the American standard of living. Although doubtless many
of these people lacked the talent to pursue a career in the arts,
on the other hand, equally doubtless, a great deal of creative
talent has been lost to the world this way.

At the present moment, however, art, which has been regarded
as a "frill," is becoming a necessity. As the work week shrinks
for the average man, and as the age of retirement is fixed far
short of senescence in many fields, thus leaving an incalculable
amount of creative energy free, leaders in government, the labor
organizations, and gerontology are urging the value of those
professions which contribute to making leisure happy and
productive.

Because drama deals with man's most inescapable philosophical problems — man's knowledge of himself, his relation to his
fellow man, and his place in the cosmos — it can do more than
merely kill time; it can build bulwarks against the detrition of
time. By revealing man's life whole and in perspective, it can
help one to live richly and to face mortality without despair.
Thus, from many sources, the director strengthens his faith in
the work he has chosen and finds justification for his own
small part in propagating the deep-rooted and wide-branching
institution we know as the theatre.

Reading List

Benedict, Ruth. *Patterns of Culture.* Boston: Houghton, Mifflin, 1931.
Coggin, Philip A. *The Uses of Drama.* New York: George Braziller,
1956.
Frazer, Sir James G. *The Golden Bough.* New York: Macmillan, re-
print, 1958.
Freedley, George and John A. Reeves. *A History of the Theatre.* New
York: Crown Publishers, 1941.

Gard, Robert. *Grassroots Theatre*. Madison: University of Wisconsin Press, 1955.

Gassner, John. *Masters of the Drama*. New York: Dover Press, 1945.

Hewitt, Barnard. *Theatre U.S.A.* New York: McGraw-Hill, 1959.

Houghton, Norris. *Advance From Broadway*. New York: Harcourt, Brace, 1941.

Macgowan, Kenneth. Footlights Across America. New York: Harcourt, Brace, 1929.

Malinowski, Bronislaw. *Magic, Science and Religion*. New York: Doubleday, Anchor Books, 1955.

Appendix A
Suggested Production Schedule

	DIRECTOR	TECHNICAL DIRECTOR	COSTUMER	PUBLICITY & FRONT
TIME	7-10 P.M.	2-5 P.M.	2-5 P.M.	IRREGULAR HOURS
JOB	3 ACTS	1 SET	12 COSTUMES	2000 SALES
DAY 1	Play agreed upon, rights cleared and whole staff begins to study			
25	Promptbook completed, budget completed	Preliminary sketches, technical drawings	Sketches and patterns	Campaign planned — Posters, display, mailing material sketched
26	General conference of all staff members to study plans and unify idea of production			
27	Tryouts	Final ground plans and elevations — Call Building crew — Order all materials — Start basic platforms and steps	Shop for fabric — Call crews	Order tickets, all material to printer — Write first news story — Arrange for photos — Call art display crew — Arrange speakers' bureau— Arrange campaign with press, libraries, display areas
28	Tryouts			
29	Tryouts / Clear grades, permissions— / Arrange late permissions for dress rehearsals			
30	Settle schedule— Block Act I		Get all measurements — Order wigs and makeup	Interview all actors with photographer — Coach speakers

	Rehearsal	Set	Costume	Publicity
31	Finish Blocking Act I		Start cutting	First news story out — Start addressing envelopes — Pick up printed material
32	Block Act II		Finish cutting	Get photos — Work on special mailing list
33	Finish Blocking Act II	Essential rigging	Fit main characters	Get display crew started
34	Block Act III	Start walls		Write second news story
35	Finish Blocking Act III			Second news story out with photos
36	Run-through	Shell of set finished	All main characters fitted, costume parts sewn together	First speaker tour—Write third news story—Check on poster crew
37	Interp I	Hang doors	Fix extras	Stuff envelopes
38	Interp II	Special problems	Fit extras	Write letter for special mailing
39	Interp III	Dutch — Start molding and trim	All costume parts sewn together	Posters out
40	Run-through	Attend rehearsals, with property master — Basic set up	Attend rehearsal	Attend rehearsal — Write feature story on rehearsal — Get pictures
41	Detail I	All backings and groundrows in place	Final Fittings and costume check by director	First displays out—Third news story

DAY	DIRECTOR	TECHNICAL DIRECTOR	COSTUMER	PUBLICITY & FRONT
42	Detail II	Finish dutching — Finish details of setting — Hand-props ready	Begin work on accessories	Send out first mailing — Check on box-office staff and ushers
43	Detail III	Start mounting lights — Make sound tape		Second speaker tour — Address and stuff envelopes for special mailing list
44	Run-through	All furniture procured — Start upholstery and drapes		
45	Detail I	Use hand-props from now on	Use any costumes that present difficulties	Fourth news story out with pictures
46	Detail II	Paint set		
47	Detail III	Finish painting — gel lights	Start work on difficult makeups	Special mailing out
48	**Run-through**	Attend rehearsal	Attend rehearsal	Attend rehearsal
49	Run-through — Detail III	Lights and sound on III	Finish costumes	Preview story
50	Run-through — Detail II	Lights and sound on II	Adjustments	Third speaker tour — New displays up

		Lights and sound on I	Adjustments	Contact reviewer — Handbills out
51	Run-through — Detail I			
52	Full Technical Rehearsal	Full Technical Rehearsal	All costumes checked by director	Set up ticket rack
53	Full Dress Rehearsal	All lights, sound, props	All costumes and makeup	Table tents and displays to hotels and restaurants
54	Full Dress Rehearsal	Polish lights	Press all costumes	Box office open — Passes to press, etc.
55	Full Dress Rehearsal — Preview	Details	Press all costumes	Final news story — Preview
56	Opening Performance	Check out all lights and sound before 7 P.M.	Press all costumes	Instruct ushers
57	During run, thank-you letters to everyone who has helped			
58	Bookkeeping	Strike set — Return all borrowed materials — Bring catalogue up to date	Return borrowed costumes — Others to cleaner	Financial report

Appendix B

Where to Get
Theatrical Supplies

Script

Dramatic Publishing Co.
170 North Michigan Ave.
Chicago 1, Ill.

Good high school plays and some
good adult material

Dramatists Play Service
14 East 38th St.
New York 16, N. Y.

Latest and many of the best playwrights; also a sizable group of
high school plays both full length
and short — Some publicity material and some sound effects.

Samuel French, Inc.
25 West 45th St.
New York 36, N. Y.
or
7623 Sunset Blvd.
Hollywood 46, Calif.

Everything from classics to latest
hits — Listed by number of characters in play

Harper & Row, Publishers
2500 Crawford Ave.
Evanston, Ill.

High school plays, some worth
doing

Children's Theatre Press
Cloverlor
Anchorage, Ky.

Playscripts for children up to teen-
age

370

Tams-Witmark Music Library
Inc.
115-117 W. 45th St.
New York 36, N. Y.

Stage Equipment

Paramount Theatrical Supplies
(Alcone Co.)
32 West 20th St.
New York 11, N. Y.

Has or can get nearly everything, including full line of makeup and cinnabex, a durable medium for coloring light. All makeup materials

Ben Walters, Inc.
156 Seventh Ave.
New York 1, N. Y.

Celastic, a quick, strong papier maché—Buy the solvent (acetone) locally

Gothic Color Company
90 Ninth Avenue
New York 11, N. Y.

Scene paint

Lighting Equipment

Century Lighting Co., Inc.
521 West 43 St.
New York 36, N. Y.

All lighting instruments, including Lekolite, a spotlight with ellipsoidal reflector, highly efficient

Kliegl Bros.
321 West 50th St.
New York 19, N. Y.

All lighting instruments — Sells an ellipsoidal spot about as good and as cheap as Leko

Superior Electric Co.
Bristol, Conn.

Makes Variak, an inductance dimmer that is cheaper and much more efficient than resistance type for small theatres

Sound Effects

MP-TV Services, Inc.
7000 Santa Monica Blvd.
Hollywood 38, Calif.

The best recordings of all sound effects

Dialecton, Inc.   Eight foreign dialects recorded
250 West 49th St.
New York 19, N. Y.

Shakespeare Recording Society   Recordings of Shakespeare's plays
461 Eighth Ave.   with name actors in the roles
New York, N. Y.

Publicity

Package Publicity Service, Inc.   News stories, posters, etc., on near-
247 West 46th St.   ly all recent plays and some old
New York 36, N. Y.   ones

Costumes and Fabrics

Van Horn and Son   Generally dependable, and cheaper
232 North 11th St.   than widely advertised New York
Philadelphia 7, Pa.   houses — Also has good wigs —
                                     Sometimes will make to order on
                                     rental basis

Capezio   All sorts of theatre shoes
1612 Broadway
New York, N. Y.

Maharam, Inc.   All theatrical fabrics—Much more
130 West 46th St.   variety and generally cheaper than
New York 19, N. Y.   one can purchase locally

Homespun House   Ten-foot wide monks cloth in a
291 South Robertson Blvd.   variety of weights and colors
Beverly Hills 32, Calif.

Glossary

Acting area. The part of the stage enclosed by the setting, in which the actors play.

Alveolar ridge. The ridge between the upper teeth and the hard palate.

Apron. The space at the front of the stage between the curtain line and the auditorium.

Arena. A stage space enclosed on two or more sides by the audience.

Articulation. The modification of the breathstream in the mouth to make speech sounds.

Backing. An element of scenery used to mask openings so that the audience cannot see backstage.

Backstage. That part of the stage which is outside of the setting and not seen by the audience.

Batten. A pipe or long board from which scenery is hung.

Beat. The division of a scene into attacks.

Blocking. Location and timing of the actors' main crosses and business.

Bookholder. The director's assistant who notes directions in the promtbook and prompts when necessary.

Border. An element of scenery used to mask the space above the set from the view of the audience. Also a row of lights hung above the setting.

Box-office casting. Assigning a part to an actor simply on the basis of his popularity, in the hope of selling tickets to all of his friends.

Brace (or stage brace). An adjustable length of wood or metal, with appropriate hooks on each end to hold the scenery to the floor in an upright position.

Business. Any stage direction that is not a cross.

Call boy. A prompter's assistant sometimes used to call the actors on stage in time for their entrances.

Character man. An actor who plays middle-aged to elderly parts.

Classic. A play that has survived from earlier times, or a contemporary play that has qualities which make it likely to survive.

Climax. The moment of release from tension after a crisis.

"Comp." A free ticket.

Consonant. A speech sound made by impeding or momentarily blocking the breathstream.

Continuity rehearsal. An uninterrupted rehearsal in which the actors gain a sense of the play as a whole.

Control board. The panel from which stage lights are controlled.

Counterweight. A weight used to balance a unit of scenery that must be flown.

Crisis. A moment of uncertainty, instability, or danger on stage accompanied by tension in the audience.

Crew. Members of the theatre group who are responsible for the technical details of the production.

Cross. A move of an actor from one point on stage to another.

Cue. The last three or four words of a speech; anything (speech or movement) that signals someone to do something.

Cyclorama. A curved drop representing the sky.

Dénouement. The solution of the plot, the event that ends the protagonist's quest for his objective.

Dimmer. A device for controlling the intensity of light.

Dim out. The gradual reduction of the amount of light until there is no light.

Double. To play more than one role.

Down (or downstage). Toward the audience.

Dress the set. To decorate it.

Effect. A term inherited from melodrama to describe unusual scenic devices such as snowfall, avalanche, house burning down, ocean waves, tempests.

Elevation. A two-dimensional scale drawing of each wall of a set.

Fade. The same as dim. Also applied to sound.

False proscenium. A frame within the proscenium frame.

Flat. A screen, one of the basic units of scenery.

Floor pattern. The system of moves made by actors on the stage.

Footlights. An obsolete row of striplights along the front of the stage.

Now used to mean a line of demarcation between stage and auditorium.

Front of the house. All the parts of the theatre used by the customers.

Gelatin. Plastic screen used in lighting instruments to color lights.

Ground plan. A scale drawing of the stage set as it would look from above.

Ground row. A masking device outside of a door or window to indicate locale.

Grid. System of girders above the stage, from which scenic units can be flown.

House. The auditorium.

House lights. The lights which illuminate the auditorium.

Jog. A very narrow flat.

Lamp. The glass-enclosed filament, with its base, which produces light.

"Lead." The role with the largest number of speeches.

Left. The actor's left as he faces the audience.

Level. A platform.

Light bridge. A catwalk just above and inside of the proscenium arch upon which lighting instruments are mounted.

Lines. (1) The words an actor has to say. (2) The ropes or wires by which scenery is flown to the grid.

Masking. A unit of scenery placed outside of openings .in the set to prevent the audience from seeing backstage.

Motivation. The character's inner reasons for his actions.

Offstage action. Action which is supposed to occur outside of the playing area and beyond the line of vision of the audience.

Olivette. A floodlight on a standard.

On stage. Toward center.

Phrasing. Dividing a speech into units of meaning by pausing between units.

Pick up a cue. To say the first word of a speech promptly after the last word of the partner's speech.

Picturize. To express visually by means of schematized drawings.

Pit. The space between the apron and the first row of seats.

Pitch pattern. The monotonous repetition of a series of tones which do not adequately express the meaning of a speech.

Platform. A part of the setting which is higher than the stage floor.

Playing time. The length of the play in minutes, exclusive of intermissions.

Project. To share the play with the audience.

Prompter. See bookholder.

Property. Any movable object on stage, exclusive of parts of the scenery or lighting equipment.

Property plot. A list of the properties and their locations, with directions for moving them on and off stage.

Props. Same as properties. Also the person responsible for moving them.

Proscenium. The arch that frames the stage.

Protagonist. The character whose objective is the core of the play.

Quick change. A costume change within a scene.

Rake. Slant.

Riding laughs. Speaking through the laughter of the audience.

Rigging. The lines by which scenery is raised to the grid.

Right. The actor's right as he faces the audience.

Run-through. Same as continuity rehearsal.

Scene dock. A rack in which flats are stored.

Scrim. A transparent drop.

Script. The text of the play.

Setting. The enclosed space in which the actors play.

Sides. Half-sheets containing one actor's speeches and his cues.

Sightlines. Limit of visibility to the audience.

Spatter. To spray or flip paint from a brush in order to texture a set.

Stage house. All the part of the theatre which houses the production— stage, storage space, shops, dressing rooms.

Stage manager. The individual who conducts the performance, cueing in all technical workers.

Staging. Same as blocking.

Strike. To remove.

Striplight. A series of small floodlights wired and housed in one unit.

Subtext. The actor's thoughts as he listens and speaks.

Talky scene. A scene in which there is much talk but nothing seems to happen.

Teaser. A drape across the top of the stage just inside of the proscenium arch.

Technique. The means by which the play is communicated to the audience.

Thickness. A piece attached to a door frame or window frame to simulate the jamb.

Trim. To mark the height of a flown object.

Type casting. Casting actors who have a great many qualities, especially visual, of the character they play.

Unit setting. A setting which, by shifting a few elements, can give an illusion of two or more places.

Upstage. Away from the audience.

Velum. A free muscle at the back of the soft palate that is used in swallowing and in making certain speech sounds.

Vowel. A speech sound made with the vocal bands and unimpeded by the articulators.

X. Cross.

Index

acting, anthropology and, 358; as emotional outlet, 248; exhibitionism and, 11-12
action, course of, 83-88; in *Playboy of the Western World*, 96-101; timing of, 258
actor(s), availability of, 22; beginner's insecurity, 252; body and voice training for, 271-297; body line of, 174-175; body training for, 274-281; character analysis by, 226-227; chart of in each scene, 68-69; in crisis tension scene, 178-179; director as emotional prop to, 255; director's acting out for, 266-267; director's driving of, 322-323; dominance of, 181; dramatist's meaning and, 8; emphasizing of in setting, 144-147; fear stimulus in, 259-260; human limitations of, 247; imagination of, 12; "imagining" of role by, 236, 238; James-Lange theory and, 259, 261, 267, 268; laziness in, 237; listening to other actors in scenes, 310-311; memorizing by, 67; motivation of, 273; moving about by, 158-160, 165 (*see also* movement); objectives and attacks for, 257; position of, 177; problems with, 251-256; proximity of, 177-178; qualities needed in, 236-240; recalling of own feelings by, 314-321; in rehearsal, 66-67; relaxing of neck muscles, 274; response to other actors in rehearsals, 308; self-control by, 12; speech problems of, 281-288; stage area occupied by, 180-181; stimulus-response

pattern in, 273; tensions in, 274-275; training techniques and principles for, 256-262; vitality in, 237; voice quality in, 239-240, 288-297; will power in, 237
Actor Prepares, An, 132
acts, reason for, 84
Adding Machine, The, 49
adolescence, motivation and, 273
adrenin, secretion of, 259
advertising, 28
Aesthetic Attitude, The, 2
aesthetic distance, 4
aesthetic experience, awareness loss in, 2
aesthetic illusion, roots of, 3
aesthetic mode, 4
affective mode, 4
age, makeup and, 348; movement and, 216-217
Ah Wilderness, 48
all-girl play, 37
American Educational Theatre Association, 36, 362
American National Theatre and Academy (ANTA), 363
amplifying system, 345
An Actor Prepares, 132
analysis, sample, 90-103; steps in, 90-91
Anderson, Maxwell, 48
Andromache, 79
anger exercises, 260
animals, imitation in, 359-360
ANTA (American National Theatre and Academy), 363
anthropology, study of, 358
Appia, Adolphe, 135, 214
arena productions, 25, 192-193
Aristotle, 79, 83, 360

6.50